THE

PUBLICATIONS

OF THE

SURTEES SOCIETY

VOL. CXCV

THE

PUBLICATIONS

OF THE

SURTEES SOCIETY

ESTABLISHED IN THE YEAR
M.DCCC.XXXIV

VOL. CXCV

FOR THE YEAR M.CM.LXXXII

At a COUNCIL MEETING of the SURTEES SOCIETY, held in Durham Castle on 1 June 1982, the PRESIDENT, Professor H.S. Offler, in the chair, it was ORDERED–

"That the edition of John Young's Diary by Mr Geoffrey Milburn should be printed as the volume of the Society's publication for 1982."

A.J. Piper, *Secretary*
The Prior's Kitchen,
The College,
Durham.

THE DIARY OF JOHN YOUNG

Sunderland Chemist and Methodist Lay Preacher

covering the years

1841 – 1843

EDITED BY

G. E. MILBURN

PRINTED FOR THE SOCIETY BY
JAMES HALL (LEAMINGTON SPA) LIMITED
1983

CONTENTS

ACKNOWLEDGEMENTS

In working on this volume over several years the editor has incurred more debts to the kindness and helpfulness of others than can be enumerated here. However he is bound to acknowledge the following: Mr Walter Crute; the staffs of the Sunderland Polytechnic Library and of the Sunderland and Newcastle Central Libraries (Local History Sections); Mr David Riley F.L.A. and his colleagues at the Deansgate Building of the John Rylands University Library of Manchester; the Archival staff at the Durham, and Tyne and Wear Record Offices; the Council of the Sunderland Antiquarian Society; the Revd Dr Oliver A. Beckerlegge; Dr David Gowland; Mr Alan Heesom; Miss Patricia J. Storey; Mrs Wendy Hawdon and Mr John Pearson. Sunderland Polytechnic has been generous in its material and financial support towards the costs of research, and in making a grant to the Surtees Society towards the costs of publication of this volume. I am very grateful to the Officers of the Surtees Society for the invitation to edit this volume, in which work I have found much profit and pleasure, and also for their patience and practical advice when the undertaking proved more protracted than had been foreseen. My most complete debt however is to my wife who not only typed and re-typed the entire text in several versions, but throughout remained a patient and cheerful pillar of support. To her the volume is dedicated.

G. E. MILBURN
Michaelmas 1982

SOURCES AND ABBREVIATED REFERENCES

Beckerlegge 1957 O. A. Beckerlegge, *The United Methodist Free Churches,* (1957)

Beckerlegge 1968 O. A. Beckerlegge, *United Methodist Ministers and their Circuits,* (1968). An alphabetical arrangement of the ministers of the various Free Methodist bodies 1797 – 1932 including those of the Wesleyan Methodist Association.

Brockie William Brockie, *Sunderland Notables,* (1894)

Corder The Corder Manuscripts, compiled by the late J. W. Corder, and containing much information on Sunderland places and people. The manuscripts, held by the Local History Section of Sunderland Central Library, have been of value in the identification of individuals mentioned in the diary.

D.N.B. *The Dictionary of National Biography.*

Directories The local directories nearest in date to John Young's diary are *Robson's Commercial Directory,* (1841); *Williams's Commercial Directory of Newcastle upon Tyne North and South Shields, Sunderland etc,* (Newcastle 1844); and *Directory of Sunderland* by Vint and Carr, (Sunderland 1844). Other directories by Whellan, Kelly *et al.* have been referred to for information on John Young's life and times later in the century.

Fordyce William Fordyce, *History and Antiquities of the County Palatine of Durham,* i – ii, (1857).

Gowland D. A. Gowland, *Methodist Secessions,* (1979).

Panton	A collection of materials relating to Wesleyan Methodism in Sunderland in the eighteenth and nineteenth centuries, compiled by members of the Panton family and held by the Sunderland Antiquarian Society.
Richardson	M. A. Richardson, *The Local Historian's Table Book,* i – viii, (1841 – 46). A chronological summary of north-eastern social history.
W M A Mag.	*The Magazine of the Wesleyan Methodist Association,* published in several parts each year from 1838 to 1857, and bound in annual volumes.
W M A Minutes	*Minutes of the Wesleyan Methodist Association,* published annually 1836 – 1857.

Other sources are quoted in full in the notes of the text.

INTRODUCTION

The diary of John Young, a Sunderland chemist, covering the period from December 1841 to November 1843, came into my possession several years ago through the kindness of Mr Walter Crute, solicitor, of Sunderland having been among the papers of his late father, Mr R.R. Crute.[1] The Crute family worshipped at Thornhill Methodist Church in Sunderland, now called Burn Park Methodist Church, which was the direct successor of the Brougham Street chapel which features so much in the diary and where John Young worshipped and occasionally preached. It was no doubt through this church connection that the diary came into R. R. Crute's hands some time after John Young's death in 1904, and its deposit in the security of a solicitor's safe must have helped to ensure its survival.

A description of the diary

The diary is a brown leather-bound volume 18½ cm. by 12 cm., and 2½ cm. thick, purchased, as a small printed notice inside the front cover informs us, at Thomas Swan's stationers shop, '2nd door below Nile Street Bishopwearmouth'. It appears to have been purchased for four shillings and three pence (21½p). The original clasp is now broken. It is not printed as a diary but is simply a substantial notebook with ruled pages, the first twenty six of which are provided with index letters down the margins. These pages are not used by John Young. Of the remaining three hundred and forty three pages, numbered by the owner, all but ten are filled with written entries, comprising some fifty thousand words in all.

1. For a general account of John Young and his diary, see G.E. Milburn, 'A Sunderland Diary', *Antiquities of Sunderland* 27 (1977 – 79), 31 – 56.

The first entry (four pages long) is dated 31 December 1841, suggesting that the diary was begun as a New Year's Resolution. The entries were at first infrequent, the second being dated 8 March 1842 and the next 19 April 1842. This pattern continues through most of 1842, with some variation. During 1843 Young kept the diary with greater regularity, once a week or more often, so that whereas the 1842 entries occupy 88 pages, those for 1843 take 240. The bulk of the diary is therefore concerned with 1843, the final entry being dated 14 November when the entries cease with no explanation and with several blank pages unused.

At first the handwriting is large and well-formed, carefully observing the rulings. On some early pages there are no more than one hundred words. From February 1843 the writing is less carefully shaped and smaller, with a resulting increase of words per page, up to two hundred or more. The change in calligraphy reflects to a certain degree a change in the emphasis of the diary. While the early entries are heavily introspective, the later ones include more objective observations of people and events. The writer's acutely evangelical self-awareness is nevertheless evident throughout.

In the very first entry Young explains that his original intention had been to use the new diary to delineate and analyse his life and character, but that after many procrastinations he had decided to plunge into 'the simple path of periodical narration'. In fact he does both in the diary, so that while parts of it are given over to extended accounts of self-examination, the narrative of everyday happenings is always sustained, intermittently at first, but gradually assuming a more dominant role. For most readers the interest of the diary will lie in the outward rather than the inward aspects.

John Young had a ready pen and a fluent style, and could depict people and events vividly. Apart from writing on his own and his family's doings he offers many fascinating vignettes of life in Sunderland in the early 1840s, which make the diary such an interesting social document. But the subjective passages have their own value in revealing the thoughts and feelings of an early Victorian evangelical. Indeed it ought not to be forgotten that it was Young's desire to record his inner life, a desire shared with many other evangelicals of the eighteenth and nineteenth centuries, that led him to begin the journal in the first place.

John Young's family background

John Young was born on 24 January 1820, the third child and first son of Thomas Brown Young and Ann Young, née Dixon. The family home was at 3 Nile Street, Sunderland,[2] in the parish of Bishopwearmouth, and the first two children, Ann and Ophelia, were baptised at St. Michael's Church in that parish. However John and his five younger brothers and sisters were taken for baptism to Holy Trinity, the parish church of Sunderland; that is Sunderland in its original meaning as the name of the compact riverside community east of Bishopwearmouth.[3] T. B. Young's sail-making workshops lay in Sunderland parish, at 89 Low Street. John was baptised at Holy Trinity on 29 March 1820, but before saying more about him some account of his family and especially his father must be given.

John's father, Thomas Brown Young (born 1794), whose name was always used in this full form, may well have been related to and named after Thomas Brown (1758–1842), an active Wesleyan businessman of Sunderland. If so this would be a small but significant indication of a feature of Sunderland's life at that time which is borne out in many other ways, namely the close interrelation of the leading Methodist families in the town.[4] The Whites, Dixons, Kirks, Vints, Dawsons, Browns, Muschamps, Tuers, Watsons, Youngs and others formed an influential clan drawn together through membership of the central Sunderland Wesleyan society, worshipping at the large chapel on Sans Street opened in 1793, and their relationship was cemented by a network of

2. This address, and a good deal of other information relevant to the diary, is found in contemporary directories of Sunderland. John Young in fact wrote neither his name nor his address in the front of the diary, but internal evidence revealing his authorship is plentiful.
3. These details are from the parish register of St. Michael's Bishopwearmouth, and Holy Trinity Sunderland, deposited at the Durham County Record Office.
4. See G. E. Milburn, 'Wesleyanism in Sunderland in the later eighteenth and early nineteenth centuries', *Antiquities of Sunderland* 26 (1974–76), and 27 (1977 –79), especially the latter volume, pp. 3–30.

chapel and Sunday School loyalties, by a common evangelical ethic, and by a complex inter-locking system of marital and commercial alliances. The Youngs were not the most prominent of these families but were related by a double link to one which was, namely the Whites. T. B. Young's aunt Jane had married John White (1763–1833), cooper, ship-owner and proprietor of the Bishopwearmouth Ironworks, and his wife, Ann Dixon, was the sister of Ophelia, who married John White's son, Andrew.

'Honest' Andrew White (1792 – 1856), an interesting figure whose life deserves to be fully investigated, was the bright star of Sunderland in the age of reform, becoming the first mayor of the revived corporation, and representing the town in Parliament from 1837 to 1841[5]. In his energy, evangelical loyalties, commercial ambition, local pride, civic zeal and liberal political views he typified many of the brash, hard-headed but not always commercially discreet business élite of Sunderland in its great age of expansion[6]. He had a major interest in the Sunderland Joint Stock Banking Company, known as the Methodist Bank, which collaped in 1852 amidst many allegations of highly dubious financial practices by the directors and officials, most of whom were leading Wesleyans in the town[7]. If true this would seem to be evidence of a strange dichotomy in the minds of these men between their personal and their commercial morality. Andrew White, as John Young's uncle, is mentioned from time to time in

5. Chapters on Andrew White and his father John White can be found in Brockie.
6. The following contemporary description of the character of early Victorian Sunderland is illuminating: "For all practical purposes, Sunderland is as new as an Australian or Yankee settlement – We like the fresh-coloured vigour that characterises everything in Sunderland. There is no dreamy, stupid, aristocratic indolence about the place. They are perfectly fierce in their money-making. They teem with self-reliance; and they love and hate with a terrible impetuosity – They like their politics, but they relish cash still more": anon., *Sketches of Public Men of the North,* (1855) p. 56. The quotation comes from an account of A. J. Moore, Mayor of Sunderland, who is mentioned from time to time in John Young's diary, and who acted as his solicitor.
7. More details are given in T. Potts, *Sunderland: a History of the Town,* (1892), pp. 320–21. See also Fordyce ii, 521–2.

the diary as a friend and adviser. John Young, with the Sunderland solicitor A.J. Moore, witnessed White's will in 1856; the small estate, of under £800, testifies to his commercial difficulties.

John's father, T. B. Young, emerges from the diary, and from other evidence, as an energetic, forceful and even domineering figure. Like so many of the able Wesleyans of his day he was recruited when young into Sunday School work and for a decade (1815 – 1825) taught in the schools, acted as superintendent of several of them, and served on the organising committee, at a time when the schools had well over a thousand boys and girls on their registers, and offered basic education to young adults also. About 1822 he began work as a lay preacher in the Sunderland Wesleyan circuit, and in addition was appointed a Class Leader with weighty responsibilities for the moral and spiritual oversight of the adult members committed to his care under the Methodist class system.[8] His class grew in numbers up to the very remarkable size of 126 by 1836,[9] a fact which indicates the magnetism and powers of leadership which he undoubtedly possessed.

These qualities, coupled with his impatience with contemporary ecclesiastical developments in Wesleyanism and a desire for the freer exercise of lay initiative, made him one of the chief leaders and inspirers in the mid-1830s of the movement in Sunderland, which had national ramifications also, calling for a more representative structure within the Wesleyan Connexion. Those demands failed, and the upshot in Sunderland, and elsewhere in England, was a major secession, from the Wesleyans, taking the name of the Wesleyan

8. Reference to T. B. Young's active involvement in Wesleyan Methodism and its Sunday Schools are to be found in Panton iii, *passim;* and in the Minutes and Annual Reports of the Sunderland and Bishopwearmouth Sunday Schools in the Tyne and Wear Record Office.

9. From lists of members proposed at the Sans Street Wesleyan Chapel Leaders Meeting, Durham County Record Office, D/X 272/2.

Methodist Association, whose local activities feature so largely in John Young's diary.[10]

There is some illuminating original material on the secession in Sunderland in the Panton collection, including the Declaration of the officers of the Wesleyans in Sunderland dated January 1835, setting forth expressions of local discontent at a number of current developments in the Wesleyan Connexion. T. B. Young's name is at the head of the list of over one hundred signatories. The controversy generated a lively pamphlet warfare, the products of which can be found in the Sunderland Local History Library and in the Methodist Archive collection in the John Rylands University Library, Manchester. The aggrieved parties in the Sunderland Wesleyan Circuit seceded from Wesleyanism in 1836, to the number of some 600, and other secessions occurred in the north-east about the same time. At first known as the Wesleyan Seceders, they formed a union with the national Wesleyan Association in 1837 and grew rapidly in numbers. The Sunderland Association published an interesting booklet in 1838, briefly describing the secession and setting forth the principles of doctrine and church discipline of the seceders; it is reproduced in Appendix II below.

T. B. Young's main occupation was that of sail-maker, which he practised on Low Street, near to the riverside quays along the south bank of the river Wear. With his sail-making he combined ship-owning, as well as activities as a ship and insurance broker. These latter activities presumably assumed a growing importance as the use of sails declined with the advent of steam powered ships. It is doubtful whether this decline was sufficiently advanced by 1852 to have provoked T. B. Young's emigration to Australia that year; perhaps the collapse of the Methodist Bank was an added factor. Whatever the reason, the fact is that at the age of 58, accompanied by his second wife Maria and three daughters by her, T. B. Young sailed to Melbourne on 11 September

10. For general accounts of the origins of the Wesleyan Methodist Association see: Beckerlegge 1957; J. C. Bowmer, *Pastor and People,* (1975); W. R. Ward, *Religion and Society in England 1790–1850* (1972); Gowland. The last book, dealing primarily with the Association in three Lancashire towns, offers interesting comparisons with developments in Sunderland.

1852 on one of the first two ships to carry organised parties of emigrants from Wearside to Australia.[11] Some fellow members of the Wesleyan Association in Sunderland sailed with him, and knowing T. B. Young's personality it is hard not to see him as the organising genius. Certainly he threw himself into the enterprise with courage and undiminished evangelical zeal.

T. B. Young's name or his initials TBY, occur repeatedly in the diary, often in connection with instances in which John, then a young man in his twenties and in business of his own, is being put firmly in his place by his father. T. B. Young's heavily paternal attitude may explain why there is not much overt affection in the diary references to him, though there is respect and loyalty. One of John's ministerial friends was quick to point out to him, when smarting from his father's quick temper, that T. B. Young's irascibility was in part due to illness and to the early death of his first wife Ann in 1832, leaving him a considerable family to care for, including John, then a boy of twelve.

There were six other surviving children, Elizabeth Mary, the fourth of the eight born to Ann, having died in infancy. The youngest two are not mentioned in the diary and it may be that they were being brought up in other homes. Most often referred to by John are his two older sisters, Ann (or Anne) aged twenty four and Ophelia aged twenty three when the diary begins. Anne, whom John refers to occasionally in slightly formal terms as Miss Anne Young, appears to have been living with the Whites either at their town house Frederick Lodge or their attractive residence three miles or so out of town, Tunstall Lodge. John seems to have been close in spirit to her, whereas there are signs of a rather edgy relationship with Ophelia. Among other things, John dis-

11. On T. B. Young's emigration to Australia, see *The Sunderland Echo* 25 August 1959, an article based on the memories of the captain of the ship, *The Emigrant,* who in fact was a brother of James Williams, the Sunderland Chartist mentioned briefly in John Young's diary; *WMA Mag.* 1853 pp. 284–5, which gives the text of a letter from T.B.Y. to the *Sunderland Herald* 24 January 1853, written from Australia; and Patricia J. Storey 'The "Lizzie Webber" and the "Emigrant", *Journal of the Northumberland and Durham Family History Society,* Vol. 5 No. 4 (July 1980), 102 ff.

approved of Ophelia's marriage to John Dixon. The two younger boys, Thomas and William, receive passing references. William was at sea at the time of the diary.

John Young's life and character, up to and including the period of his diary

When John Young died in 1904 an obituary writer said of him that 'at one time no man in the town was better known than he was'.[12] Nevertheless he did not find a place in William Brockie's *Sunderland Notables* (published 1894) and I know of no published account of his life which therefore has to be pieced together from scattered references, with much light being thrown by the diary for the limited period which it covers. The outline offered here, and in the next section, could no doubt be amplified by a more sustained study than has been possible of sources likely to produce information, such as the Sunderland newspapers over the long period of his life. But what is written, despite its limitations, will I hope help the reader to appreciate the diary and its writer with more depth of understanding than the text alone makes possible, and help also to satisfy natural curiosity about what course Young's life followed after the diary ceases in November 1843. Much supplementary information on points of detail will be found in the various notes to the diary, to which the reader is referred.

John Young grew up from birth to manhood in a medium-sized terrace house on Nile Street, Bishopwearmouth, one of those early nineteenth-century streets marking the steadily westward expansion of the urban area of Sunderland. It had the large Quaker meeting house at its southern end, opened two years after John was born, and the houses in the street were occupied by modestly prosperous citizens – master mariners, tradesmen, shopkeepers, professional folk and so on. As John Young grew up, other more attractive rows were being built further to the west, and nearer to the centre of Bishopwearmouth, so that Nile Street, while being

12. Obituary accounts of John Young are to be found in the *Sunderland Daily Echo* Friday 21 October 1904 (J. Y. died early that very day) and in the *Sunderland Year Book* 1905 p. 127 (based on the earlier *Echo* obituary). Both are quite brief though interesting in points of detail.

respectable enough, occupied a middling place in the status ranking of Sunderland housing at that time.

The Young household was steadily expanding, and the cries of babies and babble of infant voices must have pervaded the home thoughout the first dozen years or so of John's life. In these years one presumes that he and the other children were surrounded by the usual religious influences of a pious evangelical family, and that from an early age he was taken to the Sunday Schools associated with the Wesleyan chapel on Sans Street, a little lower down High Street from Nile Street, and taken also to worship at the chapel itself. How deeply evangelical religion came to pervade his own heart and mind the diary shows very clearly. His secular education was received, at least in part, at the hands of Josiah Cormack who ran a private school on Upper Sans Street. A conversation between him and John Young, recounted in the diary among the entries under the date 12 June 1843, shows Cormack to have been a religiously-minded and scholarly teacher for whom John had admiration and affection. John Young obviously became a highly literate young man with a thirst for knowledge, and the particular training he received in day school and Sunday school, together with the strong evangelical imperatives towards self-improvement, must all have played their part in moulding this intellectual development.

At the age of twelve John lost his mother. A few years later (the exact chronology here is unclear) he was smitten by a serious illness which rendered him unable for some time to walk without the help of crutches. At least twice (probably in 1836 and certainly in 1838) he was sent by sea to London to stay with friends apparently for convalescence. The theme of health runs through the diary from its start to its finish, the very last entry being a cry, 'O for health, for strength!'. In fact at the time of the diary John appears to have been quite vigorous, able to walk several miles to preaching appointments, and to sustain very long working hours, yet he expresses a constant and hypochondriacal concern for his physical state, as acute as that he had for his state of soul.

The enforced seclusion of his teenage years may well have been in part responsible for the sensitivity, loneliness, introspection, and studious habits which are revealed by the diary as strong elements in his character. It may also be that his intense love of all things nautical, his interest in military and international affairs, and his taste for romantic adventure stories all express a yearning for freedom and action unfulfilled in his formative years. The nautical connections were in any case unavoidable in a town like Sunderland and in a family whose professional links were in so many ways with the sea and sea-faring.

In considering the influences which helped to form John Young's character, at least as it appears to us in the diary, it is important to recall the social context of his life. The early decades of the nineteenth century were in Sunderland, as in the nation generally, a period of remarkable economic and social development. The town was expanding rapidly, its industries proliferating, its population increasing (to over 50,000 by 1841), its transport facilities being revolutionised by railways, its commerce booming, and its political life being transformed by emancipation in 1832 and the revival of borough status in 1835. John Young had a particular interest in many of these developments in that his family and close relations, including his uncle Andrew White, were at the heart of them. Sunderland also felt the repercussions of national movements such as Chartism and the Anti-Corn Law League, the latter being strongly supported by the Sunderland mercantile and professional classes. The upsurge of liberal ideas and the assertion of local interests, seen so clearly in contemporary political developments in Sunderland, had their religious counterpart in the Methodist upheavals in the mid-1830s leading to the secession from mainstream Wesleyanism which launched the Wesleyan Methodist Association, one of the elements in the emergence of what is known as Free Methodism. Here again John Young had as it were a ringside seat since his father was a leader of this movement in the town.

These were heady times for a young lad to grow up in, and John Young must have been the fascinated listener to many lively and heated debates in the parlour of number 3 Nile Street and in the homes of his other relatives as matters religious and political were thrashed out and some momentous decisions taken. Judging from the diary he himself was moved less by political than religious interests. The affairs of the Sunderland corporation are not mentioned in the diary but it is full of the doings of the Wesleyan Association. In so far as he had political interests they were roused more by international than local matters.

John Young's religious convictions are very evident throughout the diary as is the considerable time and energy he spent on chapel commitments. One very obvious value of the diary is the light it throws on the life and work of the Wesleyan Association in Sunderland, seen through the eyes of a committed but not uncritical member. We also get a very helpful insight into the heart and mind of a sensitive young Methodist in the 1840s, and the tensions he experienced in seeking to be true to the social and personal disciplines which membership implied. There are some frank illuminations here, of a kind not usually found in the standard Methodist literature of the day.

Much is written in the diary about John Young's work as a lay or 'local' preacher, the latter being the Methodist term used to distinguish between voluntary part-time preachers, who took appointments in their own localities, and the professional ministers, who were stationed in different circuits every few years, and who, because of their periodic journeyings, were known as 'travelling' preachers. John Young was obviously a very able preacher and some of his friends, including his aunt Ophelia White, prophesied that he would 'go out to travel'. He debated this question very seriously with himself, but the matter seems to have gone no further, and he never became a minister.

A preachers' plan for the Wesleyan Association Sunderland circuit survives, for the quarter from 29 October 1843 to 21 January 1844.[13] There are twenty seven preachers' names, the first four of which are those of the three circuit ministers and the full time circuit missionary Mr Heywood. The remainder are those of the lay preachers, with T. B. Young at the head of the list, and John's name at number twenty four. There are twenty preaching places, eight of them in Sunderland, including industrial villages like South Hylton and Southwick which were later incorporated into the town, and others in South Shields, Shiney Row, Philadelphia, New

13. The original of this plan is in the possession of the editor of this volume.

Lambton, Collier Row, Houghton-le-Spring, Hetton-le-Hole, Middle Rainton, Chatershaugh, Washington Staith, Pensher (Penshaw) and Seaham. The plan shows John Young preaching fourteen times in the quarter at nine different places, most of them some miles out of the centre of town. He did not preach in this quarter at either of the two central chapels, or Tabernacles as the Associationists liked to call them, on South Durham Street and Brougham Street, these being virtually the preserve of the ministers.

An analysis of John Young's references to his sermons shows that he used a basic half dozen texts, carefully permutated between the various chapels. Some of these texts, especially II Peter 1 vv. 5–7 and II Timothy 2 vv. 11–13, were very compendious ones offering a preacher plenty of scope and probably explaining the length of John's sermons! Despite this understandable husbanding of his resources, there is no doubt that the demands of preaching, and preparing for his oral examination, which is described in some detail in the diary, stimulated his mind and enlarged his studies. We cannot be certain how deeply he read but the scope of his reading is remarkable. It is not the least of the diary's merits that it reveals what a serious-minded and articulate young man could lay his hands on by way of reading matter in a provincial town in the early years of Victoria's reign. Some of the books were probably his father's or were borrowed from other preachers; others came from the Sunderland Subscription Library or from Burnett's commercial library, lighter reading in the latter case. The full list of books and journals referred to in the diary is set out separately at the end of this introduction.

Another stimulus to John Young's mind came from his business activities. In April 1841 he was set up, on borrowed capital, as a chemist at 210 High Street, Sunderland, the shop being on the corner of Russell Street, which ran off High Street on the opposite side to Sans Street and a little further to the east. There were at that time some eighteen or nineteen other chemists' shops along the length of High Street and competition must have been keen.[14] This proliferation may reveal a growing concern for hygiene and medical provision

14. Evidence from contemporary directories.

as a result of the cholera epidemic which afflicted Sunderland in 1831 and 1832. Of the other chemists several were Methodists and at least two were John Young's relatives. It may have been that a chemist's business appealed to the more ambitious Methodist families as an occupation for their sons entering trade because it enjoyed higher status, and offered more scope for the exercise of skill and knowledge, than say a grocery or drapery business, though these were also popular with Methodists.

In fact no qualifications were required to launch a chemist's business at that time. But it is obvious than John Young took his professional obligations seriously. He read extensively in pharmacy and medicine, and qualified as a member of the Pharmaceutical Society (which came into being in 1841) between 1842 and 1844.[15].

In addition to the dispensing side of his business he no doubt supplied medical chests and other provisions to ships. Much of a chemist's business then, as indeed today, was of a general nature and John Young's shop seems to have been as much a grocer's as a dispensing chemist's. One very lucrative sideline of his was to make spiced nuts (probably something like gingerbread biscuits) which were sold at the Sunderland fairs and maybe at other times. He held a licence to sell tobacco, tea and coffee, also one to sell pepper which was subject to duty. It was this involvement with the sale of pepper which led to the food adulteration and excise charge which is recorded at the very end of the diary.

The justice of this charge is not easy to clarify now, but it has to be admitted that it was not unknown for outwardly pious businessmen to perpetrate similar, and worse, offences in their commercial dealings in the nineteenth century and Sunderland was not immune, as the affairs of the Methodist Bank revealed. Such actions cannot be condoned but they may perhaps be understood. The very puritan business ethic, so prevalent in early Victorian England, might indeed be seen as partly to blame by placing emphasis on success in business as the God-given and rightful reward to enterprise and hard work. In an age of cut-throat competition and of laissez-

15. I owe this information to Mr William Nixon of Sunderland, former Head of the Pharmacy Department at Sunderland Polytechnic.

faire, with few restraints on commercial aggression, it is not surprising that even the righteous were lured or squeezed into accepting standard of behaviour in business which they would have condemned in private life, in order to ensure the success which they felt to be both their due and the outward mark of their piety. An entry in the diary (29 August 1843) which despite a touch of irony is very much in earnest, expresses in almost classic form the puritan work-ethic by which John Young and his Methodist fellow business men lived, indeed felt obliged to live if they were to be true to their sincere convictions.

The picture of John Young that emerges from the pages of his diary is certainly of a complex young man with a number of paradoxical features in his make-up. For example, though a strict tee-totaller he enjoyed an occasional cigar and other creature comforts; though reserved and proud enough to resist for three quarters of an hour the endeavours of some Sunderland women to carry out the Easter custom of removing his shoes, he yet could enjoy a joke, and on one occasion composed a hoax advertisement for some quack pills; though studious and somewhat critical in religious matters he could unbutton himself in a class meeting and shout his hallelujahs with the best; though confessing to a sense of loneliness he appeared to others as companionable and affable; though at times intensely introspective he would quickly turn to a lively, objective and humorous observation of the passing scene; though an astute and hard-working business man he yet longed for a different existence in which he could freely pursue his intellectual interests. These and other inner contradictions, and the way in which he frankly writes about them, make him stand out from the pages of his diary very much as flesh and blood in a way which is refreshingly different from the characterisation so prevalent in much of the religious biography of his age. At the same time it has to be confessed that some of his expressions of self-abasement, and his morbid introspections, will probably fall strangely on the ears of a modern reader.

John Young's life after the diary ceases

The sixty years of John Young's life from the end of the diary to his death can only be outlined here. It seems that for some thirty years and more his business steadily expanded.

In the early 1850s he took new premises at 130 High Street, Bishopwearmouth, from which to operate his retail business. To the rear of this new shop, on William Street, were buildings which had been owned by Andrew White as offices for his Whitwell Coal Company, and John Young at some point took these over also. By 1853 he had launched a wholesale company and was the Sunderland agent for two chemical works, at Washington and Felling. Some twenty years later (maybe less) he began the manufacture of oil and paint at the William Street premises. He carried on his retail trade all the while..

Just as his business progress can be traced in the local Directories, so can his changes of residence. Around 1850 we find him having left the family home and living on Union Street and then on Foyle Street, where he spent a few years. By 1857 he had moved to South Lodge, Roker, on the north side of the river Wear, which was to be his home for some twenty years, the period, if I read the facts aright, of his greatest prosperity. Incidentally he never married.

We know that politically and religiously he was busily occupied during the 1850s. From 1850 to 1853 he represented Bishopwearmouth ward on the Sunderland Corporation.[16] The poll books for the 1857 Parliamentary election in Sunderland show him, as would be expected, casting his votes in favour of the Liberal candidates. The Wesleyan Methodist Association continued to demand his active allegiance. In 1847 he was elected to represent the Sunderland Association at the W.M.A. Annual Assembly, as his father had done for the previous ten years, and he was a representative again in 1850, 1852 and 1853. In 1853, 1854 and 1855 he was also chosen as a member of some important connexional committees of the W.M.A., including, in 1855, the special committee set up to negotiate a union of the W.M.A. with a later secession from Wesleyanism, the Wesleyan Reformers.[17] The two movements came together in 1857

16. Tyne and Wear Archives. Sunderland Corporation Minutes Vol. ii, p. 194, 1 November 1850. John Young was not re-elected three years later (*op. cit.* p. 546).
17. This information on J. Y's connexional commitments with the W.M.A. is based on the Association's published annual *Minutes*, of which copies are held in the Methodist Archive at John Rylands University Library, Manchester.

to form the United Methodist Free Churches, though local mergers had taken place before this date, as in Sunderland in 1854–1855. John Young was the chairman of the grand meeting marking the completion of the union in Sunderland, held at the Brougham Street Tabernacle on New Year's Day 1855, and spoke, according to the accounts, with his 'accustomed eloquence'.[18]

Obituary tributes to John Young speak of his having suffered a commercial crash but without any details of exactly when this occurred. It would seem that it happened in the mid-1870s, or slightly afterwards. Certainly by 1877 he had left his residence in Roker and was living in a relatively modest terraced house, apparently let as lodgings, on a street known as The Royalty, off Chester Road, Sunderland. He carried on business but at different premises, first on Fawcett Street and then Bridge Street. When he finally retired from business in 1897 he is said to have had so few resources that his friends were obliged to support him. He did in fact move back to Roker in 1889 but at some point, maybe on retirement, he returned to Bishopwearmouth where he was to die. In his latter years he is said to have been a familiar if somewhat eccentric figure about the town, wearing a small old-fashioned cap and a shawl about his shoulders.[19]

His death took place early in the morning of 21 October 1904 at number 2 Crowtree Terrace, Bishopwearmouth, a street of older terraced houses occupied at that time by lesser trades people and lodging house keepers. He was buried the following Sunday in Bishopwearmouth Cemetery, in an unpurchased grave in common ground and with no stone erected to mark the spot. Later two other men, of no known family connections, were buried above him in the same grave.[20]

The contradictions and complexities which were observed earlier in regard to John Young were certainly there at the end. Despite the reputation he once had enjoyed in the town, as his obituary noted, it seems that no-one took the trouble to purchase a grave and erect a stone. Was it that his com-

18. *WMA Mag.* (1855) 98–101.
19. See the obituary reference note 12 p. xviii above.
20. I owe this information to the staff at the Bishopwearmouth Cemetery, Sunderland.

mercial troubles, as well as affecting his material circumstances, also caused personal rifts, even a break with the church, leaving him lonely in old age?

The memories of him recorded at the time of his death are oddly variant too. On the one hand he was recalled as having been exceptionally well-informed on public and national issues, especially the naval defences of Great Britain, and of having spoken publicly on these matters and corresponded on them with leading statesmen. On the other hand there was a memory of his shop-front brightly illuminated to attract trade, and of the immense popularity of his ginger nuts, sold in enormous quantities at what sound like expensive prices at the old Sunderland fairs. It seems that John Young may never have resolved the tension within himself, characterised by these two memories, between the intellectual and commercial sides of his character and perhaps it was over-ambition in business which proved his undoing in the end.

Editorial practice

The diary has been reproduced entire, with the addition of two appendices. The sectional headings are the author's. He wrote them across the head of each page and for this printed edition they have been transferred to the body of the text. John Young used hyphens very liberally in place of punctuation marks. For the sake of clarity many of these have been replaced by standard punctuation. Spelling errors, of which there are a few in the manuscript, have been corrected. Abbreviations used by Young are explained at the first use but not generally thereafter. Round brackets in the text are the author's own; square brackets contain editorial insertions. Biblical references have been provided in square brackets for all the identifiable scriptural quotations and allusions. An asterisk against a biblical reference indicates an imperfect quotation, perhaps made from memory. The notes to the text have been made as full as possible in order to identify and illuminate for the reader the people, the incidents, the books and so on which John Young refers to, and to fill out the details of the context of his life; persons and places included in the sections 'Summary biographies', 'Notes to the Area Map' and 'Notes to the Town Plan' are marked in the text with an obelus †.

JOHN YOUNG'S READING

Books and journals which John Young read, or which are alluded to in the diary. Fuller details on some of the books listed are given in the footnotes.

I Books on the Bible, theology and the religious life

C. Leslie	A *Short and Easie Method with the Deists,* (1698)
Wm Burkitt	*Expository Notes . . . on the New Testament,* (1700)
M. Henry	*The Pleasantness of a Religious Life,* (1714)
J. Wesley	*Explanatory Notes on the New Testament,* (1755)
G. Campbell	*Lectures on Systematic Theology and Pulpit Eloquence,* (1807)
Joseph Benson	*The Holy Bible . . . with Notes,* (1810)
Josiah Pratt	*Life Character and Remains of the Rev. Richard Cecil,* (1811)
Richard Watson	*Theological Institutes,* (1823)
G. C. Storr & C. C. von Flatt	*An Elementary Course of Biblical Theology,* (1826/1838)
I. Taylor	*Natural History of Enthusiasm,* (1829)
A. Clarke	*Christian Theology,* arr. S. Dunn, (1835)
I. Taylor	*Physical Theory of Another Life,* (1836)
John Harris	*Union; or, the Divided Church made one,* (1837)
T. H. Skinner	*Aids to Preaching and Hearing,* (1839)
Joseph Barker	*All War Anti-Christian,* (1840)
J. T. Conquest	*The Holy Bible . . . with . . . emendations,* (1841)
G. Borrow	*The Bible in Spain,* (1843)

John Young also reveals considerable familiarity with Methodist hymns.

II History and current affairs

Wm James	either *A full and correct account of the chief Naval Occurrences of the late War between Great Britain and the United States of America,* (1817)
	or *A full and correct account of the Military Occurrences of the late War between Great Britain and the United States of America,* i–ii, (1818)
J. Fenimore Cooper	*Gleanings in Europe,* (1837)
J. H. M. d'Aubigné	*History of the Great Reformation,* i–iii (1838–41)
V. Eyre	*The Military Operations at Cabul,* (1843)

III Literary, linguistic and critical studies

James Harris	*Hermes: a Philosophical Enquiry Concerning Language and Uriversal Grammar,* (1751)
L. Murray	*English Grammar,* (1795)
Wm Lennie	*Principles of English Grammar,* (1816)
Wm Cobbett	*A Grammar of the English Language* (1819)
Wm Cobbett	*A French Grammar,* (1824)
	Autobiography of Sir Walter Scott, (1831)

IV Fiction

Ann Radcliffe	*The Mysteries of Udolpho,* (1794)
J. Fenimore Cooper	*The Last of the Mohicans,* (1826)
M. Scott	*Tom Cringle's Log,* (1835)
M. Scott	*The Cruise of the Midge,* (1836)
F. Marryat	*Mr Midshipman Easy,* (1836)
C. J. Lever	*The Confessions of Harry Lorrequer,* (1837)

V Scientific and general

John Mason	*Self-Knowledge,* (1745)
Wm Kitchiner	*The Art of Invigorating and Prolonging Life,* (1821)
Richard Whateley	*Elements of Logic,* (1826)
A. Combe	*The Principles of Physiology,* (1834)

VI Journals

Various newspapers
The Wesleyan Association Magazine, The Arminian (Wesleyan) Magazine, Dublin University Review, Tait's Edinburgh Magazine, United Service Magazine and Naval and Military Journal, W. Morgan & A. Creuze, *Papers on Naval Architecture, Fraser's Magazine, The Westminster Review, The Quarterly Review, The Monthly Review.*

JOURNAL

Thoughts on keeping a journal

Friday Dec. 31, 1841

It is remarked by Sir W. Scott in the introduction to his autobiography that he had 'always considered the best mode of conducting a private journal to be to put down ideas, facts, or occurrences spontaneously in the order of time, without reference to any positive systematic arrangement'.[1] When I first bought this new Journal I felt ambitious to commence with certain elaborate ideas, or the expression of some comprehensive remarks respecting moral, mental and physical cultivation. Again I felt desirous to institute a general review of the past, to attempt to delineate with some degree of accuracy all the leading features of my life; to trace the influence of circumstances of the formation of character in order to attain right conceptions of my capabilities, and attainments; and lastly to gather from the whole lessons of future practical interest. This subject has occupied my attention from time to time, and yet I have never been able to decide on what would please my fancy as the *best introduction,* thus suffering time to creep away and with it the recollection of a thousand incidents which, if seized and noted at the time, would have proved fruitful in pleasing and improving retrospect. Weary of indecision, I have at length resolved to go straightforward in the simple path of periodical narration.

1. *The Autobiography of Sir Walter Scott Bart.,* compiled from his introductions and notes to the editions of the 'Waverley Novels' and 'Poetical Works' published between 1827 and 1831, (Philadelphia, 1831).

Record of gratitude and estimate of my religion

The last day of the year 1841 finds me in very altered circumstances from any previous period. *First* I would here devoutly record, before men and angels, the sincerity of my gratitude to God that I am still a member of his church, that I still am spiritually enlighted to understand my true position as a moral and accountable being. This is of God's mercy. *Secondly,* I would also express my sense of Divine Goodness for the Restoration of my Health, so that I am enabled to discharge with personal comfort those various duties which arise from my position in society.[2] *Thirdly* my thankfulness that in the generous arrangements of Divine Providence there has been allotted to me so favourable a station in social and civil life, which station affords me enviable opportunities for promoting God's Glory and serving my own salvation. *4th.* If I judge rightly of my sincerity, I desire above all things daily to feel my responsibilities and daily to be assisted to fulfil with faithfulness every indication of duty. *5th.* If there is one lesson which I feel ought to be more deeply imprinted on my mind from the experience of the past than another, *It is to distrust myself.* Alas who can know himself? J. Young.

2. On John Young's health in the years prior to the diary see various references in the text, e.g. under p. 88, 97, 138-9 below.

Improvement of time

March 8th, 1842.

What a disposition there is in the mind to allow the present moment to glide away, extinguishing the remonstrances of reason and conscience by the vain confidence of doing something in the indefinite future.

I have some object of pursuit, some plan, something which I feel to be desirable or essential to my success in life; it may be the attainment of a language, the knowledge of some science, facility in the practice of some Art; it is a settled point with me that it must be accomplished, of this I have no doubt. How long is it since I first began in earnest their pursuit? Has not sufficient time elapsed to have secured all those objects? Might I not have been able *Now,* to have considered them as part and parcel of the attainments of the mind? But I am still found looking to the *future.*

This day, nay only *this moment* is mine, the morrow may never come. In spite of dear-bought experience, the uniform testimony of others, I am still trusting my best and most important interest to the vicissitudes of other days. Reason convinces me that it would be true wisdom to live today as though there were no tomorrow and yet I detect myself in suffering the present to pass in easy enjoyment, in busy idleness and worthless trifles.

To feel the value of this moment; to suppress each wandering thought; to quench the risings of passion; to rise superior to the allurements of sensual gratification; to concentrate the attention on the object which ought to engage the powers of the mind; this is the first requisite, and most certain guarantee of success.

How invaluable the attainment of such a power. Wealth cannot purchase it. Desire cannot reach it. And yet it is within the grasp of all. The obstacles to its acquisition are powerful – but they are not in outward circumstances. It is equally accessible to the poor, as to the rich. The Discipline of the Heart, its affections, its propensities, and its passions. The Discipline of the Mind, its noble powers, its stupendous faculties, to subject *this* to the guidance of reason, and *that to* supremacy of conscience, is an arduous Victory and a *triumph* worthy of commemoration.

Time is an aggregate of moments following in constant succession. To live the present, to seize, and to consecrate *this moment* to the best of purposes is therefore to live every moment, to live always satisfactorily, and well. If this were graven on the heart; if this could be kept instantly before the mind; then might we expect to lay the foundation of a sound intellectual and moral character, to realise our most sanguine wishes, and we should not die before we had felt that we had not utterly failed in fulfilling the objects of our existence.

Such are my views, and such my feelings – Shall they direct my conduct? Devoutly do I pray that my life may attest the sincerity of my convictions. Constant watchfulness is necessary. Care lest any object should so interest the affections as to lessen and withdraw the attention from these principles.

First speech. Public speaking

On Shrove Tuesday Feb. 8th a Public Tea Party was held in the upper School Room adjoining the Tabernacle, S. Durham Street.† At this meeting I spoke for the first time in public, except an occasional invitation in prayer meeting, &c. I felt more confidence than I anticipated. At one time nearly confused, I saw clearly some of the difficulties which beset, and the emotions which agitate, the mind of a speaker. Perhaps the great point is a clear and collected mind; this *inspires* confidence. A good voice, strong, and clear is highly necessary. If you feel you have got something to say and that you can say it, you are in small danger of being confused. Respecting Public Speaking one can scarcely underrate the value of physical qualifications. Do I wish to acquire facility in speaking, setting to one side mental ability, I ought to pay strict attention to the voice. Though the strength of the lungs will depend in a good degree on the health of the whole system, they are yet capable of receiving great improvement from judicious exercise. Speaking is a faculty which must be cultivated. The lungs may be strong, and vigorous, and yet be inefficient in oratory. We must acquire the *habit* of speaking correctly on all occasions. The due modulation, and inflection of the voice, the correct pronunciation of words, all are greatly influenced by habit. Mental ability being equal, the best orator will always exert the greatest influence. How far superior mental powers may yield in influence to bodily qualification is a question.

Self-examination

April 19th, 1842.

By the mercy of God I am still the subject of religious feeling. I am astonished how I have been brought through a thousand difficulties and temptations, would to God that I could say unharmed and unsinged. Alas! the consciousness of guilt hangs like the dark brooding of a storm over my conscience. Disquietude and uneasiness mar my peace. Where that delightful calm which filled my soul, and made my hours to flow like the even progress of the quiet brook? The eruption of unrestrained and unsanctified passion has created a stormy turbulence within, which, like the brook when swollen by the rain, has swept before it the restraint of conscience and propriety and involved me in misery and remorse. Remorse! Ah; that I could feel it as deeply as I have once felt it. Oh! that it would prey upon my heart, until its very load might drive me to the feet of the Saviour, that my soul might be dissolved in a flood of tears, that I might

Weep my life away
For having grieved his love.

I am a sinner, it is stamped in my inmost nature. Sin is stereotyped in every faculty of my soul and on all their manifestations. Literally I cannot accomplish any 'good thing'. Or at least the effort is but transient. I do not continue in well doing. 'To will is present with me but how to perform I know not.' [Romans 7:18].[3] *I know what ought to be.* There is no need of conviction. I've before trodden the path of duty, and know well its landmarks. It is but an idea, a mere impression, which was in the mind, and again passes from the grasp of consciousness. Comformable to the law of association, incidents which strike its chord cause a train of painful reminiscence to pass through the mind, which may perhaps lead to renewed vows to return again to the once dearly loved paths of peaceful enjoyment when the soul *'walked with God'* [Genesis 5:24]; or it may be that remembering the futility of older resolutions, the soul has at once gone to the Cross and, casting itself on the mercy of God through the atonement has obtained pardon and peace and, thus justified from all past delinquencies it has burst into rapturous praise, firmly convenanting never more to forsake, but rather to give all diligence 'to hold fast its profession', [Hewbrews 4:14*] even to the end. But, all that is meant and felt by Christians when they speak of the world, *The World.* Its seductive influence. What is not comprehended in the emphatic *world.* Alas!!! the world has gradually and smoothly coiled itself again around the heart. There is no sudden departure from the ordinary duty. Such a dereliction would stand revealed, to be steadfastly resisted with holy indignation.

It is some little today, and more tomorrow. The slight

flaw widens imperceptibly into an enormous rent. The first opening caused a momentary smart, but the entire separation would appear to have destroyed the susceptibility of impression.

It is in the spirituality of Religion as in the human body; the flight of its vitality renders it impervious to all sensibility.

3. From the Authorised Version of the Bible, as are all the references in the diary. The actual quotation reads: 'For I know that in me (that is in my flesh) dwelleth no good thing: for to will is present with me; but how to perform that which is good I find not.' John Young appears to quote from memory here, and his memory lets him down, as in instances below. An asterisk against a Biblical reference in the text below indicates an imperfect rendering of the original.

The nature of Religion

What a contrast between bodily and spiritual disease; one bodily disorder passes through the progressive stages which terminate in dissolution. The patient becomes more acutely alive to the torture and harrowing suspense; whilst the most melancholy feature of a morbid soul is that spiritual death and spiritual insensibility retrograde [*sic*] or advance together. The maintenance of life does not more depend on the constant and regular circulation of the blood, than the health of the soul on the plenteous and continuous supplies of the Spirit of God. As the stagnant and exhausted blood receives renovation and vitality from its exposure to the atmosphere in the lungs, so the soul is daily renewed and invigorated in the genial atmosphere of Heaven; and as the blood in its periodical return to the lungs throws off those impurities which it has gathered on its revolution through the system, so the soul in its constant approach to God throws off those stains on its fair and lovely image, which attach themselves to its surface on its passage through the world, just as the breath disappears from the polished mirror by the warmth of the surrounding air. The intense Holiness of God must scorch up and destroy every thing that is repulsive and antagonist [*sic*] to its nature. There is no such thing as two substances having no affinity for each other, but rather being mutually repulsive, yet remaining in undisturbed and harmonious contact unless forcibly bound by superior pressure; neither can sin and holiness reign in one soul at the same instant.

No figure, no metaphor, could be employed to express too powerfully the opposing nature of these qualities. Pleasure and pain, light and darkness, are less distinct. Do I want to dwell in light? 'To walk in the light as he is in the light, that the blood of Jesus Christ may cleanse me from all unrighteousness?' [I John 1:7*]. What should hinder but that folly which is 'bound up in my heart?' Have I any doubt as to the certainty of my admission into the family of God? It may now for ever be resolved. He, the Lord, is anxious that I may be brought to 'know that the Son of God has come, and that he has given me understanding, that I may know him that is true, and that I am in him that is true, even in his Son Jesus Christ' [I John 5:20*].

O that from this moment I might renounce all ungodliness and worldly lusts, and live soberly and righteously in this present evil world, looking for that blessed hope, and the glorious appearing of the Great God, our Saviour Jesus Christ.

Lord I cry to thee 'I am thine, save me, for I have sought thy precepts.' [Psalm 119:94].

Christian experience

Among other symptoms which give satisfaction to my mind I feel more pleasure in prayer, greater delight in the assembly of the church, less of weariness and irksomeness in the reading of the scriptures. As I give diligence to these, life becomes sweeter and peace steals over my frame.

April 20th, 1842.

Last night I had a refreshing time at my Class.[4] My soul was drawn out in stronger desire and I cried to God in earnest – *in earnest* – 'O then is the time of joy, of mercy, of love' [Jude 2 etc].

We 'love him because he first loved us,' [I John 4:19] and when his Spirit takes the things of Christ and shows them unto us, when we see that glorious love which is commended unto us, 'in that whilst we were *yet sinners* Christ died for us,'

[Romans 5:8] there is kindled in my soul a flame of ardent gratitude, which irresistibly impels me to cry 'Thanks be unto God for his unspeakable gift.' [II Cor. 9:15].

Revelation declares *'If any man* love not the Lord Jesus Christ let him be anathema, Maranatha' [I Cor. 16:22].

Yes, let them be accursed – my soul acquiesces in the righteousness of that doom. Nay, there are times when, taking deeper and broader views of man's guiltiness, I wonder at that longsuffering and forbearance, which stays in its descent the arm of God which I seem to feel ought at once to crush the sinner.

4. John Wesley introduced the system of dividing up the members of each Methodist society into classes which met weekly under their leaders for spiritual fellowship and mutual discipline. The class meeting was in fact the basic cell of the Methodist system of organisation.

Ashamed of Christ

'Whosoever shall be ashamed of me, and of my words' – [Mark 8:38]. Ashamed of the Son of God – Ashamed of the light and loveliness of nature, ashamed of the fragrant rose, or the meek and drooping lily. Ashamed of those Heavens which declare the wisdom of Goodness of their Creator – Yes I have been ashamed of Christ. The fear of ridicule, the smile of contempt from a fellow worm, and I have disowned in silence the *Son of God.* Have I now attained that strength of grace which leads me at all times to make mention of his righteousness 'and of his only?' The Lord save me from the fear of man. It is a low, base, dastardly emotion unworthy a noble and elevated soul. *In this also* I recognise my want of that 'Holiness without which no man shall see the Lord' [Hebrews 12:14].

Commonplace Book

April 20th, 1842.

I have long felt the need of a commonplace book in which I could register those ideas, original or drawn from reading, and observations which interest the mind but often elude its memory when most wishful to recall their images. How often, when I have sat down to write on a subject, facts and ideas illustrative of its principles have occurred to the mind that had occupied its attention previously, but now, owing to the want of habit of association, or of reviewing, or of writing at the time in such a book as this, those ideas are indistinct and confused, and the facts, if used at all, it is with a painful fear lest they should prove incorrect in some of their details. Perhaps, indeed, a great mass of knowledge which has passed through the mind, and might now have proved a powerful auxilliary and a mighty weapon to the intellect in its labours, is now not touched. It has faded into such dim perspective that the utmost efforts of the memory serve but to render the looming blank more painfully and tortuously confused.

I sometimes think that if all that I have thought and known were now substantially present in the mind I should vainly fancy myself an intellectual giant; but again I recalled that when I have glanced over the surface of the universe, when the mind has thrown itself on the vast ocean of knowledge, and brooded over its infinite and seemingly ever-extending expanse, I remember it is at such times that the mind feels most humbled, and shrinks in its own estimation to the most atomic minuteness, and consequent insignificancy.

Literary Diary

I propose to use it to all intents and purposes as a sort of *literary diary.* To note down in the order of time all that I may read that appears worthy of retention, especially to keep an exact account of any book I may read, and thus I shall gradually accumulate an interesting store, from which at a future date I may draw *material* for successful labour, a pleasing review. 'The diligent hand maketh rich' [Proverbs 10:4*] is pre-eminently true of literary labour.

Church Journal

Independent of this Book I have thought of a *'Journal of Religious Affairs,'* having special reference to the history and circumstances connected with the church to which I am united.[5]

How useful might this prove at another time, in reviving old impressions, and giving *certainty* to opinion and recollection. How useful in the discussion of questions of doctrine and discipline. Things which will ever be mooted, long as humanity exists. Reference to authority will generally settle any disputed fact in the history of things of general interest, but in the little minutiae connected with one church, the interest of which is necessarily local and limited, it is only by the individual recollection of those who have been associated with it in its progress, that any point can be ascertained. My intention is simply to aid myself in life, to cultivate the habit of attention, at the same time not knowing how useful such reminiscences may prove in some of the strange and unexpected vicissitudes of this changing scene.

5. On the Wesleyan Methodist Association see the introduction pp. xv-xvi, xx-xxii, and Appendix II below.

Philadelphia

April 25th, 1842.

Yesterday, I visited Philadelphia† having been invited by Mr. Harrison† of Bunker's Hill†. Father[6] preached in the morning from 'The opening of a door of utterance' [Colossians 4:3]. A Lovefeast[7] was held in the afternoon. Mr. Pattison preached at night. The Missionary Services.

I went in company with Mr. Forster† and Mr. Longstaff†, two faithful pious men of our church. Half way we stopped under the canopy of heaven, and poured out our souls in fervent prayer for God's blessing on the services of the day.

6. On Thomas Brown Young see the introduction pp. xiii-xvii above.

7. Lovefeasts were symbolic religious meals much practised by all Methodist groups, in the eighteenth and early nineteenth centuries in particular, Water (drunk from large two-handled cups) and food (biscuits or cake) were shared by the congregation, and the meal was the occasion for prayer, hymns and testimony. Though not a sacrament, it is hard to believe that the love-feast did not develop some sacramental significance in the minds of many Methodists. See Frank Baker, *Methodism and the Love Feast,* (1957).

Indulgence in profuse diet, supper etc.

I did not feel so much at those services as I expected. How is this? I think the cause to be heaviness and sluggishness of body, arising from having indulged in late reading last week to a greater extent than usual; and further from having overloaded my stomach the last evening after the exhaustion and fatigue of a late Saturday night.

I am constantly wishing and resolving to pay more attention to regularity in diet, sleep, exercise, &c. and just as constantly reproaching myself for instability. Am I never to grow wiser by experience? I have, I comfort myself, improved greatly in these points, but I am still far from possessing that command over myself, and that decision and resolution, which might enable me to withstand the insidious influence of sensual propensities.

I manage well at every meal but supper, as this is the only period when I can partake in comfort and quietude. It is also the hour of social relaxation after the anxiety and toil of the day. There is therefore a great temptation to exceed the bounds of prudent temperance, the result of which is a heaviness and dulness in the place of that cheerful alacrity with which we ought to rise in the morning. I also in general find supper to be very cheering and exhilarating to the mind, enabling me to sit down and read or study with more buoyancy and wakeful attention.

Newspaper Reading – Its effect on the mind

Reading the London papers every day, I have long felt it possible to let the mind too eagerly seek stimulus and amusement from these sources. This I have guarded against, and can now read as usual without feeling the tone of my mind disqualified for more serious and sober study. It is I think absolutely necessary in order to keep up with the spirit of the age to read its embodiment in the press. I know there are some who fancy it *sinful* to give any ordinary share of attention to newspapers.

It may have an injurious effect on the spirituality of some weak or peculiarly-constituted minds, but in moderate degree, not to beget a political mania and induce such a morbid state as to lead a man to the neglect of his ordinary duties, the reading of the newspaper is essential to that growth with the progress and information of the age, which every man pretending to education and intelligence ought to possess.

If a man in his eagerness for news shortens his prayers, and forgets his bible at the beginning of the day, it will then certainly act on his frame of mind most injuriously, but it springs not from any natural bad effect of the newspaper but from suffering it to occupy the place and exclude the attention which was primarily due to those other subjects.

Class meeting: no sympathy for sinners

April 27th.

Last night we had in our little assembly a most blessed influence. I did not feel much at first, and it was also late when I arrived, but we found the reality of the importance of the command to continue in prayer. Slowly and surely, whilst we cried to God, our hearts melted, we bowed to the sceptre of Jesus and found that he waiteth to be gracious [Is. 30:18*].

Our meeting continued to a later hour. Brother Forster† led the class. Mr. Wolstenholme,† the superintendent of our Circuit, visited us. Two or three souls were encouraged to trust in Christ. Blessed be God.

It is a lamentable feature in my Christian experience, that I feel *so little* for that world which lieth in the arms of the wicked one.

I know that the world is estranged from God, and under his curse. I profess myself to be saved by the mercy of God from that ruin. O how is it I care *so little* for my fellow men? Did I rightly estimate the goodness of God in my own salvation, surely I should not be so indifferent to that of others?

The Lord search my heart – discover to me, in the light of his truth and spirit, what it is that leads to this apathy; and thus I shall be humbled for past negligence and pray for such an abiding sense of the responsibility involved in the Christian character as shall lead me at every opportunity to beseech sinners to be reconciled to God.

May 6th, 1842.

On Tuesday I was again at Class and I must say that I cannot remember any period within the last two or three years, when I have been more the subject of subdued and hallowed feeling. O for more firmness of purpose, and decision of character.

Depression of mind &c.

At night, after coming home I felt faint, and ate heartily; feeling no disposition to sleep I sat reading till 2 o'clock.

In the morning I rose dull and inanimate, and went forth to business with scarce a feeling of gratitude to God for his mercies, or prayers for his guidance and presence during the day. Not to mention that, by sitting up so late, when I went to bed I could hardly mumble a few words of prayer to satisfy conscience.

The result of this was that I could not read the scriptures with pleasure, neither enter into communion with God in prayer, and throughout the day my mind was unhinged, and I could not settle to calm thought or serious study.

I felt glad to seize a newspaper, or some book of light reading, to dissipate *ennui.* It were well if this continued no longer than one day; on the contrary I am affected and deranged generally during the whole week. Such fits are of periodical occurrence. The seasons are not more regular in their return than these periods of alternate depression and elevation. At such times the body is incapable of any active exertion. Every thing is wearisome and fatiguing; and the mind is dull, heavy and stupid; everything is insipid – as if some dense cloud had set in upon the mind, and involved its faculties in a palsied darkness.

What time is lost on such occasions, when, incapable of application, the only desire felt is to get easily through the necessary occupations of the day, devoting the rest to a monotonous idleness.

It is misery. Deprived of the buoyant spirit of healthful enjoyment, that which Dr. Andrew Combe[8] beautifully describes to be 'the joyous consciousness of existence,' life is bereft of all its delightful pleasures, and becomes literally a *burden.*

It is not surprising, this having been the painful experience of months and years of suffering regret, that I should anxiously labour to ascertain the cause, in order to successfully anticipate the recurrence of such disagreeable feelings. Indigestion is the friend who thus roughly nags my happiness. Happily in me it is not confirmed; a little care has hitherto proved omnipotent to deliver me from its fangs. My occupation is sedentary, and though not braced by exposure to the air, I yet have the disposition to indulge in eating too freely.

I am resolved to be more watchful; to shun the road which, once entered into, almost cert. ends in misery. I am persuaded that nothing but the permanent sense of the presence of God, and strong conviction of my responsibility for the fruit of every moment, can keep me from indulgence.

May God help me! For Christ's sake.

8. Dr Andrew Combe (1797 – 1847), surgeon, physiologist, phrenologist, and author of popular treatises on health, including *The Principles of Physiology applied to the preservation of Health and to the improvement of physical and mental education* (1834); *The Physiology of Digestion* (1836); and *Phrenology* (1846).

Ayre's Quay Sabbath School

Saturday, May 21.

On Monday 16th, I attended Sabbath School tea party, Ayres Quary,† and addressed the Meeting extempore. Very agreeable season – returned at 8 o'clock to a Lovefeast in Brougham St. Chapel.† On Tuesday visited Mr. Backhouse's† Garden and then the Class. We had a precious time, I felt powerfully. Oh that it may continue!

Love

May 26th

What is it to feel the emotion of love. It is indescribable. It is oppressive. It is soul crushing. It is an intense sensation, before which all other crouch in vast disparity. It seems to gradually coil around the heart, and imbed it in a lambent flame, ever glowing, withering, and dissipating all minor sensations. We gaze on the object of our love, until it fills the eye, the brain, the heart. As a German writer has observed, the history of the world turns on the conjugation of the verb Amo, Love. To love, and to be loved, is indeed the *sum of life* ['height of bliss' *crossed out*]. Love unreciprocal is hell, is the demon of despair rioting in the overthrow of the most sacred of human feelings. To love with ardour, to experience that ardent devotion to the object enthroned in the affections, which would lead us to sacrifice life itself to secure its happiness, and still to witness a cold eye, no smile to thaw the chillness of the heart, is like the shivering damp of man's last home to the warm and cheerful buoyancy of youth.

First Sermon – and Preaching

May 29th 1842.

Threw myself on the sofa last night and slept till dawn of day. Staggered to bed, and rose about ½ past 8 o'clock, weary and jaded. My Father said, 'You must take Monkwearmouth† this night, there is no one at liberty.'[9] I replied 'I can't.' He said 'You must begin and this is a favourable opportunity; never mind preparation, go and exhort sinners to flee from the wrath to come.' [Matt. 3:7]. I considered, and resolved to go, though I felt little confidence in my resolution.

In company with a young man, John Moffitt,† I went, and spoke 40 minutes from the 32nd verse of the 2nd of Joel, first clause.[10]

I stood up in expectation of God's blessing. I felt myself much fettered and confined. A want of confidence caused me to feel as though I had but faint glimpses of ideas. I am deeply impressed with the necessity of preparation. It is possible to *speak* extempore; but to speak with effect must require the concentration of all the energies of the mind. Instead of painfully racking the mind for ideas, the attention ought to be directed to the state and feelings of the auditory. *Shall I preach, or not?* is the question which has agitated my mind several years. In the consequence of health, business situation, and especially a feeling of incompetency to discharge its duties, I have hitherto refrained. I am now constantly urged by friends and members of the church, and, in reply to all my difficulties alleged, I am told *to try.* God help me, I am in a strait. I dread the responsibility of the office. I fear lest I should, even if able to go on at the first, grow weary in well doing. And then Business presses on, and occupies my attention. Then I am told 'God requires us to do simply what we can.'

I have thought of delaying another year, but when I think, I know not that I shall not be more favourably situated then than now; it [is] therefore perhaps fear, or slothfulness; again if I throw myself into the work, I shall be under a necessity to pay attention to study, in fact it may act as a stimulus to the mind. I have felt at other times its energies rise superior to the occasion, and in this cast 'necessity' may oblige me to live by rule, to live all the hours and days of life to purpose, and thus the end will be blessed. I mourn especially that I cannot feel for the sinful state of the world, as a Christian ought to feel. If I engage in this work, it is with a profound conviction that the Gospel is the Salvation of Man. I desire above all things that I may be instrumental in some measure in diffusing a knowledge of its truth.

I should like to give myself in Spirit and soul and body to the interests of the church, but oh! I feel a dread lest my desires should prove evanescent, the transient caprice of a moment, to be forgotten in disgraceful indifference. May God keep me. It is only in Him that I find strength. Trials new and peculiar I may expect. Temptations more forcible and dangerous, yet God is the strength of my heart, what shall I fear? 'I am thine, save me.' [Psalm 119:94]. Here I record my prayer.

9. T.B. Young meant that John must lead worship and preach at a service of the Monkwearmouth Wesleyan Methodist Association, as no other preacher was available.
10. 'And it shall come to pass that whosoever shall call on the name of the Lord shall be delivered.'

Sister's voyage

On Thursday last, May 26th 1842, Ophelia [J.Y.'s sister] and Misses Mary Ann & Sarah Harrison† embarked for London and sailed at 5 o'clock in the Brig Princes of Wales, Capt. Welch, belonging to Mr. White.† Misses Harrisons came down on Tuesday, but in consequence of want of water and swell on the bar they did not sail till Thursday.

Joseph Barker's Peace notions

Joseph Barker's† Lectures on 'War antiscriptural and unreasonable' were delivered on Monday May 30th and June 1st in Brougham St.† on the Monday and S[outh] Durham St. Tab[ernacle] † June 1st. I heard part of the 2nd lecture. At the close questions were asked by Chapman and Williams [? James Williams†].

I have also read two tracts which he has published to unfold his views. I am strongly inclined to think that many of his arguments are very superficial, and sophistical.

His views appear to be carried to most unjustifiable extremes. That all war is most criminal and unnecessary no Christian can doubt. The real point at issue is, who is the party on whom the responsibility rests? The aggressive nation, or the peaceful and unoffending people who strive to preserve their lives and liberties? The assassin, or the victim? It is sinful and unnecessary for that nation to seize on the possessions of its neighbour, or for that assassin to deprive his victim of life, but I cannot see anything in common sense, or revelation, to prevent any people or individual from exercising the right of self-defence, a principle which seems to be of the first obligation. J.B. would carry the principle of passive resistance or entire submission to an extent which would prohibit Christians from obtaining the protection of Civil law or government, either for the maintenance of property or life.

On his principles, no Christian can be a Magistrate, or vote for a Representative in Parliament, or in any way countenance and support authority. For, says he, 'Christians are prohibited in the Scripture from using constraint, violence or punishment, either to induce wicked men to obedience, or as a penalty for offences,' – and for *good men* no law is necessary.

This fancied logic, this conclusive reasoning, all rests upon the hypothesis that the Scriptures do not allow Christians to countenance and support social order by the institution of law and authority to enforce regularity and obedience.

The pivot on which this whole system rests is simply the words of Christ, *'Resist not evil'* [Matt. 5:39]. Laying this as the foundation stone he rears upon it a fabric which is to overturn the ideas and convictions which are the growth of thousands of years. To this every other passage and example is twisted and distorted, that it may agree with his fancied interpretation of the Sermon on the Mount.

I purpose to examine this subject and when I have more leisure to write down my views. There can be no doubt but the maintenance of such doctrines amounts to *Sedition,* and *Treason.*

First Written Sermon

June 14, 1842.

Last week, and the previous one, I have been trying to live nearer God in the exercise of prayer and self examination. I have composed a sermon on 'And ye will not come unto me, that ye might have life' [John 5:40]. Thank God for spiritual influences. I may call this my *first sermon,* as it is the first I have fairly written out. After the toil of thought, and perplexity of composition what a pleasure it gives to the mind when having overcome difficulties, and put the finishing stroke to the subject, we gaze on *that* which we feel to be part of ours inasmuch as it is of our own creation. I feel encouraged, and truly thankful.

Great God! give unto thy disciple meekness and wisdom [cf James 3:13] – If thou givest talent and ability, graciously vouchsafe grace to preserve me from temptation, and guide one in all the paths of youth and inexperience. Impress my mind with the importance of constantly directing my attention to Jesus, and the Atonement. May I never forget that I am as nothing and vanity, for every good and perfect gift cometh down from the Father of lights with whom there is no variableness neither shadow of turning [James 1:17]. Lead me to the Rock that is higher than I [Psalm 61:2] Amen.

Sermon Composed

June 28th, 1842.

I have just finished a sermon on *'Decision a necessary element of Character.'* I have not enjoyed that health these last few days which I in general possess. I have not yet fallen into the habit of rising at 5 o'clock. My time is about ¼ to 7, and I retire about 12 or 1 o'clock.

Proposed as a Local Preacher

On Wednesday last my leader Mr G. Longstaff† proposed me at the Leaders' meeting.[11] It was agreed to. On Monday at the Quarterly Meeting I was received along [with] 6 others, four from South Shields, 1 (John Moffat†) in the town, and 1 from the county.

11. The 'Leaders' Meeting' was the quarterly meeting of leaders of the various classes into which the members of Methodist societies were divided. It acted *inter al.* as the disciplinary court of each Methodist society. The Quarterly Meeting referred to is that of the circuit ministers and lay representatives from each Methodist society within the circuit. See Appendix II.

Misses Naylor

July 26th 1842.

Thank God for unspeakable mercies!!! Amen!!!

On Sunday the 17th Father preached in Hull, and ret[d] on the Tuesday. Monday June 11th [recte July] Miss Eliz[th] and Miss Maryann Naylor arrived on a visit from London. On Tuesday the 19th they came down from Tunstall,† where they had been stopping with Mr. White,† to our house expecting to get to sea, but owing to want of water and swell on the bar, they did not sail till yesterday the 25th at 3 o'clock in the morning in the brig Prince Albert, Capt. Barry. I accompanied them out to the river. I have been very much pleased with their conversation, manners, and piety, especially with Miss Mary Ann in whom I confess I feel a particular interest, more so than any young female I ever had the pleasure of knowing. God preserve and guide them. Can I analyse my feelings, or dare I? I declare I feel a vacuity of heart, and find my mind overturned, and can think only of one subject, 'Guide me with thy counsel' [Psalm 73:24].

Oh! I am happy to think that I can appeal to God on the purity and sincerity of my heart. I come to thee!!! 'I am thine save me!' I am weary of the world. Here is no peace. Here is no rest. 'O let me catch a smile from thee, and drop into eternity.'[12]

12. The final couplet of a six-line verse, beginning 'In age and feebleness extreme', composed by Charles Wesley on his death-bed and dictated to his wife, who copied it into her hymn-book. The correct reading is 'O could I catch one smile from Thee, and drop into eternity'.

Sermon completed

On July 15th I finished another sermon, the subject 'And beside this give all diligence, add to your faith virtue &c.' II Peter 1 ch. 5.6.7 vv.

Oh what shall be my fate here, and beyond the valley of death? The soul is crowded with fancies, tossed by hope and fear.

My mind is going forth in speculative prognostications, and such like mazes of imaginary ratiocination. It is well the future is dark, that the credulity of the mind may seize on some ray of hope, to give to its dark presages something of consolation.

Preached at Ballast Hills

August 4th, 1842

For about a fortnight my habits have been broken up, and my time invaded by business. I have had a press of business and much anxiety. O that I could learn to cast my care on him that careth for me [I Peter 5:7].

On Sunday evening I preached at the Ballast Hills [i.e. Ayres Quay†] at 6 o'clock p.m. from V John 40 v. I felt by no means so much of fear as I anticipated. I endeavoured to prepare my mind as much as possible. In order to [achieve] that I went down on to the sands, and recited my sermon over once or twice. I also wrote down the succession of heads and laid it on the pulpit for reference. I did not need to look more than once, but the knowledge that it was at hand materially sustained my confidence.

I felt softened towards the close and the tears fell from my eyes as I hounded sinners to Jesus, the fountain of life, and reproached them for their indifference to his love.

May God help me. This was not an appointment of my own but taken up at the request of Mr. Wolstenholme.†

Father goes to the Assembly

On Tuesday July 26th father went as delegate to the Annual Assembly of the Association, convened at Rochdale.[13]

13. The Wesleyan Association chose to call its annual gathering an Assembly rather than a Conference, the old Wesleyan term, in order to emphasise its different character. Whereas the Wesleyan Conference was clerical, authoritative, and secretive, the W.M.A. Assembly was intended to be none of these – laymen such as T.B. Young could be freely elected to it, its meetings were deliberative not legislative, and the public could attend. Rochdale, where the 1842 Assembly took place, was a stronghold of the Association. T.B. Young was a representative at the Assembly 1837 – 1846, and again in 1849 and 1851. See *WMA Minutes* for those years.

Mr Reed's visit

Mr Wm Reed† arrived this day from Darlington (Aug 4) bringing with him Mrs Reed, the late Miss Gunstone of Hurworth, to whom he was married this morning in Darlington at the Independent Chapel.[14]

He is invited, and appointed to stay another year in the Rochdale Circuit.

Aug. 9th

On Sunday W. Reed preached in the morning at Brougham St.† from the first clause of the 8th v. of the IV ch. of Luke, and in the evening at South D. St.† from the parable of Lazarus and the rich man [Luke 16: 19–31]. Mr. Wolstenholme preached his last sermon at night in Brougham St. He has left this morning for the South.[15] Mr & Mrs Reed left yesterday morning by the steamer for Stockton. The boat having been engaged by the singers of South D. St. Tab. they embraced the opportunity. The same day the singers of the Brougham St. Tab. went to Newcastle by steamer.

14. The Independent (i.e. Congregational) chapel in Darlington was built in 1810, though the cause was much older, and enlarged in 1824. Since the Dissenters' Marriage Act of 1836 marriages could be solemnised in licensed nonconformist chapels.
15. Woolstenholme's next circuit on leaving Sunderland was in Liverpool.

Preached at Monkwearmouth

August 16th

On Sunday morning I heard Mr Paterson for the last time. Text "I change not; therefore ye sons of Jacob are not consumed –" [Malachi 3:16].

I spent the afternoon in study and in the evening preached at Monkwearmouth. Text II Peter I ch. 5.6.7. vv. I was much encouraged and felt the presence of God inspiring greater confidence. I feel that I need every day to confess my sins, and confide in Him who is faithful and just to forgive my sins, and to cleanse from all unrighteousness [I John 1:9].

Preached at Southwick

Aug. 25.

On Sunday last I preached at Southwick,† at 6 o'clock from Eccles. XI 4 v. *'He that observeth'* &c.

During the previous week my mind was much dissipated – and I neglected preparation, until the two last days. I went without the spirit of prayer, without piety. Is it therefore surprising that it proved hard labour and discouraging to the mind? True there were few there, and no zeal amongst them, but still had I wrestled in prayer the word might have proved refreshing. The Lord make me watchful. I am only safe when I embrace thy cross. May I cling to Christ, – Believe in Christ, – Love Christ, that my soul may be the habitation of God through the Spirit.

Duke of Cambridge

Yesterday the Duke of Cambridge[16] and the Marquess of Londonderry[17] visited and dined here.

16. Adolphus Frederick (1774 – 1850), seventh son of George III, Duke of Cambridge from 1801. This visit to Sunderland was made when he was a guest of the Marquess of Londonderry at Wynyard Hall on the occasion of the coming-of-age celebrations of Lord Seaham, the Marquess' eldest son. The Duke spent two weeks in the north east, commencing Monday 22nd August 1842. On Wednesday 24 August he visited Lord Londonderry's colliery villages at Rainton† and Penshaw†, where an enormous dinner for pitmen was held, and then travelled to Sunderland for dinner at the Exchange† Rooms (on High Street), arriving there three hours late, at 9 p.m. Other guests included the Duke of Rutland, the Marquess and Marchioness of Exeter, and the Marquess of Blandford. A ball at the Athenaeum† followed at about midnight, continuing 'to an advanced hour': Richardson v, 397–400. The Sunderland Corporation presented an address welcoming the Duke "to our maritime and populous borough." Sund Corp. Mins. (i) 269–270, Tyne and Wear Archives.
17. Charles William Vane Stewart (1778 – 1854), Lord Stewart from 1814, third Marquess of Londonderry from 1822, following the suicide of his half-brother Lord Castlereagh, the second marquess. Through his marriage to Frances Anne Vane-Tempest in 1819 he acquired extensive estates and coal mines in County Durham. In 1828 he founded Seaham Harbour† for the export of his coals, having purchased the Seaham Hall estates in 1821: see R.W. Sturgess, *Aristocrat in Business,* (1975).

A. Keene's first Sermon

Sept. 7th 1842.

On Sabbath Aug. 20. Revd. Aquila Keene† preached for the first time in South D. St. Tab^{n}. [on] "created in Christ Jesus unto good works" [Ephes. 2:10] in the morning, and the Prodigal Son in the evening – good impression. On Sabbath 4th Sept. Mr Peters† at the Brougham St. Tab.† The gospel preached to the poor in the morning and in the evening *'This do in remembrance of me'* [Luke 22:19].

I have received the Revivalist[18] for September in which there appears a little piece of mine entitled *"This moment."*

18. I have been unable to trace this magazine.

Instability of Character

My mind has been sadly disorganised and deranged lately. I have in an evil moment suffered the helm of self-government to slide from my grasp, and suffered ship-wreck on the sands of sloth, and folly. There has been no serious and diligent application to study – mere trifling – and where I might have accomplished something valuable time has been frittered away in idle excitement to dissipate stupidity and ennui. How is this? Whence arise the influences which repeatedly drag my mind from a state of peace, order, and activity down to a miserable uneasiness?

Have I been diligent in reading the word of God? No! In my closet? No! In shunning idle conversation and levity? No! In refraining from the perusal of books and newspapers calculated to give a morbid excitement to the soul? To all these I plead guilty in thy sight, O God. I have sinned, what can I now say, I have sinned.

I am ashamed of my weakness and childishness, once crying *'Thou art mine'* and at another time, exclaiming, 'Where art Thou?'

Reflections on Unfaithfulness

O that the time past might more than suffice wherein I have done iniquity. It is thy work, God only can keep me, but I have wilfully, and deliberately sinned. I am worthy of death, but God in Christ is merciful. What did I resolve? Did I not vainly imagine immense progression in wisdom, and yet I have not yet learnt to know myself. When I have fancied myself acquiring an acquaintance with human nature from the observations of others, I have yet to learn the character of my own spirit. O for humility, meekness and self abasement. 'So teach me to number my days that I may apply my heart unto wisdom' [Psalm 90:12].

I need watchfulness to arrest the first approach of evil. In eating, in drinking – sleep – business – conversation – and above all intercourse with God.

Here is the mainspring, the magic key to the whole – with my heart holy and my soul unspotted, what should disturb my quiet? At peace with God, I shall be at peace with all.

O! I am vile – I am wicked – how true – *'the whole head is sick.'* I look to thee for help, save me.

I dare scarce think of the past, its recollection overpowers me – I gladly revert to the hopes of the future.

I am mad. I am foolish, or insane; or surely, in the face of all the verities of my position, all the obligations of my relations, I would never act so mad a part.

Eternal prince of underived and independent life, in infinite care bestow one glance of merciful consideration upon one of the most contemptible of thy creatures. I bring into thy presence no other plea than my weakness, the interposition of thy Son; for the sake of his redeeming love raise my spirit from the depths of depravity to thy spotless purity. Break the last tie which binds me to sensual gratification and let my soul rise in immortal and eternal aspirations to thy ineffable and resplendent perfections.

Preach at Deptford

Sept. 19th Monday.

Yesterday I preached at Deptford† in the morning. Text Psalm XC 12 v. "So teach us to number our days & c".

I felt very comfortable. My mind calm, and unruffled. Brothers W. Dixon† and Lillyfoot accompanied me. In the evening I attended South D. St.† Aquila Keene†, "Which of you is willing this day to consecrate, & c" [I Chronicles 29:5].

In the afternoon I read in the house.

My experience in the pulpit confirms much that I had previously imagined to be the sensations of the mind.

John Moffat's departure

Sept. 22nd

I this day bade farewell to J. Moffat.† He expects to sail in the afternoon for the West Indies – or rather to Demerara. His deportment has endeared him to my heart. I am reminded of the dramatic character of life. I feel that I must remember that the most enduring association on earth is but transitory – it passes away, and thus my attention may be directed to that everlasting rest where the career of friendship shall be contemporary with eternity.

J.M. came on to our plan to preach by note as No. 28 this quarter, but will be left off the next plan. He has for some time past kept a school, but, not succeeding according to expectation, he, principally I fancy at my own persuasion has gone to sea. For this there are many and sufficient reasons which cannot find a place here.

J.M. is a young man who has had innumerable trials and many disadvantages to contend with.

Sept. 28th 1842.

On Sabbath morning I heard Mr T.B.Y. [Thomas Brown Young, John's father] from "follow on to know the Lord" [Hosea 6:3]. In the evening I heard Mr Moffat – Missionary from Africa.[19]

In the afternoon got tea with Mr J.S.M. On Monday our usual quarterly meeting was held. Nothing of interest, but a motion by Mr Milner[20] that a Committee be appointed to work on Mr Clare [21] to ascertain his doctrinal opinions, and advise him respecting his abilities.

I have lost much time. The attention requisite to be given to business has been more pressing, and then the fatigue necessarily the greater; in fact it begets such lassitude and apathy that it [is] impossible to accomplish anything valuable. Thank Heaven!!! in the day when the secret thoughts of men are brought into judgement and every man gives an account of himself to God, the Righteous judge will not require an improvement of time never possessed, and opportunities never enjoyed. I want a steady flame of love to kindle and burn on the altar of my heart – a calm and collected frame of mind, removed from that levity of which I may truthfully complain.

I am naturally of a sanguine temperament though perhaps chastened and modified by a dash of the *melancholies* of a self.

19. Robert Moffat, (1795–1883), pioneer missionary in S. Africa, on leave in England 1839–43.
20. Probably the same Milner that John Young talked with at South Hylton after preaching there, p. 134 below.
21. Probably the Mr Clare, 'our missionary', mentioned in the entry p. 34 below. Clare was succeeded by Edward [recte Edmund] Heywood†.

First sermons at Philadelphia

Monday Oct. 10th

Yesterday, I preached at Philadelphia.† Text 12v. XC Ps. I left home at 25m to 12 and reached Mr. Harrison's† at 1 o'clock just in time for dinner. Owing to the unusual walk, and fatigue from confinement, and want of rest, I felt very unwell and could eat little. Mr. Harrison pressed, and urged me to eat most perseveringly. Surely this is an abuse of hospitality. Kindness in excess becomes unkindness. Mrs H. very kindly made me a cup of coffee, which refreshed me considerably. One and all they are a nice family. I felt rather nervous but felt encouraged as I proceeded. I got through without any very great blunders, and felt exceedingly thankful. I did not get *loose,* so to speak.

I want a deep impression of the value of souls, that I may be directed in all my thoughts to aim at their salvation as the great object of my labours. Without this my pulpit preparations are weak, and spiritless. With this I shall feel the ardour and sincerity which will inspire me with zeal and affection and enable me to discharge the duties of my office with comfort to myself and satisfaction to the church.

The walk home in the dark was dreary and cheerless; this is one of the difficulties or inconveniences incidental to my duty. If I have really at heart the interests of God's cause this will not daunt me – God give unto me a heart steady of purpose, and resolute in heart in the paths of duty.

My need of piety

I want regular systematic habits of study, if not in business, and still more I need system in my religious exercises. How few, and barren, they are! What dryness of soul when at a throne of grace. Where that melting heart, that fervent struggling for divine influence, that self-examination, that diligent and serious perusal of the holy scriptures in humble expectations of divine assistance. It is here I come short. Did I there obtain the baptism of the spirit then should my life flow in a calm and even current, labour would prove a pleasure, and duty a consolation. Help! and redeem me for thy mercies sake, O God of my salvation!

Ballast Hills, Monkwearmouth

Nov. 14th 1842.

Nov. 6th I preached at Monkwearmouth,† and on Sunday 13 at Ballast Hills.† At MW. from John V. 40 and at B.H. II Peter I ch. 5.6.7. verses.

Repeating sermons

When I first commenced preaching I thought I should make a point of preaching a new sermon at every appointment. This I fancied would give me experience in the composition of sermons, and secure a stock against any emergency which might arise from business or what other cause might deprive me of time. When I stand up to preach I am not conscious of preparation, I become nervous and confused. Indeed unaccustomed as I am to speak in the Sanctuary, uninitiated into its habits, and acquirements, without a prior arrangement I cannot speak with confidence or edification. Ay and that arrangement must be written on the mind not merely in its outlines, but in all its particulars down even to the very identical phraseology of the original. What labour! What a task! Yes, it is a consumer of time – and nothing but a more extensive discipline of the mind, enjoined with greater experience in the pulpit will remove the burden.

I dare not stand forth without such a preparation, and therefore I occupy in its acquisition time sufficient to write a new sermon. In addition to this, and flowing from this, when delivering a new sermon there is so great an effort necessary to call distinctly to recollection the succession of language that it withdraws the attention of the mind from the ideas themselves and those impressions which it is so necessary to cultivate.

These two considerations have shaken my original intention, and I shall not scruple to re-deliver the same subject in places apart from each other.

My want of Time

I have been much in the habit of complaining lately of a

want of time. Is it with or without reason? The Business of the day may be said to commence with me about ¼ to seven o'clock and to conclude at 9 or 10.

There is about 15 hours in which the mind and body is engaged in business; here is no opportunity for study without neglect of those things which ought to be accomplished. And then here are 9 hours to be consumed in sleep, supper, &c, to say nothing of relaxation and exercise.

Was ever a poor fellow so beset? Yes many. Suppose I sleep six hours, allowing 1 hour for the many little things which are to be attended to, here are two hours – two hours at the close of a long and weary day. What are they worth? After 15 hours close confinement and monotony the mind cannot be brought to serious and successful study. It needs rather something to cheer and console and revive its depressed energies; something to give a stimulus to its inanition. Let those who are ignorant of the lethargic effect of an ever-lasting routine of daily confinement tell me of the importance and value of one hour in an evening given to studious thought. Give to me the freshness of intellect which flows from the buoyant elasticity of a healthful physical organization – an organization whose powers and functions are vigorous from a conformity to those provisions of nature which impose on man the necessity of exposure, aye an active exposure, to the genial air and light of heaven.

My spirit at the close of a day's labour seems to crave social intercourse with some friendly heart. How many little sorrows and how many mutual incidents of experience in life's rough passage to communicate, to ease by benign sympathy the irritation of the chafed mind.

Destitution of friends

I have had few friends, meaning by the term not the friends of blood and connection but the youth of the same age, with the same classes of feelings, purified and ennobled into generous friendship. I have often been overcome with a feeling of solitariness – alone and unloved. What a dreary dampness it gives to the world's community. I gaze on its throng, and I see here arm locked in arm, and there the smile of reciprocal enjoyment dimpling the lips of countenance on which easy confidence appears to repose. I walk in the streets, or turn down some sunny lane, my eyes wander over the many groups that stroll slowly along each with his comrade in delightful communion of spirit, but for me there was no eye of joyous recognition, no feet lightly to trip across the path, no hand grasped with kindly feeling or voice to shout a welcome. No, though my person might brush past many whose features were known, and with whom perchance I might exchange the nod of formal acknowledgement there was nothing to gratify the forlorn and starved sensibilities of the heart, for between such association and that civility there seemed to be interposed a strangeness as unsurmountable as a mountain of granite. To be utterly unknown to all mankind would certainly be misery. Better to be known to be hated, or feared than such an estrangement. But it is the expression of esteem which we covet. Not the testimony of selfishly interested feelings, or the formalities of cold politeness, but the *homage of the heart.*

S. Hodgson & Rippon preach

Nov. 21st

On Sunday in the morning I attended S.D.St. Tab. [South Durham Street Tabernacle†] and heard S. Hodgson† from 'Thou has redeemed us to God by thy blood' [Rev. 5:9]. In the afternoon at Brougham St.† Rippon† of Shields from 'Good Master what shall I do to inherit eternal life' [Luke 10:25] – and in evening I accompanied Mr John Dixon† to Southwick.† He preached from 'Neither is their salvation in any other' &c. [Acts 4:12].

Disposition of Time and Improvement on the Sabbath

At the close of the day I frequently involuntarily ask myself what have I learnt? In what am I wiser or better than the previous day? *One thing* is much against me, and that is the late hours which I am kept on the Saturday evening.

It is generally 12 o'clock when I reach home and then I am so jaded and fatigued that am loth to retire to bed, so that I do not rise early on the Sabbath morning. To this I may add a want of previous arrangement and decision in fulfilling any prior schemes. I am apt to think, well here is a whole day, I must first read this, and then study that, and thus my time is squandered in the intervals of worship in first peeping into one book and then another, and having no opportunity to give any one thing a satisfactory consideration. I want system, and unity of purpose.

I am afraid I do not consecrate the Sabbath sufficiently to devotional purposes. I begin it without serious prayer and perusal of the scripture. True I read and pray but it is mere formality simply to ease my conscience. Were I under deeper impressions of God's love and God's mercy I should be compelled to live to his glory. I want the 'mind of christ' [I Cor. 2:16; Phil. 2:5]. I want to feel the holiness and sincerity required in those who profess to be his disciples.

If I ask myself, do I habitually and momentarily live in reference to eternal things, what shall I say? I am driven to and fro with tempests of life. Who can save but God? Unless his power is enlisted in my behalf I shall perish. I shall be in the condition of those who are 'ever learning and never able to come to the knowledge of the truth' [II Tim. 3:7].

None but God can give to me steadfastness of purpose, and decision of character.

Early rising

Nov. 24th

Those last three days I have retired to rest at 10 o'clock, and risen at 6 precisely. If I can persevere in this newly-formed habit it must prove of great value. So soon as I have performed the needful ablutions I have gone down to the pier and walked for an hour.

This has had a happy effect on my spirits and health all the day. Those three mornings it has rained, and blown half a gale, which in addition to the darkness of the season renders recreation unpleasant at an early hour. But after all, to the courageous and enterprising soul *these* are but little things. Is there not something in the wild storminess of the ocean to enkindle an emotion of romantic or at least unusual enjoyment. I sometimes delight in exposure to a storm especially if that exposure be voluntary.

Reflections on the Pier

There is pleasure to be drunk when, shivering and chattering, you watch the heaving of the water, the appearance and disappearance of its snowy ridges of foam. How pleasant to see the ships careering on the billows, their sails and ropes bending on the breeze, the whole vessel conveying to the mind an impression as though some huge monster were struggling and straining every nerve and muscle to gain the port.

I was interested in following the progress of a pilot coble with six hands and oars. She seemed to cleave the water as if conscious of superior and skilful guidance, now in an hollow, and again perched on the summit of the seas.

A vain world

And then how many seasonable reflections are the birth of that hour. Alone on the extremity of the pier you look back on the town over-hung with darkness and you think of its slumbering inhabitants, their occupations, their hopes, their destinies. Can you forget yourself or refrain from reviewing your own position and prospects – thus I have felt.

I have thought of its busy denizens each led on by some specious bauble glittering before their vision, and [which] alas, in the vast majority, [has] deluded them to the neglect of those things which really constitute happiness.

Ah! when my imagination has passed over the town I have sometimes stumbled on the graveyard. I have remembered that everyone of these poor sinners must shortly repose there. Nothing can delay Death's triumph. How mournful, and yet such is our true position. *Mine* – have I not asked myself, wherein dost thou differ?

Has not memory raised the picture of the past, the portraiture of my life and has not my heart throbbed, my whole frame shuddered, when the conviction has irresistibly fastened on my mind that I long had been identified in character with that community of the vain, and the depraved. Really what shall I do? These are my impressions, and they are to my conscience the conviction of truth. I must live another character. The diligence of every future day shall attest my sincerity.

My Illness

Thursday Jan. 5th 1843.

'How weak the thought, and vain
Of Self-deluded man.'[22]

Such was my exclamation after the perusal of the foregoing remarks.

Those very circumstances in which I seem to have delighted appear to have been the fruitful source of misery. I caught cold by my early and unaccustomed exposure on the pier and at present am but recovering from a severe illness. I was suddenly seized about 12 at night with a severe pain in the right side. I sent down to the shop and procured leeches and applied them. I thought it to be an attack of inflamation of the chest. I recovered, but [am] suffering from a dull heavy pain between the hip joints and the ribs which increased to a great fulness and soreness, extending round to the stomach. I fancied it to be a liver complaint and treated it with calomel, blistering, &c.[23] With this I was much better but still retaining some little pain I called upon Dr. Brown,† who stated it to be Muscular pains and since the application of his medicine I have been gradually recovering.

My mind was the subject of strange feelings during this affliction. How clearly I felt the vanity of the world, and the necessity of continual preparation. What inward resolves, and vows!! O that the strength of grace may keep me.

22. From no. 67 in *A Collection of Hymns for the use of the People called Methodists,* (1780), in the section entitled 'Describing Heaven'; the hymn is by Charles Wesley, and the correct reading is 'How weak the thoughts and vain, of self-deluding man'. See note 58 below.

23. Calomel is an aperient and stimulates the liver. Blistering refers to the use of some external poultice or plaster, probably of mustard, or of capsicums (peppers) – see Appendix II pp. 160–161.

Heaton's Case

Quarter Day

On Monday Dec. 26th our Quarterly meeting[24] was held

at which I attended. Mr Heaton was excluded from the Preachers' Plan because he refused to pledge himself to teach no other doctrines than those received amongst us. Mr Clare our missionary took his leave.

Increase of about 46 members. Took tea, and in the school room Mr Peters† at the Church meeting preached a superior sermon. A series of meetings were held every night and addresses delivered, excepting Wednesday night when a tea party was held in Brougham St.† School, A White† Esq. in the chair. A large company. Mr Stoney†, N[ew] Connexion, Messrs. Peters,† Keene† and Mules†, and T.B.Y. spoke.

Miss Harrison of Bunkers Hill† came down on Tuesday the 27th and stayed still Monday Jny 2nd.

24. Methodist Quarterly Meetings at that date lasted for most of the day and to hold one on Boxing Day would allow more to attend. It was not unknown for December meetings to be held on Christmas Day; such in fact was the case in 1843. The meetings were occasions for worship, fellowship and hospitality, as well as business, so that such choices of day were not as unnatural as first appears.

Preach at Houghton, Collier row

On Sunday I took Mr Heaton's appointments, at Collier row† 2 o'clock and Houghton† 6 o'clock. I rode out in the gig at 12 o'clock and came home with G. Elliott, James Thompson,† and J. Hutchison.[25] I got tea with a Mr Charleton, and supper with Mrs Matthew at Houghton.

I preached at Collier Row from John V 40. & at Houghton from II Peter 1. 5.6.7.v. I felt much better during the evening service.

25. Three W.M.A. lay preachers. John Young seems to have been quite closely associated with G. Elliott, both in preaching and in other ways, pp. 50-1, 72, 91, 150.

Visit to Newcastle. Centrifugal Railway

I went to Newcastle on Monday at 11 o'clock.[26] Dined at 2 o'clock with Mrs Muschamp.† Before dinner I walked out with Mr John M. & J. Tuer.† I saw the newsroom, and then the centrifugal railway.[27] I rode round the circle in the car.

it was a most strange sensation. Admission and ride 1/–d.

I returned at night in compy. with Mr Tuer, and children. I then went to a lovefeast we had at B.St.T. [Brougham Street Tabernacle] School.†

26. Travelling presumably on the 11 a.m. train from Monkwearmouth stations to Gateshead on the Brandling Junction Railway.†

27. I have been unable to trace any other reference to the Centrifugal Railway operating in Newcastle, or indeed to discover what it actually was. However the London *Times* 24 November 1843 reported an accident which had occurred, apparently in London at the 'exhibition' of the Centrifugal Railway. I owe this reference to Mr Frank Manders of the Newcastle-upon-Tyne City Library.

Sunday School Committee

On Wednesday night Jany. 4th I attended the above meeting at B.St.T. This is the first meeting since they have separated the B.St. School from S.D.St. [South Durham Street]. Messrs T.B. Young, Wilson† & Coxon chosen Superintendents, also a financial, visiting, and Library Committee. Messrs John Dixon† & John Young chosen as Religious instructors. G. Elliott Librarian.

Looking over the past few weeks I am deeply humbled – but to what use are my confessions if there are not *'fruits meet for repentance'*? [Matt. 3:8]. Do I feel contrition for unfaithfulness? O God! let its truth be attested in my life. Let me not 'love in word only but in truth, and in deed' Amen [I John 3:18*].

Partnership in Business

Jany. 1843

During my illness I need hardly remark my business suffered from my absence. Mr White† repeatedly advised me to think of taking a partner and recommended J. Taft† as a suitable party. By their advice I wrote J. Taft on the 17th of Dec. 1842, and rec'd. his reply, which was judicious. I feel no desire to enter into such a compact provided I could ensure a fair prospect of Health.

Confinement such as mine must inevitably break down the strongest constitution and of what avail is life without health?

Previous to Mr J. Dixon† entering into business he proposed to me in kind terms, but none of my friends were agreeable and at that time I was much prejudiced against any such alliance. I wish ever to remember that the business of life is but the secondary object of existence, and that the primary obligation is to seek first the Kingdom of God, and all other things shall be added unto me [Matt. 6:33*].

Preach at Southwick

Monday Jany. 9th, 1843.

Yesterday being the sabbath I did not rise until ½ past 8 o'clock having retired very late the previous day. In fact Saturday night is invariably uncomfortable and late. I was much refreshed during the morning in reading God's word. Light shone on its revelations, and I drank consolation. It is always best with me when my mind delights in the simple naked statements of the Bible. How foolish ever to be straying to the productions of men for information and peace when the sublime precepts and holy truth of Scripture may be perused in all its comprehensive fulness. In the afternoon I preached at Southwick† Text II Peter 1 ch. 5.6.7. verses. I was enabled to discharge this duty with considerable pleasure.

At night I heard Mr Mules† in S.D.St. Chapel† for [sic ?from] 'Happy is this people whose God is the Lord' [Psalm 144:15].

I am another Sabbath nearer eternity, and how my time is wasting. Indisposition of body clouds and stultifies my soul. Dulness and heaviness wither my aspirations. God help me! Give vigour to my body, elation to our minds, and let their strength be devoted to thee!!

Monday Jany. 16th.

Sabbath morning I felt unwell and walked on to the seashore. The afternoon I attempted to study a little. At night I heard Mr Mules preach at Brougham St.† from 'As it is appointed unto man once to die, and after death the judgement' [Hebrews 9:27*]. In the afternoon I drank tea with A. White Esq.† How did I spend this day? Did I feel nearer to Heaven at his close? O for the mind of Jesus [I Cor. 2:16. Phil. 2:5].

Preached at Ballast Hills

Monday Jany. 23/43.

I desire to record my gratitude that 'hitherto the Lord hath helped me' [I Sam. 7:12]. On Saturday night I left business at 20m to 12, then went home and read until past 2 o'clock. I awoke at 7 and lay in 'dreamy thought' until 12 o'clock. In the afternoon I spent some time in pulpit study and then, going to the S.D. St. Tab.,† found assembled a 'General Meeting of the Schools' which I attended.

In the evening at 6 o'clock I preached at Ayres Quay† from 2nd Tim. 2nd ch. 11.12.13 verses. I had some calmness, and felt much blessed.

My health is improving by dint of care, and exercise. If I wish to impart efficiency to the mind I must train the body to healthy vigour.

Mr Heywood† of Heywood who has come on trial as a missionary preached last night at Brougham St. 'He that winneth souls is wise' [Proverbs 11:30] – youthful zeal!!! Anniversaries were preached at Southwick† yesterday. Mr. Peters† is at Whitby. Miss Anne Young[28] is very unwell.

28. John's sister. Anne appears to have lived with Andrew and Ophelia White at the time the diary was written.

Birthday

Jany. 24th 1843.

Twenty and three years have been registered in heaven since the hour at which I became one of the human family. They are gone! But their influence cannot be estimated until the day of retribution. May I live for eternity.

Death of John Moffat

On Wednesday evening the 25th of Jany., I was called out from my tea to speak to an old man in the shop. His stooping gait, and mumbling tones made me suppose him to be a pauper. It was only when he said 'Woodpecker' that my attention was aroused and when he murmured 'John Moffat† died in November' what a revulsion of feeling I experienced.

Alas, my friend, thou art gone – so young so full of hope. Thy trials apparently just surmounted by thy indomitable perseverance. The dawn of day peeping above the horizon to raise in thy ardent heart the bright visions of meridian enjoyments. Years of suffering and of poverty about to disappear. Disappointment and despair about to give place to competence and health. But thou art gone.' The film of death has shaded the eye that beamed with confidence and hope. Cold and impassive is the countenance that in time past radiated kindness and sympathy. Thou art gone – But it must be to a better world. I mourn for thee with that heart's agony with which thou wouldest have mourned for me. Painful was our separation but bright the revelations of the future – 'Let us' said I, and he responded to the expression, *'meet in heaven'*. 'Heaven is our home.' Far from my mind were any doubts of our reunion. We shall meet each other no more till we stand at the judgement seat of Christ.

Here is another link to connect one with eternity. When my eyes light upon his glorified features in the rest of the righteous, I fancy how I shall thrill with delightful rapture when we greet each other with an emotion which will not as now be inexpressible but will burst forth in thanksgiving to *'our Father the guide of our youth'* [Jeremiah 3:4*].

Memoir of J. Moffat

I have been impressed with the duty of composing a memorial of my friend for insertion in the magazine, or in such manner as may prove practicable.

I am sorry that my memory does not charge me with much of the information I gleaned in my intercourse with J. Moffat. Still I am persuaded that if God give me resolution, grace and ability I might draw up such a memoir as must prove impressive and improving in its influence.

Situated as I am at present I have not time to devote daily to this object. I shall therefore get a book, draw up an analysis, or arrangement of subjects, and under each head enter such material as I may gather, and thus by and by I shall be able to cast them into the mould of memoir.

Address of the owner of the '*Woodpecker*'.

Mr. Wm. Williams
Cheltenham Road,
Bristol.

Monday Jany. 30th 1843.

On Sabbath I rose at ½ past 7 o'clock and breakfasted on hasty pudding after which I went on to the sands. Owing to my not having left the shop until ¼ past 12 and not retiring to rest until ½ past 1 a.m. I felt sleepy during the day. I heard Mr Mules† at B. St,† in the morning, 'What went ye out into the wilderness to see' [Matt. 11:7], and in the evening 'Because judgement is not executed against an evil work speedily' &c. [Eccles. 8:11]. In the afternoon I visited my sister Miss Anne Young at Frederick Lodge.† She has been ill for some time. Messrs John† and W.† Dixon took tea with us this day, my father being present.

I feel grateful that my mind is under increasingly serious impressions. I desire to live near to a throne of grace and in the perusal of God's words. It is then I shall be safe and peace shall possess my mind. I pray thee Father of mercies graciously to give to me the aid of thy Holy Spirit that I may daily be led into an increasing and abiding communion with thee!

Mr & Mrs Good's Accident

Monday Feby 6th 1843.

On Sabbath I rose at ½ to 8 o'clock, breakfasted and went on to the sands – very stormy – the remnant of the gale of wind we had yesterday morning – sudden, and continued squalls – great damage done to the houses. Mr and Mrs Good, South D. St.,† were o'erwhelmed by the fall of a chimney through the roof and though their bed was covered by bricks and rubbish they providentially escaped unhurt. About 600 bricks and other material came through the ceiling to the amount it is stated of about 2 tons.[29]

I heard James Thompson† at Brougham St.† in the morning. Text [left blank].

29. The storm did extensive damage throughout the north east, e.g. a woman was killed in South Shields, and the whole of the Brandling Junction Railway† sheds at Brockley Whins† were swept away by the violent wind: T. Fordyce, *Local Records 1833 – 1866*, (1867), p. 174.

Mrs Nesbitt. Dixon Aunt

After dinner, I visited and prayed with Mrs Nesbitt who last week had a boy. From 2 o'clock until ½ past 3 I studied my sermon and perused an outline for pulpit use. This is my practice, it inspires confidence, and has proved a resource of value in a moment of forgetfulness. I went to Mrs Dixon's to tea, this is the first time I have been there for along period – some years. Hugh D.† invited me, I have a great esteem for cousin Hugh, and the whole family, but somehow or other there has been a lengthened coolness between us which I have often wished to overcome, and though often invited I have delayed and again delayed until I have been ashamed to go at all. I spent the time very agreeably for they are an intelligent family.

Dr Paley's pulpit

I learnt that the present pulpit in the Wesleyan Chapel at Ayre's Quay† is the very same in which *Dr. Paley*[30] used to preach at the Bishopwearmouth Church.† Just as the pulpit of the Ayre's Quay Wesleyan Association Chapel was taken from the old chapel in Number's Garth,[31] and is therefore supposed to be the same in which *John Wesley*[32] preached.

30. William Paley D.D. 1743 – 1805, rector of St. Michael's Bishopwearmouth 1795 – 1805, and also archdeacon of Carlisle from 1782. Author of several successful works, including *Principles of Moral and Political Philosophy* (1785), *Evidences of Christianity* (1794) and *Natural Theology* (1802). See *D.N.B.*, Brockie, and M.L. Clarke, *Paley : Evidences for the Man,* (1974).

31. Numbers Garth was a small close between High Street and Bishopwearmouth Pans. It is clearly shown on Rain's Eye Plan of Sunderland c. 1790. The Wesleyans built a chapel here in 1759, which served until the opening of the larger Sans Street Chapel† in 1793.

32. John Wesley (1703 – 1791), the principal founder of Methodism, visited Sunderland on over thirty occasions between 1743 and 1790, preaching often in the Numbers Garth chapel. See F.F. Bretherton, 'John Wesley's Visits to Sunderland', *Antiquities of Sunderland* 20 (1951), 129–141.

Mr Peter's Corn Law lecture

Rev Mr Peters† delivered a lecture at the Athenaeum† on Friday the 3 at 8 o'clock, on the Corn Laws,[33] to a crowded audience. It was listened to with attention, but at the conclusion a Chartist[34] moved a resolution to the effect that "the repeal of the corn laws under existing circumstances would be a positive injustice to the shopkeepers, and labouring classes". Then ensued a most dreadful confusion and uproar. The Chartist persisted in speaking, and would not suffer a reply. At length the leaguers withdrew and they were left to themselves when the gas was extinguished which put an extinguisher on their violence. Shame on men, advocates of liberty.[35]

The lecture was good. He spoke of the effects of the Corn laws – Physical, Mental and religious, Moral, Commercial. There is a combination in the town in connection with the Great Manchester League. There is evidently a great movement in public opinion.

33. Those laws, primarily the Corn Law of 1815, imposing a protective duty on foreign corn, which as a result was imported free of duty only when the price of wheat reached eighty shillings (£4) a quarter. Modifications aimed at lessening the distress caused to the poor by the high price of bread were introduced in 1828 and 1843. The Anti-Corn Law League, launched in Manchester in 1839 and led by Richard Cobden and John Bright, organised a nationwide campaign to achieve complete repeal of the Corn Laws. This campaign received much support among the urban middle classes, many of whom were dissenters. Bright was himself a Quaker and he imparted a strong religious tone to the campaign. He addressed a meeting in Sunderland 14 July 1843. The Corn Laws were repealed in 1846. At a meeting of the Sunderland Corporation in March 1843 a resolution, proposed by A.J. Moore, to petition Parliament for a complete repeal of the Corn Laws was passed by a considerable majority.

The Sunderland Anti-Corn Law Association held weekly 'soirées' at the Bridge Hotel† and at one time contemplated the production of a Sunderland Free Trade Journal. See *Newcastle Chronicle*

11 March 1843, 27 May 1843 etc. In South Shields an Anti-Corn Law lecture by Colonel T.P. Thompson was held in the Salem Chapel belonging to the Wesleyan Methodist Association, *Newcastle Chronicle* 7 Oct. 1843.

34. The Chartist Movement was more or less contemporary with, and in some senses rival to, the Anti-Corn Law League. It sought major political reforms to enact the six points of the People's Charter of 1838, which included universal male suffrage. The movement was seriously divided, and lacked the clear united purpose of the Anti-Corn Law League. Some Chartists opposed the League partly because they saw it as diverting interest away from Parliamentry reform, and partly because they feared that cheaper bread would be an excuse to depress industrial wages. The movement failed at the time (c. 1838 – 1848) but several of its demands became law in due course. Two of the most active Chartists in Sunderland were James Williams and George Binns. See Brockie pp. 267 – 272, and Patricia Storey in the *Sunderland Echo* 12 May 1981. James Williams in fact supported the Anti-Corn Law League and Free Trade. A report in the *WMA Mag.* 1840, 39–40 described the detrimental effect that Chartist excitement had had on membership in the Sunderland Circuit.

35. The *Sunderland Herald* 10 February 1843 carried a lively account of the meeting, which was well attended by an audience of working men. The trouble began at the end of the lecture when a '"whole hog" Chartist' named Connell Murray tried to put questions to the speaker. When it was made clear that this would not be allowed he and some 'brother O'Connorites' made a great row and endeavoured to put a resolution. At this point Mr James Williams 'made his way to the platform, an angry altercation ensued between him and the "whole hog" fraternity. Ultimately the gas lights were extinguished, and this also extinguished the uproar of the Chartists, who went away very sure they had not had all their own way'. The role played by Williams in this is a revealing one. (I am grateful to Mr John Pearson for drawing my attention to this reference.)

The Revd John Peters gave another lecture in the Athenaeum† on 7 April in favour of total and immediate repeal of the Corn Laws, which is not mentioned in J.Y.'s diary, and the following Tuesday there was another meeting at the Athenaeum, not addressed by Peters, at which the O'Connor Chartists (the followers of Fergus O'Connor who believed in the use of physical force to gain their ends) again tried to gain a hearing, apparently without success. *Sunderland Herald* 14 April 1843.

Newsroom – influence on minds

On Thursday last a News Room called the Borough News Room was opened in the room above my shop.[36] Subscription 10/– per annum, I have joined. It will be peculiarly convenient for me for I can step up first thing in the morning for half an hour, for I must not be seen there in the day. I am in the habit of paying one halfpenny per day for the Gazette so that I shall save 3/– per year and have access to many papers viz. Times, Sun, Gazette (Shipping), Dispatch, Examiner, Britannia's Manchester and Leeds papers, and all the local papers &c. Dublin University, Tait's &c Magazines.[37] It must be a great advantage to keep pace with the intelligence of the day but there is a danger lest a young man in any situation should be led to neglect business, lest the mind should become unduly interested and excited. I must strive to rise above these influences, and what can be so effectual to keep a right balance as to labour for communion with God, the witness of the Spirit? – a tender conscience, then I shall be kept in safety, for a monitor within will keep watch over the vagaries of the mind. Incessant occupation is the best preservative against dissipation.

36. At 210 High Street.

37. *Dublin University Magazine,* a literary and philosophical review, published in Dublin 1833 – 1877. *Tait's Edinburgh Magazine* was published 1832 – 1861.

Selling of Tobacco

It is about two years since I commenced business or it will be so the 14th day of April. During this time I have forborne dealing in tobacco because I have not been able to make up my mind as to the Christian lawfulness of encouraging such a practice. Notwithstanding, I have never sold it habitually across the counter, yet I have had and paid for a *licence* because I have sometimes sold it to ships with bonded stores.

I am not a smoker myself, though I have taken a cigar sometimes, especially when given one. I am inclined to think more favourably of the lawfulness of retailing the article – but still I have not commenced to sell it for fear my opinions should arise rather from a desire to secure the profits which may accrue by its sale than from a sincere conviction of its propriety. I wish I were decided. I have asked the opinions of wiser and judicious men, and they have been favourable. May I act with conscience towards God – freed from selfishness and sin.

Need of System
Inf[luence] of circumstances on the Mind in Study

I see every day more clearly the necessity of living by system. May I not say that "I am ever learning, and never able to come to the knowledge of the truth" [II Tim 3:7] first seizing one book, and then another, and thus gathering a superficial stock of information. I certainly cannot blame myself for being so dissipated in mind as in the past hours of existence. Thank God my efforts at self-discipline have not been so utterly fruitless – but how many little portions of times I lose because I neglect to keep constantly before the mind the great objects to which I ought now to devote my energies. How frequently I have an half hour to spare which I perhaps lose in idle conversation. This in my situation as a shopkeeper is a sore evil. I have people intruding themselves, sometimes for hours, on one's attentions, for whom civility must be shown. Alas! that there are so many whose feelings are so obdurate that hints are thrown away.

In addition to this, fatigue and indisposition frequently render thought impossible. Of what infinite value is a sound bodily constitution. Health smooths the path to knowledge. The vigour of the mind must depend in an important degree upon the state of the brain – and if that be depraved, weakness and imbecility must be the result.

I have seriously considered – What are the objects which it is now my duty to accomplish? I have determined to draw out a list of these, and keeping it constantly at hand for reference I have but to glance at its enumeration when I am at a loss how to improve a vacant hour and I can at once devote myself to that which is most convenient and suitable. Then all these objects will be moved onward and advantage taken of every opportunity.

List of Present Objects

As in less than two months I will have to undergo an examination preparatory to being received as a full and accredited preacher on my views of those subjects which are connected with the Theology of preaching, now, as I have given of late little attention prior to commencing preaching to such subjects, I propose to draw an outline of views, which I imagine will refresh my mind, and imprint the truth more indelibly on the mind. As the period rapidly draws near, this must occupy my primary attention. I find I shall not be under the absolute necessity of preparing any new sermons until after that time, so that I trust to be able to bestow considerable attention.

I. **'Preparation for Examination'**

Blank book into which enter 'An arranged view of opinions or Brief Statements of views,' and concise enumeration of the arguments by which they are supported. [Marginal note:] Accomplished.

Since I heard of the Death of my friend John Moffat†, I have thought that it might be of considerable advantage to my own mind, and of use to the public if I could draw up an outline of his character and life for insertion in our magazine.[38] At present, I have no time to give to the subject but, to lose nothing, I purpose gathering all the information that I can glean and entering it in a book, together with such ideas as may occur to my mind, and thus the work will afterwards be very materially facilitated.

38. The *Wesleyan Association Magazine* published at the Association Bookroom, Ludgate Hill, London from 1838 to 1857, when the Association merged with the Wesley Reformers to form the United Methodist Free Churches.

II **'Memoir of John Moffat.'**

Blank book – Arrangement – into which enter matter for subsequent discussion.

As I am necessitated to pay constant attention to the preparation of sermons and as at present I have not time to give to their composition will it not be wise to carry out the principle alluded to in reference to John Moffat's Memoir – that is to have a book in which to enter those ideas which may occur to the mind. How often flashes of brilliant thought rush through the mind, which if not penned instantly are lost in succeeding darkness, like the momentary glare of the lightning bursting from the dark cloud.

III Sermonising

I have frequently, when reading in the morning some portion of the Scripture, felt passages to be presented to the mind with peculiar light and beauty. And at those periods that I am more than usually under the influence of spiritual impressions trains of thought have flitted across the imagination which I have afterwards sought in vain to recall. Now if I draw but some skeletons, and add from time to time such ideas as may be the result of accident or study, I shall have materials at hand for future arrangement while I am still giving attention to the chief object.

Blank books, in which enter skeletons, and materials.

IV French Language Review past attainments

In the year 1840 I resolved to commence the study of the French. I purchased old Cobbett's Grammar,[39] and went very diligently through the first part and prepared to advance, when I left my situation and began to prepare to enter into business. This so completely occupied my attention that its study was abandoned, though with the the intention of returning to the pursuit at the first opportunity. When I began to have a little time to spare, preaching came between to arrest my mind, but now that I have conquered first difficulties I wish to start again with redoubled diligence.

I know that to acquire a correct knowledge of the language a master is essential, but that I may be prepared for engaging with a master I propose to review my past acquisitions, and thus my labour will be relieved.

39. William Cobbett (1763 – 1835), *A French Grammar, or Plain Instruction for the Learning of French,* (1824, etc.)

V Latin Language. At school from the age of 9 or 10 until 12 I learnt, according to school [? purpose], Latin.

I had not been at business more than 3 years before I forgot all I had known from which it will be inferred it never had a very deep seated foundation in the schoolboy's brain. In fact, I never could construe latin sentences by the rule of Syntax.

At the business of Chemist and Druggist I felt the necessity of an accurate acquaintance with the language, and, especially when I read in the various branches of Medicine and Chemistry. Of the Mathematics I felt myself destitute. Now a knowledge of the principles of language and of a number are the foundation of all sound attainments in Science. I read a great number of books connected with Natural Philosophy in its various branches, and Medicine and Chemistry, and though I thus filled my mind with a considerable amount of general information yet I never possessed or acquired that accurate and profound knowledge which can be secured only through this medium of thorough preliminary education.

I made several attempts to acquire the Latin, and then I discovered I needed the grammar of my own language. I studied several grammars until I became conversant with its structure – Harris' *Hermes,* Murray, Lennie, Mylne, McCulloch, Cobbett &c. &c.[40]

I know, and am thoroughly persuaded, that if I wish to succeed in the strife of intellect and usefulness I must have some acquaintance at least, if not profound at least elementary, with the Latin and other languages. I therefore propose by the blessing of God to devote if possible some little time to the Grammar.

40. Some of the books referred to here are: James Harris, *Hermes : a Philosophical enquiry concerning language and universal grammar,* (1751), William Lennie, *Principles of English Grammar,* (1816), and Lindley Murray, *English Grammar,* (1795).

VI Book of incident and Reflection

Many facts and illustrations of Human Nature are presented to the notice in an ordinary intercourse with Society, and further many schemes and notions or phantasms pass in one's own mind which if noted might prove of value. Get therefore a Blank Book, and enter in the order of times.

VII Book of the Church

Record of matters of interest which belong to the religious party with which I am connected, and facts of similar interest in the universal church.

Illustrations of many things connected with the material of the church. Its officers, Preachers – Itinerant and Local,

Leaders, Prayer do., Ordinances, Worship and many little things of real interest which escape observation, or in themselves alone are not deemed worthy of attention.

VIII **Book of the Business of Life**

'Ways and means of living.' Shopkeeping – The Mysteries of buying and selling. *'Drug Business.'* Give prominence to what is related to personal experience.

IX **Health** The most important of all, because on this depends the preceding. General Health. Attention to diet, and daily exercise. Regularity in retiring to bed, and in rising.

Another point of importance – Health *and efficiency of the Lungs.* This is essential to success as a speaker. I believe my lungs are sound though not strong, or at least the voice is not so *deep, sonorous* and *clear* as I could wish. A good voice is of inestimable value – the same sermon delivered by 2 persons who shall possess good and indifferent voices will be felt as different productions by the same audience.

The former will have credit for superiority of intellect. Many, says a writer, many popular men have nothing but their voices to recommend them.

'Health in the Lungs' For some time I have been in the habit of visiting the sands, and shouting to the noise of the waves. I feel already some benefit from this practice and I have no doubt but I shall secure a large increase of voice if I persevere. Exercise is the only physic which memory suggests – but I have not been regular and indefatigable. By visiting the sands every morning I shall improve both my health in general, and in this particular.

Sometimes I feel such an overflow of energy that I could shake the house with my voice, and utter thought in a clear and commanding tone, and again I have hardly power to pray in my class, or prayer-meeting with sufficient energy to contend against the murmuring supplications of the brethren. Shall I give up in despair? No! I must try! and try! and try! again until I conquer.

X **Moral Improvements**

The consummation of the design, and struggle of existence. Here everything terminates. To this every passing thought and flitting action must look as the great objects of the momentary being. Let me secure this, and then all other objects and pursuits may perish. This is the rest of the soul, the satisfaction of the intellect. Apart from this nothing can bestow the peace and joy which fill the heart with happiness and love.

If I could retain every instant in all the engagements of life that consciousness of rectitude and purity – if in every hour of existence the presence of God illuminated my heart and sanctified its affections – how delightfully the glass of time would run to its last grain, and the fall of its last atom would be soft and sweet for it would abide in the stillness of peace.

I am sensible that nothing but ordinary diligence is requisite in order that I may arise in the morning with the freshness of love, and lie down in the evening in the calmness of faith. When the day is begun with simplicity of heart and confidence of integrity of purpose, then its trials and temptations and allurements are impotent and vain to seduce the soul to sinful indulgence – but when restlessness and wandering of temper mark the commencement of our avocations, then our spiritual steadfastness is shattered and remorseful impressions cast their dark misery on the tranquility of the day.

The instrument of all moral improvement is the *'truth of God'*. Religion can only teach wisdom, and the wisdom which is sown in the heart by this 'word', and germinates under the kindly influences of the spirit of God, will prove the architect of consistent and enduring virtue. Have I not sought in forbidden objects the delight which harsh experience proved to be very disappointment and misery. Let me be taught to come to Thee, the *'fountain of life'* [Psalm 36 : 9 et al.] to learn at Thy feet the meekness of true wisdom.

I have thus sketched a brief list of objects, which seem at present to claim primary attention. Is it vanity and presumption O Lord, that leads me to aim at *'vast knowledge'*. 'Search me and try me, and see if there be any wicked way in me, and bid it hence depart, and lead me in the way everlasting.' [Psalm 139: 23–23*].

I feel it to be of the first importance to *consider,* and *pause,* and *Review* my progress. I have satisfied myself with noting down what appeared at the time to be the chief occurrences of the week, but matters of thought and feeling if not placed on paper before their impressions are succeeded by others of interest will be forgotten in their more minute details.

Besides, if I give five minutes at the close of each day to enter in the Journal its occurrences, it must closely urge home the important query – "What have I accomplished this day?" And thus a happy barrier may be placed in the way of a gradual descent into slothful inactivity.

After all there is the Business of Life!! The toil to gain the bread which perisheth, which in these dreadful times of depression are continually forcing themselves on one's attention. I will not be wise to be so eager in pursuit of grace, and knowledge, as to neglect *'to oil the mill'*. This must be done just as the other must not be left undone.

Harrisons. Preach at Philadelphia and Shiney Row

Monday Feby. 13th

I left home yesterday in company with G. Elliott, and N. Atkinson[41] about ½ past 9 o'clock. They set me down in Newbottle.† Mrs H. [Harrison] † I saw first and had some chat about sundries. Has a strong esteem for Mr Keene.† Conversation Spiritual. Miss H. then came down and her brother Thos. and we had a long conversation upon indifferent subjects. Inspection of Album – perusal of poetry. Dinner – Miss S.H. came down at dinner. Mr. Harrison as before most awfully hospitable.

Eating and cramming by compulsion, was left for 20 m. alone, thought over my sermon, and asked divine aid. Preached from II Peter 1 ch. 5.6.7,v. Throat dry, and parched – voice *par consequence* – body felt pretty well, and there appeared to be a good feeling. Returned, had some conversation with Miss S.H. and then had tea. Interesting talk with Mr. H. at the table. Retired upstairs, and thought and prayed for half an hour. Saw Misses H. in their room, called me in when passing the door. Miss H. laid down, bad of rheumatism in face. Saw Mr. Keene downstairs. He had come over from Shiney Row† to preach at Philadelphia† at night.

They pressed me to come out on Tuesday first to Collier Row,† to speak at the Missionary Meeting.

Arrived at Shiney Row chapel in good time, very good company. Some children squalling annoyed me very much. Preached from V ch. John 40 v. Never felt calmer and more comfortable. Praise God!

The people listened with great attention. Supped with Mrs. Smith and remained until ½ past 9 o'clock waiting of the gig. Mr. Lewins[42] came to wait, also Messrs. Smith, Humphrey and Hedley were there to converse. Got home safely in the gig with Messrs. Atkinson, Elliott and Lewins at ½ past 10 o'clock.

I am thankful that I was by divine grace enabled to pass with some degree of comfort and satisfaction through the labours of the Sabbath.

At the first day of another week, let me begin afresh to serve God, and buy up every moment. May I be diligent.

41. W.M.A. lay preacher.
42. Frank Lewins, a W.M.A. lay preacher.

Back Room

Friday Feb. 17th.

What have I done this week?

I have been engaged in cleaning, and improving my back room.

Many happy hours I have spent in its precincts. How delightful to have some spot, however beggarly, to which we can retreat, and call it one's own. There the foot of intrusion and the voice of rebuke cannot enter. There in conscious security after the labours and nonsense of the day I retire, and draw my chair to the fire, and just employ the mind as I choose. About ½ past 8 o'clock the business of the day is or ought to be done – but I have been in the habit of burning the gas, and shutting the doors so that parties seeing the light above the door come and buy. This plan though profitable, is harrassing. I sit down to study but the mind is kept on 'the listen' to notice if anyone comes into the shop. I am resolved to close up finally about 9 o'clock to 'freshen my way'. The weather is too cold yet to rise early. I trust when the summer advances I shall form the better habit.

Dr. Clarke's 'Theology' by Dunn

This week I have risen at ½ past 7 o'clock, taken some hasty pudding, and instead of at once proceeding to the sands, in consequence of the stormy weather I have gone to the shop. At the close of the day I have done nothing but read Dr. Clarke's 'Theology' as arranged by S. Dunn.[43] I have read on the 'Scriptures', God – Man – Christ. Dr. Clarke is a loose writer – there is a heaping together of words, and lack of conciseness.

It has struck me that the greatest deficiency of Dr. C's attainments lies in his apparent ignorance of mental philosophy. ,This strikes me forcibly in the want of precision and force in his language. His experience of human nature and information is most extensive but still the want of Science and philosophic arrangement is very apparent in his statements.

43. Adam Clarke (? 1762 – 1832), Methodist preacher and scholar. The book referred to is *Christian Theology selected from his published and unpublished writings, and systematically arranged with a life of the author* by Samuel Dunn, (1835).

Divinity of Jesus, Dr. Clarke on
Wm. Reed. d'Aubigny's Reformation

On the proper Divinity of Jesus, Dr. C. having shown that Creation is the work of Christ from the testimony of the Apostle in 1st Colossians, infers his Divinity. 'Because creation is the work of omnipotence, therefore as Omnipotence cannot be delegated Jesus must be God.' The doctor assumes as the basis of his argument that to create, nothing short of omnific energy will avail. I cannot see why omnipotence [? should be] essential.

On a similar question I find the Unity of the Divine Nature inferred from the impossibility of the co-existence of two omnipotent beings. But what evidence have we that Omnipotence is a necessary attribute of God except from the pages of inspiration?[44]

No other book has engaged my attention except Tait's magazine for 1838, and a glance at d'Aubigny's *'Histoire de la Reformation'*.[45]

Newsroom. I go upstairs in the morning for 20 m. I find no indisposition to seriousness engendered.

I wrote today to *Wm. Reed*† my old friend, and beloved brother in Jesus.

The last few days the weather has been severely cold, and I have had a troublesome catarrh.

44. John Young is here alluding to a protracted theological controversy regarding the 'eternal Sonship' of Jesus Christ, roused by Adam Clarke's writings. See J.W. Etheridge, *The Life of Adam Clarke,* (1858), pp. 328 – 332.
45. Jean Henri Merle D'Augbiné,| (Swiss Protestant divine and historian 1795 – 1872), *History of the Great Reformation of the Sixteenth Century in Germany, Switzerland etc.,* trans. D. Walther, i–iii, (London 1838–41). Another translation available to John Young was that by W.K. Kelly, (London, 1842), but he may have read the work in its French edition, since he quotes the French title.

Mr. Keene and Miss Harrison

Mr. Keene,† I hear, is going to marry Miss Marianne Harrison† of Bunker's Hill.†

I highly esteem his character as far as I have had the opportunity to observe its complexion. Miss H. has many good properties, and if enriched with the grace of Jesus would be an ornament to society. Without divine wisdom she can never, however amiable, and talented, become a suitable wife for a minister of the gospel. Miss Sarah H. is as far as I have had opportunity to observe a very superior, and intelligent girl. Perhaps her intellect may not soar above mediocrity, but I judge her to possess the higher and nobler qualities in woman, that softness and feminine sensibility which constitutes the charm and spell of domestic intercourse. Hem! Hem!!

Spirituality

I am making some headway – Thank God I am not given over to sinful affections. [cf Romans 1:26]

Monday Feb. 20th.

Another Monday. Alas! how many are gone! Never to

return. I have had a severe cold all last week, which together with the extremely cold weather has hampered and frustrated what little energy I possess.

Mr. Ward Preached

Yesterday afternoon Mr. Ward minister of Gibson Street Chapel, Newcastle[46] preach[ed] in the aftn. at B. St. Ch.† from, 'There is joy in the presence of the angels' &c. (Luke 15 : 10).

46. Foundation stone laid 12 March 1837 (Richardson iv, 347) and opened 3 Dec. 1837 (*WMA Mag.* 1838, 79) when T.B. Young was among the preachers. The building accommodated about 1000 hearers in a first floor chapel on an amphitheatre plan, with a schoolroom for 800 below – i.e. it was similar to, though slightly larger than, Brougham Street chapel, Sunderland. There is a problem about the W.M.A. in Newcastle: no reference is made to it, nor are any details given of ministers 'stationed' there in the *WMA Minutes,* after 1837. However the Chapel obviously continued in use, though the members may have severed their links with the national Association. There is no reference to Mr Ward in the W.M.A. records.

Reflections

Help me O God! to live this week in more intimate union with thee! Oh call in each wandering thought. Centre in thyself the waywardness of youth. Let me breathe the atmosphere of Heaven. Let spiritual and divine affections be kindled in my heart, that sin may be destroyed, and 'grace reign through righteousness, unto eternal life by Jesus Christ our Lord' Amen, and Amen. [Romans 5:21]

I have lost much time this day by the interruptions of friends, chatting and wasting my precious time. I dare scarce think about it. Oh! for the devotion of the Apostolic Spirits.

Studies

Wednesday Feb. 22nd 1843.

On Monday I began reading Part 1 of the 'Biblical Theology' by Storr and Flatt on the 'Evidences of Revelation'.[47] I finished its review last night with much satisfaction. Remained each evening in my 'Dormitory' until ½ past 10 o'clock. Last night I took home the 1st vol: of Watson's *Institutes*[48] and reviewed until 12 o'clock with a clear head his summary of evidence.

I propose to confine myself this week to this subject, and to finish by putting on paper a short abstract or general view of 'Testimony'. I am thankful for continued health, and spiritual refreshment. 'My soul, wait thou only on God'. [Psalm 62:5].

On Monday night Mr. Peters† preached at Brougham St.† and the annual examination of the children took place.

Friday 24th.

By the grace of God I have been able to prosecute the above plan, and I propose to bind it, that is my abstract with blank paper, into one volume so that from time to time I will be able to add to my material. I now go on to the first great doctrine of the Christian Faith, the 'existence of God'. My present review is but cursory, necessarily so, for my object is to refresh my memory preparatory to the examination. But I shall return to their deliberate consideration after that ordeal, though perhaps not immediately for I must compose some sermons – and then if I secure a sufficient number to serve me for some months I intend to write a subject on the various 'Divisions of Biblical Theology' as I proposed. For instance, first I grapple with the Evidences. Here I may have a sermon on the 'Inspiration of the Scriptures', 'Miracles of Jesus' &c.&c. for I shall accumulate materials suitable to be wrought into composition. And when the topics are new to the mind it will be of easier accomplishment than afterwards.

Then, all that is connected with the 'Being, and Attributes of God', 'The Atonement and its kindred subjects' will furnish abundant room for disquisition; besides if a sermon is to be written the mind will be compelled to think, and to digest.

To perform this properly is a work of time – therefore I think I ought to have first of all a number of sermons to keep me from being obliged to break off every now and then to hurry up a sermon. The sermons I compose in this course of study ought to be prepared with great care. Now is the period for labour. I know not how soon the day may arrive when some cause or other may break in upon my studies, and leave me timeless.

Besides I must, if possible, nay I must, give time every week to the study of language &c. Once fairly on full plan, with sermons for a year, I may sit down with a calm mind and pursue systems.

I have no doubt that every year for many succeeding years, in fact for all the valuable portion of my life, will be increasingly occupied, and of necessity afford decreasing opportunities for mental cultivation.

Great God! let this conviction not be a mere transient emotion but an abiding conviction, such a conviction as will lead me to seize and to consecrate this moment to thee! Amen Amen.

47. G.C. Storr and C.C. von Flatt, *An Elementary course of Biblical Theology translated from the work of Professors Storr and Flatt with additions by S.S. Schmucker*, (Andover, U.S.A; 1826. London, c. 1838).

48. Richard Watson, (Methodist preacher and divine 1781 – 1833), *Theological Institutes or a view of the evidences, doctrines, morals and institutes of Christianity* i – iv (1823), was for many years the standard Methodist theological textbook.

Ghost

Last night at midnight a large crowd of people assembled at the Sunderland Church Yard, expecting to see a *Ghost.*[49]

49. This ghost scare (apparently a hoax) was caused by a young sailor who prophesied that his sister's ghost would appear in the Sunderland church† yard at midnight on the 23 February 1843. When the crowds assembled he explained to them that his sister had appeared a day earlier! (*Sunderland Herald* 24 Feb. 1843. I am indebted to the staff of the Local History library at Sunderland Central Library for this reference.) An earlier ghost scare at Sunderland church yard (in the 1820s) had resulted from the nocturnal doings of body-snatchers. (Taylor Potts, *Sunderland – A History of the Town, Port, Trade and Commerce*, 1892, pp. 244–249.)

Toothache

On Wednesday night I was seized with a severe toothache which caused me to lose my rest, and obliged me to come down to the shop at 4 o'clock in the morning for some *Creosote.*[50]

I received on Thursday a letter from W. Reed.†

50. Creosote, or Kreosote, was the name applied in 1832 by Reichenbach to an oily fluid distilled from wood tar. Purified creosote, especially that made from beechwood, was discovered to have extensive pharamaceutical uses, including antiseptic and local anaesthetic properties, explaining J.Y's uses of it for toothache.

Hetton

Monday Feb. 27th.

S. Hodgson and I left the Inn with the phaeton yesterday morning at ½ past eight o'clock. We rode to the Newtown[51] to wait of J. Thomson, and then with J. Hutchinson & Frank Lewins rode up Durham Lane. We set the two last down at Newbottle† Lane end, and proceeded towards Renton [Rainton]† when L.H. and J.T. left the former for Collier Row,† and the latter for Rainton. I took the phaeton to Hetton and put it up at March the publican's, and then inquired for Ann Speates. I dined there and then went to chapel and preached to about 25 from II Peter 1 ch. 5,6,7. Returned to Pen[shaw] †, and afterwards preached from V John 40 verse, 17 present. I remained at the Class in the afternoon, old Willy Robinson led it. Very strange, and amusing. In the afternoon I stood beneath the pulpit on the forms but in the evening was obliged to ascend the rostrum for want of light. The great fault of pulpits is that they are so high. Let us have no pulpits at all and be content with a simple reading desk, and platform. How much easier to develop energy – and what freedom of movement!

Ann S. has been afflicted for 5 years, and unable to walk. Grace has been her stay, and guide. She read me some letters from Wolstenholme.† They breathe an admirable spirit. In the evening the Revd. George Thompson from America gave a Lecture in the Primitive Methodist Chapel at Hetton† to a crowded audience on *'Slavery'*. This thinned my congregation. Mr. Thos. Hutchinson, a Baptist, who took tea with us at Speates, called when I was at supper and asked if I would give Mr. Thompson a ride to Houghton.† I agreed. Mr. Thompson came – a stout, hearty looking man. He said he had preached one Sabbath afternoon in the Tabernacle, Sunderland and delivered a lecture in Sans St. Chapel [Sunderland] † about two years ago.

It was very dark. We could hardly see our way, but arrived, thank God, safely at Houghton.

S.H. and J.T. were waiting at Miss Short's. We got home about 10 o'clock.

Mr. Thompson was introduced at Hetton on Saturday by Mr. Heywood.† He was to lecture on Monday evg. at our Houghton Chapel.

Mr. Mules† when last at Hetton took the vote of the congregation, prior to the annunciation of his text, to ascertain by show of hands whether the majority were believers or unbelievers. He told them that he had two subjects impressed upon his mind and that he was at a loss which to speak from.

51. The newly developed urban area of Bishopwearmouth,† where many of the more affluent citizens of Sunderland were taking houses at the time John Young was writing, a process of westward migration which had been in process for some time but had gathered pace in the second quarter of the century. See Town Plan, p.203 below.

Sunday School Tea

Wednesday, March 1st 1843.

Last night I attended our annual Sabbath School tea in the upper school room S. Durham Street.† The attendance was scanty. The speeches excellent. T.B.Y. in the chair. Mr. Mules spoke first with considerable tact, and ability. Then Mr. Heywood, and Milne† the Seaman Missionary. Messrs. Moore and Dixon were called upon to give a practical acct. of the schools, but refused. S. Hodgson† was their substitute. Mr. Peters† delivered the best speech. It was very excellent. I was pleased with all the sentiments save that part in which he advised the bringing together of the sexes in one school. 'Why' said he 'should boys be prevented from learning to demean themselves with courtesy towards their little sisters with whom in a few years they would enter into a more intimate association, when God had said "It is not good for man to be alone"? I could not understand the propriety of such language in reference to children.

This day being Shrove Tuesday we closed our shop at ¼ to 2 o'clock.

Monday March 6th.

Last week I felt great difficulty in restraining the 'wandering thoughts', and applying my mind to the object of study. Fancy would indulge in a range through imaginary and delusive fairy castles. I have read Storr & Flatt *'On the Existence and Attributes of God'* and I am now busy with Watson's *Institutes.*

Library Committee

Saturday March 11th.

Interrupted, I have now had opportunity to return to my notes. On Sunday I walked in the morning, and heard my Father preach in the afternoon on the church in Thyatira [Rev. 2 : 18-29]. Mr Mules at night on, 'Let a man examine himself' – Corinth'ns [I Cor. 11:28]. Sacrament, at which I stayed and then went to Mr. Coxon's where I remained until ½ past 10 o'clock. I visited and prayed with Mrs. Nesbitt in the morning. On Monday night we had a meeting of the Sub-Library Committee in my back room. Present S. Hodgson†, W. Dixon†, I. Bruce. The same night there was a meeting of the B. St. Ch. S.S.† committee in the vestry. On Tuesday I had a joiner. On Sunday March 5 I took tea with Andrew White Esq., † our present Mayor, at Frederick Lodge.†

Preach Silver Street

Mr. Triffet busy in the shop. On Wednesday the same. And on Thursday night I preached down in Mrs. Butcher's, Silver Street,[52] at 7 o'clock to a crowded place – from II Peter 1 ch. 5,6,7. This was Mr. Keene's† duty but he persuaded me to take it for him on consideration of his depression from frequent preaching.

52. A preaching place was later opened in Silver Street in a converted sail loft, see pp. 145-6 below. Lofts for the making and repair of sails 'as a rule occupied the top flat of a large house, extending sometimes over two or three houses'; T. Potts, *Sunderland: a History of the Town,* (1892), p. 20.

Trustee Meeting

Last Friday evening, that is March 3rd, we had a Trustee Meeting of the S.D. St. Ch.† to consider the propriety of buying out our 3 shares in the Building Society, and in the manner in which it should be applied. We could not agree. My Father wishing to purchase the whole of the shares, and Messrs. Philips, Dixon & Coxon wishing to buy out, and then settle at once and be done with the Building Society.

Preach at Southwick

Monday March 13th.

I rose late on S. morning and heard Mr. Heywood† from, 'Say ye to the righteous it shall be well with them' [Isaiah 3 : 10*].

In the afternoon I went to Southwick† with Mr. Triffet and preached from XC Psalm & 12 v. *So teach us* &c. I had greater compass of voice than on any prior occasion. I led a class of 3 persons, Messrs. Ball, Cowell, and an old man at the finish. A good time.

Returned, and took tea with Mrs. & Mr. Taylor, Union Street. Came home, and intending to study, took up Cecil's *Remains*[53] and spent the greater part of the evening in reading them with much interest. Sat up late talking with Ophy [Ophelia, J.Y.'s sister]. Went to rest without any sensible manifestation of the divine presence. Have mercy, mercy. Rose this morning with a languid breathing to God for devout feeling. Oh, to begin the day and to continue well, to lie down at night in peace and safety. This week I am resolved to live nearer to God. To strive to rise earlier, and live holier.

53. Richard Cecil (1748 – 1810). Evangelical divine of the Church of England. *The Life, Character and Remains of the Revd. Richard Cecil,* collected and revised by Josiah Pratt, (London 1811).

Notice of Trial Sermon

Wednesday March 15th 1843.

I have health today, thank God! Halleluia!!

S. Hodgson† called this afternoon to inform me that the Circuit Committee had agreed at their meeting that I should preach my Trial Sermon[54] on Friday evening the 24th March, in the Brougham St. School† at 7 o'clock, and be examined afterwards [at] the adjourned meeting of the Circuit Committee.

The Lord help me, and give me grace to discharge this duty, and sustain this scrutiny with calm self-possession, and reliance on divine assistance. May vanity and self-confidence be put far from me. May I speak as to Christ, think of Christ, do it as to the Lord, and not unto men.

I ask myself, should I be afraid? Should I go up with trembling knees, and palsied hands. In the recollection of my poor dismal sinfulness I might shrink to nothing – but let one eye glance to Heaven – see Jesus – His smile – recognition and approval – and thus I shall in his strength fearlessly pronounce the will of God.

It seems to be an impression on many minds that a young man on such an occasion ought to manifest symptoms of timidity and backwardness. I shall strive to appear in my true character – no assumed hesitancy. If possible I will speak with *all the boldness* I can summon to my aid. Much will depend upon physical health – clearness of voice, and accurate preparation; these secured, the rest, in the mercy of my heavenly Father, will be easy. Let me labour. But how deficient I am in spirituality – where the zeal, the once unaffected devotional breathing?

I come to a throne of grace, I abide there until I receive renewal, and vigorous piety.

54. Part of his examination for recognition as a fully accredited lay preacher.

Mr. Keene's marriage

Mr. S. Hodgson states that it was notified at the Quarterly meeting that Mr. Keene† would marry this conference – and that, if invited, he would stay at Bunker's Hill† another year at a young man's salary.[55] Mr. Peters† refused to pledge himself either to stay or go.

My Father is recovering. My sister Anne is recovered.

Mr. Peters preached on Monday evening to commemorate the deaths of the seamen who have been took during the late gale who were members of our society.

55. Aquila Keene was due to be 'received into full Connexion' at the Annual Assembly of the W.M.A. in the summer of 1843 and as his probationary period would then cease he would be eligible to marry. However he offered to stay on another year in Sunderland at a probationer's salary, i.e. at a rate less than that of a fully accredited minister. The Service of Reception into Full Connexion of the W.M.A. is described in Beckerlegge 1957, p. 53. One notable and typical feature was that 'each candidate's acceptance was . . . moved and seconded by members of the Assembly and carried by the vote of all present including the general public'.

Gratitude for Mercies

Friday March 17th.

'It is of the Lord's mercies I am not consumed' [Lamentations 3 : 22*]. I am at present labouring under very severe temptation from a quarter to which I have a bias, and at which I am most readily, and successfully, overcome. Is this a wile of the great enemy of our race to humble and prostrate me at this juncture? O how weak I am. I ought to tremble if I was alive to my danger. I am so ungrateful for God's mercies, so feeble, and apathetic that I am incapable of a vigorous effort to throw off this demon incubus, and struggle with every energy for liberty. Lord save or I perish. I perish. Awake O my soul. Awake to all thy past convictions, awake to my present folly, and grasp the throne of God.

Trust Deeds, S. Durham St. Ch.

I have this day March 17, 1843 signed the Mortgage Deed to the Building Society for South D. Street Chapel.† Mr. A.J. Moore's† brother brought it to the shop. I also signed two notes at six months date for the loan of £50 each to the Trustees of Brougham St. Chapel† by Mr. Ralph Elliott of Shiney Row.† These notes were brought down by my father. This £100 is now held by the trustees of S. Durham St. Ch. and will be transferred to us of B. St. Chapel when we take the money out of the B. Society.

On Wednesday evening at 8 o'clock we had another trustee meeting at which on my arrival I found Messrs. T.B. Young and T.R. Wilson.† Later on Revd. J. Peters† and Mr. Coxon arrived, and then Mr. W. Dixon.†

My Father stated that he had called the meeting together simply to say that he could not accept the office of steward in conjunction with Messrs. Wilson and Bolton after its resignation by Mr. Alexr. Philips if he was expected to carry out the resolution of the previous meeting, viz. – to buy out only two shares. He showed that instead of there being only £63 floating debt to pay there was in reality £100, so that after having payed Mr. C. £100 and Mr. Bolton's £80 there would be a pressing debt of £40 to commence with, the amount of the shares being £240, i.e. debt £280 – 240 = £40.

He would not take office without the 3 shares were taken out to pay the above, and Mr. E's £100.

At the same time he would sign the deed for 2 shares, and offer no obstruction if they would appoint another secretary.

Mr. Peters with the most Christian calmness laboured to reconcile the parties. After an investigation, and reconsideration of the whole financial statement, it was agreed that if six individuals would guarantee £5 each for the term of the Building Society the 3 shares might be bought out. Mr. Wm. Dixon dissented, Mr. Peters urged him to consent for the sake of peace, and union even at the sacrifice of his own opinion. He refused. Mr. Peters rose and said he would go and bring Mr. Philips. I offered to go for him. After 10 o'clock I brought him from his house in Nicholson Street and after a long discussion he consented if a guarantee were obtained. Mr. Peters continued to entreat W.D., nay he sought his consent, as a personal favour. 'Will you', said he, 'consent to sign the deed if six can be had and will you agree to be one of the six?' He assented at last about 11 o'clock. Thanks to Mr. Peters.

Monday March 20th

On Sabbath I rose at 8 o'clock having retired to rest at

2 o'clock. I got home from the shop about ¼ to 12 o'clock and took up the United Service Magazine[56] for February 1843 and continued to read until 2 o'clock. I heard Mr. Heywood† preach in the morning from 'Come thou with us and we will do thee good: for the Lord hath spoken, &c.' [Numbers 10 : 29].

In the afternoon Mr. G. Elliott 'And thou Bethlehem of Judah' [Matt. 2 : 6]. At night Mr. Milne†, Seamen's Missionary, 'The kingdom of God is not meat and drink but righteousness, &c.' [Romans 14 : 17].

56. *The United Service Magazine and Naval and Military Journal,* published 1842–3 as a continuation of the *United Service Journal* 1829 – 1841. It continued from 1843 as *Colburn's United Service Magazine* and later simply as the *United Service Magazine* to 1920.

Sir John Fife

Father was very ill today of his piles. Could not get out. I wrote to J. Muschamp† to request him to enquire at what period Sir J. Fife† could be seen for I have pressed him to go over to Newcastle for that purpose. It is no use bothering with every man who sports a diploma or certificate, and dubs himself with a high sounding appellation! I visited and prayed with Mrs. Nesbitt after tea, she still continues very ill, though seems better today.

Last night I asked my father 'Why my trial sermon had not been announced?' He replied that he was surprised at the wish, for young men generally strove to shun rather than court observations. Ophelia said 'Oh! you want a crowd'. I answered, 'It must be a very unenviable position for a young man in a private manner to preach before a few of the circuit Committee and Preachers who come especially as critics. How can he exhort sinners to repentance, should he be prepared with such a subject, if there are none present? Let the congregation be of a similar complexion to those which he is expected to address in future, and then he may be able to address them in his usual and proper mode, which must be impossible where the usual elements of assembly are excluded'.

In the afternoon I added a conclusion to the sermon I intend to preach. I have felt some more confidence in my approaches to God this day. The Lord help me and cause the light of his face to shine upon me for his mercies sake, Amen!!

On Saturday I stepped down before breakfast and had some conversation with W. Dixon† and feel sorry that his mind should be so irritated at the result of last Trustee Meeting.

Catlin's Lecture

March 23rd. 1843.

On Wednesday evening I attended a Lecture in the Athenaeum by Mr. Catlin[57] of America on the 'Red Indians of North America'. It was crowded. I called of my sister at Mr. White's.† Admission 1/-d. I was exceedingly gratified. 20 living figures in costumes personified their modes and manners.

On Thursday March 23rd I remained in the shop until ½ past 11 and drew up a brief abstract or synopsis of views on the genuineness and authenticity of the scriptures. Existence of God, Attributes, Trinity, Deity and personality of Jesus, and the Holy Spirit. Depravity, Repentance, Faith, Justification, Regeneration, Adoption, Witness of the Spirit, Sanctification, Resurrection, Judgement &c. &c. in order that I might not be utterly unprepared for the next evening.

On Friday 24th. My Father this day visited Sir John Fife†; he told him that he was troubled with a liver complaint, and that his piles had not degenerated into fistulas.

57. George Catlin (1796 – 1872), an American lawyer and self-taught artist who from 1832 devoted his life to discovering and preserving as much as he could of the languages, customs and modes of life of the American Indians, whom he realised were dying out at an alarming rate. In 1840 he came to Europe with an immense museum of objects and his collection of paintings, many of which are now in the Catlin Gallery of the National Museum, Washington; a permanent exhibition was mounted in the Egyptian Hall, London, while Catlin undertook tours with part of his collection. His lectures were illustrated, as John Young mentions, by 'Tableaux vivants', for which the actors were dressed in full Indian costumes and demonstrated Indian 'councils, games, religious ceremonies, dances, songs, signals, war-whoops etc'. Catlin was anxious to present the North American Indians at their best – a high-minded people

threatened by modern civilisation. He published a number of books including the *Manners, Customs, and Condition of the North Americn Indians,* i – ii, (1841). His book *My Life among the Indians,* ed. N.G. Humphreys, was published in 1909. He toured the north of England in the spring of 1843 and there are reports and advertisements in the *Newcastle Chronicle* 4 March, 11 March and 25th March 1843, which speak of his lecture as realising 'most completely the idea of travelling without leaving home', which would appeal strongly to John Young.

Trial Sermon

March 24th. 1843.

During this day Friday 24th of March I felt very unwell, but wisely took every precaution which experience could suggest to husband my strength for the evening conflict. I left the shop about 6 o'clock, retired home, and dressed, and then took a circuitous route for exercise to the Brougham St. School.† I took with me a paperful of Mint Loz[enges] Liquorice, and coffee berries to stimulate and clear the voice. Arrived at the School, I got Harker to bring out the Bible in which I pinned my notes and then went into the [word missing]. I found the gas scarce half-lighted, so I came out again and requested Mr. Harker to let us have additional lights.

Then ascending the desk I gave out:

Lord of the worlds above
How pleasant and how fair
The dwellings of Thy Love &c.[58]

In the morning I walked up to the School to see if the desk was secure and comfortable. I prayed with little liberty. Sung again 'When I survey the wondrous cross';[59] during this Mr. Peters† came in, Mr. Keene† having previously arrived.

The attendance was about 150, many more would have been present but it was never announced except once the previous Wednesday at S.D. St. I preached from XC Ps. 12 v. 'So teach us &c.' Thank God, as I proceeded I gathered confidence and my voice was wonderfully strengthened. I preached about 35 minutes, and then sang 'Happy the man who wisdom gains'[60] &c. Prayed short and this trial was done.

Mr. Keene requested the brethren on the plan to retire into the vestry which was a mistake because the examination belonged exclusively to the Circuit Committee.

Present: Messrs. Peters, Keene. W. Moore,† Draper, Simpson Hodgson,† Elliott, Forster.†

After prayers, Mr. Peters, who conducted the investigation, inquired what evidence I could adduce to prove the Being of God apart from Revelation.

I instanced 1st. The instinctive voice of conscience.

2nd. The Consitution of nature, quoting illustrations.

Mr. Peters asked if I had read Paley's *'Natural Theology'*. I replied No! He said 'I would advise its perusal, it will give clearness to your views and statements'. This hint I thought was unnecessary for I was not informed in what I had failed to please.

There can be no other evidences than the above without we say 'The existence of God is confirmed by the miracles of Jesus'. The tendency of the above remark must have been to produce an impression on the minds of the Committee that he (Mr. Peters) considered my reply unsatisfactory. Then: The attributes of God as known by the same process, which I stated to be 'Power' 'Wisdom' and 'Goodness', which was received as satisfactory.

Authenticity and genuineness of the Old Testament. I replied that I rested my proof on these two grounds –

1. That the books we possess are the same as existed in the time of Jesus, and the Apostles, and Josephus, and Philo &c. and the essential agreement of transcripts, translations.

2. Their Divine authority on the recognition of Christ and his Apostles.

3. The confirmation of the earliest antique remains Mr. P.: 'Did I know of no other arguments? J.Y. –'There is the evidence of Prophecy and the remarkable prophecies connected with the Jewish Nation and those connected with Jesus and His mission.'

Mr. P.: 'But do you know of no other important Branch?' There was a dead pause in which I wondered what he could mean, and stole a glance at the countenances of my neighbours and they in return exchanged glances among themselves. Mr. P.: 'Does it not occur to your mind that God not only sent messengers but authenticated the messengers He sent?'

It struck me immediately that he must allude to the miracles of the Old Testament. So I replied, 'Certainly. Moses and the prophets performed miracles in confirmation of their authority.' 'Ay' said Mr. P. 'I thought you would see you had omitted a very important evidence, and not only this but that most important evidence from Profane History, Monuments & Coins. Have you read Leslie's *Short and Easy Method?*'[61] J.Y.: 'No Sir, I have not.' J.P. 'Well then I would advise you, it will be desirable to give clearness to your views.'

S. Hodgson: 'Have you Leslie, Brother Young?' J.Y. 'No Sir, I have not.' S. Hodgson: 'Well then I'll lend it to you,' in quite a patronising mode. J.Y.: 'I am much obliged to you Sir, but with respect to the miracles of the Old Testament, I did not consider them as proof of the divine authority of the writer, but as resting on that authority as proved in another way, and with respect to the new and important branch of evidence of which Mr. Peters has just spoken I meant to include that under my 3rd General Head, the confirmation of the earliest antique remains, of which I was prevented at the time from speaking more explicitly, but I am now ready if necessary to state more largely.

I here remark that I considered Mr. Peter's mode of proposing these queries confused and his exhibition of evidence unsatisfactory.

III Without any further discussion Mr. P. proceeded at once to ask the previous question as applied to the writings of the New Testament.

1. The early existence of Christians and Christian writings I proved from the testimony of Tacitus, Suetonius, Pliny, Celsus, and Porphyria, &c.

2. That those writings were truly written by the disciples whose name they bear, at least with what are termed the Homologous or Universally received books, from the fact that they were acknowledged by all authorities, Christians and their adversaries, Heretics &c.

3. The Style of the New Testament.

Here I was interrupted by Mr. P. asking about the miracles, just as I was going to state –

4. The miracles of Jesus and

5. His general character and mode of procedure.

6. The impossibility of deception, and others which I had no opportunity to enlarge upon. Peters: 'My Brother, to what miracles do you allude?' I instanced, Lazarus, Blind

man, the calming of the seas, multiplying of Bread, creation of hands, arms, &c. We speedily came to a close with this and then proceeding at once [to] the 'Doctrines of Revelation'.

Depravity, Man's original state, His Fall, Its results, Their universality, quoting passages of scripture in support of each proposition which I was, thank God, able to do to my own satisfaction.

The mode of Restoration.

J.P.: 'My Brother have we any intimation of God's design to bless mankind? J.Y. – 'In thy seed shall all the nations . . .' [Genesis 22 : 18]. J.P.: 'Nothing earlier, the seed of the . . .? J.Y.: 'Shall bruise the head of the serpent' [Gen. 3 : 15]. Upon the Substitution, Atonement and works of Christ he was only brief and went [on] to enquire sixthly –

The Conditions of man's Salvation. This is an illustration of what occurred frequently in the examination. An indefinite way of proposing a query. He had been as indefinite and brief on the Interposition of Jesus that I concluded he wished for a further explanation of my views respecting the atonement, and was therefore obliged to enquire whether he meant that or the duty of man himself.

J.P.: 'Our duty certainly, we have a work to do, what is that work?' J.Y.: 'To repent.' J.P.: 'Well, what is repentance?' Here I explained my views, and adduced my quotations, Faith, Justification, Regeneration, Sanctification, Perseverance, Judgement, Resurrection, &c. &c.

It may be necessary to remark that I see I have omitted a large part of that part connected with the Divinity and Humanity of Jesus, Personality and Deity of the Holy Spirit &c. &c.

II Disciplinary Rule and Church Economy &c. I here stated my acquiescence in the views entertained by the Society [See Appendix II]. The question was put, 'Do you know of anything in which you differ from us?' I replied 'No'. Mr. S. Hodgson asked 'Will brother Young be willing to take his work regularly on the plan?' J. Peters, 'Of course, Brother Hodgson, I believe our Brother Young will do so to the utmost of his ability.'

The above is but a bird's eye view, to suggest to my mind the various features of the process and is by no means a fair summary of all that passed in review.

58. A paraphrase of Psalm 84 by Isaac Watts, number 591 in *A Collection of Hymns for the use of the People called Methodists* by John Wesley, with supplement. The W.M.A. used Wesley's collection of 1780, with its later supplement, as their hymn-book, and published an edition at their Bookroom late in 1838 or early 1839; I owe this information to the Revd Dr Oliver Beckerlegge.
59. *ibid.* number 700, also by Watts.
60. *ibid.* number 14, a paraphrase of Proverbs 3 : 13–18 by Charles Wesley. The verse quoted is the last.
61. Charles Leslie (1650 – 1722), *A Short and Easie Method with the Deists, wherein the certainty of the Christian religion is demonstrated,* (1698). Leslie, a non-juror, was a prolific writer on religious questions. His *Short and Easie Method* was popular and continued in print in various editions up to John Young's day; it was included by the Wesleyan Thomas Jackson in *The Christian Armed against Infidelity,* (1837).

Preach Southwick

Sunday March 16th.

I was very unwell on the Saturday and also on Sunday. In the morning I took a walk with Wm. Dixon† to Monkwearmouth.† In the afternoon I attended a Lovefeast held by Mr. Mules† in South Durham Street Church.† In the evening I preached at Southwick† from John V. ch. 40 v. It rained and blew very heavy on coming home.

Received at the Church Meeting

On Monday I still felt unwell, laid on three chairs much of the day. In the evening I went to Brougham Street Church† at which the Quarterly Church meeting was held. I arrived there at ½ past 8 o'clock. Mr. Mules had preached at 7 o'clock, and Mr. Keene† was engaged with the financial statement when I arrived. I sat down beside the door. When I went in all eyes were turned upon me.

After Mr. Keene had finished Mr. Peters† introduced me to the meeting, requesting me to state my Conversion Experience, Call to the Ministry, Views of Doctrine and Discipline.

I very briefly stated the two first and then my conformity with that 'Code of Doctrine and Discipline' which was published by the Society.[62] It had been usual for our young men to repeat a whole catalogue of 'I Believes' but this I thought unecessary. Turning to Mr. P. I said 'Is there anything Sir, that I have omitted?'

Mr. P: 'Yes, yes, your call to the ministry' [i.e. the part-time lay ministry of local preaching].

I then stated that as brief as possible, and then said again 'Is it necessary to particularise doctrines?' 'Oh no!' he replied. I was perfectly able to have done so if needed, for I felt quite composed. A show of hands was taken, and the contrary, when it appeared unanimous. Mr. P. gave an address to me and the church.

When he first introduced me he stated that I had passed through a faithful and highly satisfactory examination.

62. *The Principles of Doctrine and Church Discipline held by the Methodists of the Wesleyan Association in the Sunderland Circuit,* (Sunderland, 1838). A small pamphlet of 16 pp. See Appendix II below.

Opinions on Examination and Trial Sermon

On Tuesday Mr. Keene† called and smoked a pipe in the back room. He said, 'I have one thing to say respecting your trial sermon, and you must not be offended'. J.Y.: 'I will be most happy if you will give me advice, you will find me willing to be instructed.'

Keene: 'I highly admire your style, and was exceedingly pleased with your sermon, but there is one fault I would advise you to guard against – and that is a very common one with a fruitful imagination – too great a profusion of images, or illustrations, which tend to confuse the common hearers &c. &c. Apart from this I was much pleased, indeed I felt quite ashamed of myself to see you figuring off in that way.' J.Y.: 'Oh, Mr. Keene.' Keene, 'I am not flattering, it is quite contrary to my mode. I am happy to think the character of our plan is now likely to be improved.'

In the afternoon I took a walk down and saw Mr. W. Dixon, and talked over the whole affair. In the evening he came up and sat until ½ past 10 o'clock.

On Wednesday I rose with a continuance of sore throat which has continued until now, Thursday 30th inst. with very general depression, headache, &c. Oh for health, but I have reason to be grateful. What shall I render unto Thee for all thy benefits? [Psalm 116 : 12*]. Inspire me with love, faith, and charity.

Thus I have accomplished the first object in my list – 'Preparation for Examination &c.' May thy grace render all other objects equally successful. Thursday March 30th 1843.

Preach Houghton and Collier Row

Monday April 3rd.

The whole of last week I laboured under a degree of lassitude arising from a sore throat, and headache. I did not expect to be able to preach till I used every measure which experience could suggest to prevent my recovery. I tried to get a substitute but was not able. I went in the phaeton with Messrs. Cook and Atkinson taking G. Elliott, to give out hymns and pray, and if necessary to preach.

It was a most delightful day. I went to Mrs. Matthews, and left my coat, and saw Mr. Peters,† and then G.E. and I went over the hill down to Philadelphia,† calling at the chapel and then at the House. After chatting with the Miss Harrisons† we returned to Houghton† and dined with Mrs. Matthews. I preached from John V. 40. After tea finding my throat and voice not much injured, I proceeded to Collier Row† with G.E. and spoke from II Peter 1 ch. V, VI, VII. Supped with Jacob Dowel, until Atkinson called with phaeton.

On Friday night Mr. Keene† called and remained until 10 o'clock. We had a very interesting conversation on various topics connected with Study, and Preaching.

Methuselah's Pills

Monday, April 10th.

O for a grateful heart. During the week I have been troubled with a sensation in my throat as though it had been strained. I have accomplished little this week in study. Read a good part of the Iliad of Homer, which I bought in vols. for 8d. Drew an outline for a sermon on *'And this I pray that your love may abound'* &c. [Philippians 1:9].

I also wrote a fictitious advertisement for some Quack Pills for a hoax.[63] Read a good deal of the New Testament.

John Moffat's† Father called to tell me that a young man came here who had been with him two hours before he died. He brought a letter written a few days before his death. Mrs. Foster also received a letter by the same person, written two days before his death.

The young man states that 'He never saw anyone die so happy. When he went into the room two hours before his death he just glanced his eyes towards him and said 'I will never leave Demerara'. May I meet him in Heaven.

63. J.Y. was no doubt inspired by the many quack remedies on sale in his day. The *Sunderland Herald* for instance carried advertisements for 'Henry's Magic Pills for the Cure of Gout', 'Parr's Life Pills', and 'Kearsley's Original Widow Welch's Female Pills' among many other medical aids all vouched for by columns of testimonials.

Preach at Deptford

On Sunday heard Mr. Mules† on the 'wedding garment' [Mark 22:11]. Visited the S.D. St. School† in the afternoon, and preached at Deptford at night, from II Peter 1 c. 5,6,7, v. I begin this week with prayer for divine aid to enable me to consecrate every moment to God. Lord answer, I beseech of thee, for Christ's sake.

Wire Model of Canvas Boat

Wednesday April 12th

One half of the week has passed and what have I done? Nothing but a bare attendance on the shop.

Yesterday I made a wire model of a boat to be covered with canvas. Monday and Tuesday evening W. Dixon† has been here in my back shop till late. I have not got exercise for I have been up so late that I could not find time in the morning to walk. This must be reformed. Well I ask, what can I do this week? Oh, what time I have lost in idle talk? Lord save me.

Business.

Jaunt up to Lambton. Visit Shields

Wednesday April 19th

On Good Friday April 14th I enjoyed a pleasant trip up

the water as far as Lambton Castle† in company with W. Dixon†, J. Bennett† and M. Young – we tea'd at Biddick Inn, having left home about ¼ to 12 o'clock in W.D.s coble, returning by 20m to eight p.m.

Saturday I felt as usual. On Sunday I was in the house the whole of the morning until ½ past 12 when I left to accompany the Revd John Dunning† to Shields† who was going to preach the Missionary Anniversary Sermons. We arrived at Mr. Moffat's and then proceeded to the chapel. I prayed and read the lesson for Mr. D. We returned by the 5 o'clock train. Mr. D. to preach in South D. St. Chapel† and I at Monkwearmouth.† I had great trouble in finding the place. I preached from XC Psalm 12v. and my congregation consisted of about 8 or 9 of all sorts, old and young. I afterwards went over to the S.D.St.C. Saw W.D. and walked with him until late. I have sat up an hour or so with Mr. Dunning every night he has been here and have enjoyed much interesting conversation.

Missionary Meeting, Brougham Street

On Monday we gave up business about 1 o'clock. In going home I was entrapped into a house and detained prisoner for ¾ of an hour because I refused to let three women have my *boots,* or pay forfeit for them. This is an old custom here, the men seizing the women's shoes on the Sunday, and the women the men's on Easter Monday.[64] In the evening I took the Misses Harrisons† (who just arrived about ½ past 6 o'clock) to our Missionary Meeting at B. Street Chapel, A. White Esq., in the chair. Mr. Mules† moved the 1st Resolution, 2nd by a Primitive Methodist preacher. The 2nd by Keene† supported by the Revd Law Stoney† of the New Connexion in this place, and the 3rd Resl. moved by Mr Peters and supported by Mr. Dunning.† The vote of thanks to the chairman and ladies by Mr. Peters and T.B. Young. The report was read by Mr. Cosen, the financial accounts by Mr. T.B. Young.

64. The custom is referred to by J.R. Boyle, *Comprehensive Guide to the County of Durham,* (1892), p. 133, though with a slight difference, in that he says that on Easter Monday the women took the men's caps, not their shoes. Fordyce i, 563 also refers to

the same practice, which he appears to think was confined to the Bishop Auckland area, although he says that in the eighteenth century the women had attempted to snatch the men's shoe buckles, rather than their hats as in the nineteenth century. George Hudson was a victim of the custom on one occasion: Brockie pp. 351–2. Easter shoe-snatching in Sunderland is mentioned by another local diarist, W.B. Ogden, writing in 1817: R. Hyslop, 'Sidelights from an old Sunderland diary', *Antiquities of Sunderland* 20, (1951), 42.

Misses Harrisons

Mr. Dunning spoke exceedingly well, and has proved himself a clear ingenious advocate. At the conclusion of the service I went with the Harrisons† and Keene† to the Londonderry Arms to get their gig and await the arrival of Mr. Clark who was to drive them home. They called for biscuits and whiskey, and warm water, of which Miss Marianne and Sarah partook with Mr. Keene. I am a teetotaler, and tasted nothing.[65] I scarce know what to say of this, it is painful to my feelings especially as I feel deeply interested in every one of these friends. Sad would it be if this dangerous habit should insidiously and stealthily creep onward until ruin and misery should attest its fearful, its demoralizing tendency. I should wish to speak against it but I feel unable, my confidential position precludes my revealing it to any. I must do my utmost to influence all at once to abandon the practice. What will be Keene's feelings if the habit thus encouraged in the person destined to be the companion of his life should then prove the fell poison, the dark serpent curled at the bottom of the cup of domestic bliss, diffusing through every streamlet of the current of life the bitterness of death.

65. Opinion within Methodism on the consumption of alcohol was mixed at the time John Young was writing. Many still regarded moderation as an adequate rule, but the supporters of total abstinence were making their views more strongly heard from c. 1830 onwards,. especially among the non-Wesleyan Methodist groups who were eager to advance the cause of religion and morality among the working classes, and who saw drink as a major obstacle. The Primitive Methodists for instance adopted teetotalism in the early 1830s and Hugh Bourne, one of the founders of Primitive Methodism, became an active preacher on its behalf. He toured the north of England early in 1843. H.B. Kendall, *Origin and History of the Primitive Methodist Church,* [c. 1905], i, 469–487. The Free

Methodists, including the W.M.A., took a leading part in advocating total abstinence and the second Assembly of the W.M.A. held in 1837 urged all members to support the temperance societies which were then being established in many places. Beckerlegge 1957, pp. 56–57, Gowland pp. 157 ff. John Young obviously accepted this position, no doubt being influenced by his father, whose name appears as a temperance speaker on a plan of interdenominational temperance meetings in Sunderland in 1837, a copy of which is held by the Sunderland Antiquarian Society. A Teetotal meeting was held at the Salem W.M.A. Chapel in South Shields 4 October 1843 addressed by a well-known Newcastle temperance lecturer, George Dodds, *Newcastle Chronicle* 7 October 1843. The eighth anniversary of the Sunderland Total Abstinence Society was held on 29 November 1843 in the W.M.A. South Durham Street Tabernacle when Revd John Peters was in the chair and Dodds again one of the speakers *Sunderland Herald* 1 December 1843. Aquila Keene took a liberal line on the question of drink, more typical of the Wesleyan Methodists of that time than the W.M.A.

Missionary Meeting at Shields
First miss[ionar]y speech

On Tuesday Ms. Keene, Heywood† and Dunning† tea'd at our house and then proceeded over to Shields† per Railway to attend the Missionary meeting. We called at Moffat's house where the resolutions, and arrangement of speakers, were prepared. To my surprise I was put down to second the first resolution. I said, 'Are you serious?' Mr Moffat replied, 'Didn't I ask you to come over for the very purpose?' 'Why' said I, 'But you gave me no intimation that you desired me to speak'. 'Of course not', said he, 'If I had said so you wouldn't have come, I left it to be inferred'. Thank God I had in my mind a train of thought which I hoped, if I were able to muster confidence, I should be able to get through with decency.

I left there and came with Mr. Heywood to the Chapel and went on to the platform. Mr. T.B. Young in the chair. Mr. [? Cotes] gave out a hymn, and called upon me to pray. This was kind, it gave me confidence in a degree. Father was then voted into the chair, and having spoken, Mr. Coxon read the report, after which Mr. Keene was called upon to move the 1st Resolution. He spoke near to half an hour. All this time I was cramming my mouth with lozenges to help the voice and stimulate the frame. I had a piece of paper on which were noted the main heads of my train of argument and on the other side I put down two or three additional ideas which occurred to me. Oh how I watched Mr. Keene knowing that when he was done I should be called.

'I cordially move the adoption &c' at last fell from his lips, and then my Father said, 'Mr. John Young will 2nd the Resolution'. I rose paper in hand and, deliberately walking to the table, drank some water, and calmly setting the glass down I commenced with the awful prelude 'Mr. Chairman, Sir' I felt self-possessed – obtained command over my voice and gradually rose until I sat down with a thankful heart, having been kindly received by the people with considerable applause. O Praise the Lord for his goodness! I am satisfied that I succeeded much better than I had reason to expect. Halleluia! O for a thankful heart!

Afterwards Mr. Peters† spoke, and then Mr. Dawson of Shields, and then Mr. Dunning.† It is strange that neither last night nor tonight did Mr. Peters soar to his wonted brilliance. Mr. Dunning exceeded himself; what happy and felicitious strokes! The audience convulsed with merriment. Then came a ludicrous farce enacted by Messrs. Mules† and Heywood in proposing a vote of thanks to the ladies. Mules talked about the ladies and complimented them very highly, and then Mr. Heywood got up and declared that no such word as ladies was to be found in the resolution. Mr. Mules protested that his resolution was different. The chairman demanded that they should be compared, when it appeared the word 'ladies' was in neither, all the difference being the intrusion of the phrase *'Missionary Boxes'* on that of Mules; Heywood then said that the reason why Mr. Mules had thus dragged the ladies into his motion, must be *'because he was fond of the ladies'*, – and some other ridiculous remarks. After the meeting we had supper at the lodgings of Mr. Mules, and then rode home in a chaise, setting down Mr. Rapier and Heywood at Cleadon. Home at last. Had the events of the day discussed after supper when my father had retired to bed.

Dunning's Flattery

Mr. Dunning was pleased to compliment me in a very flattering terms on my speech declaring that six out of seven of the travelling preachers of the Association could not make such a speech. He has urged upon me my duty to go out to travel [as a full-time minister of the W.M.A. Connexion].

Ophelia was indignant at the proposition, declaring I would never do anything of the kind if I were wise. I assured Mr. D. that I entertained no such intention, for I did not conceive myself physically constituted to labour successfully in such a sphere. He replied, 'You do not mean to say that you are less strong than I'. Mr. Dunning thought I had a good voice, that the speech could not be mended, &c. I had some conversation with him about my studies &c. and his own speech and those of the others &c. &c.

At last I bid him farewell, for he proceeded to attend Shiney-row† on the following night, and thence on Thursday (sleeping at Bunker's Hill)† to Darlington.

Ophelia thinks he flattered me grossly. Of course she did not hear me, nor has she ever heard me. How difficult to distinguish between the flattery of professed friendship and the sentiment of esteem.

Mrs. White thinks I'll be a Minister

I wrote today to Reed† at Rochdale.

I was invited to tea at A. White Esq's last night, that is Tuesday 18th April, but owing to my going to Shields I could not go. My Aunt White called today and in conversation expressed her opinion that, sooner or later, I would be going out to travel. What an unaccountable notion to enter their heads. I am perfectly unconscious of having done anything to give birth to such an idea.

I had thought it quite possible to continue the two together. Said I: 'My intention has been to give the mind to business, during its regular hours, and then to devote the surplus of time, morning and evening, to sacred purposes. I do not attend any meetings during the week. The Sabbath is the only day on which I venture to do anything for God'.

Am I to go into the ministry? The Ministerial Character

I regret such a feeling exists. I am sensible that if I were in the work of the ministry I should have much better opportunities of improvement, and might expect to make correspondent progress – and did I believe that I were qualified for the work I might willingly engage to give my life to the gospel of Jesus. But what will be the consequence if, after having given up business, I should return broken in health, without resources, no competence to fall back upon? Yes, had I a strong constitution I would rejoice to dedicate my humble soul in sacrifice to the Lord. I trust my piety is not of that superficial character to lead me to desire to rest in my nest when the voice of God should say *'Stand forth'.* Father of mercies by thy grace may I live even now to Thee, and however my future lot may be cast, may the result be Thy Glory! If I thought of going out, I should wish, after having sold my business, to go down to Edinburgh or Glasgow to apply myself to study. Oh! how necessary is preliminary discipline to discharge at this advanced state of society the duties of the ministry. If the world is to be converted the Church must have men whose piety and learning are of a much higher order than at present. I believe the Church is culpably negligent in sending out men who are scarce competent as creditable local men. This lowers the standard character of the sacred office, and brings it before the eyes of the people in a very contemptible view. The people are not to be suffered to look on the preachers with mere sufferance but must be taught to look up to them as men able to give the light, and truth necessary for Salvation.[66]

66. Ministerial training was a much debated, and divisive, issue within all branches of Methodism over many years. The W.M.A. secession arose in part as a result of opposition to the launching of the first Wesleyan theological institution (1834–5) and many seceders had a resulting prejudice against college training, believing that the gifts needed for an evangelical ministry were such as could not be taught in college. On the other hand there was a growing body of opinion, voiced here by J.Y., that, without improved education, ministers would prove inadequate to serve their congregations. See W. Bardsley Brash, *The Story of our Colleges 1835 – 1935 : a Centenary record of Ministerial training in the Methodist Church,* (1935).

Religious Impressions

Saturday April 22nd, 1843.

The following extract from a letter written this day to Mr. Wm. Dixon,† will best record my present feelings.

'I feel this morning deep gratitude to God for mercy. "Thou hast covered my life with lovingkindness and with tender mercy." [Psalm 103:4*]. O for a spirit of humble prayer, and devout reliance on the atoning blood. Yesterday, and this morning I have been blessed in prayer. Light streamed upon my heart, and I seemed to see at a glance that all my *'conversation'* of the past, has been full of wickedness. I am just now trying to look to the Cross, and lay my hand upon my heart and say "Lord Thou knowest all things, Thou knowest that I love Thee" [John 21:17]. Oh! There is an awful possibility of going down to Hell in the very midst of the people of God. Save us Lord. I have often lamented that you and I have not had more of spiritual conversation. Perhaps we are both to blame. We are ignorant of Him from whom we are to derive our strength. Depend upon it, if we had been in the habit of meeting together once a week especially for prayer, wrestling prayer, we should have made much greater progress in the grace of God, saved ourselves from many sins and temptations, grown much more rapidly in moral and intellectual excellence, and above all might have possessed that greatest of earthly blessings, "Entire resignation to God and full assurance of our personal acceptance in His sight". Oh! that your heart may be as mine at this moment. Let us begin at once, let us put aside our shamefacedness and commence on those exercises which we hope to consummate in heaven.'

Reading of light literature

Last night I felt so wearied in business that I sent to three libraries to procure 'Harry Lorrequer'[67] but failed. I got from Burnett's 'Cruise of the Midge'[68] which I read until ½ past 10 o'clock. Beautiful imagery, and descriptive scenery.

I do not spend time over books of this class. This I believe is the first I have read this year. I once entertained strong feeling against the occasional or habitual perusal of fiction. I now entertain a modified sentiment.[69]

I believe that occasionally read to give zest and stimulus to the mind they are useful, and still more to [? inspire] the imagination into chaste, yet fiery, and graphic description. By this I may learn in reading to write with more power and beauty of illustration.

In conversing with Dunning he told me he had read most of the popular light works of the present day, Dickens, Ainsworth, Bulwer, 'Harry Lorrequer' and others, periodical literature – 'Dublin University', 'Blackwood', 'Bentley's Miscellany'[70] &c. &c. We agreed that the moderate perusal of this sort of literature might prove beneficial.

Said he, 'I durst not tell every person that I devoted any time to such reading. Many of our grave brethren shake their heads, and declaim against what they assert to be a shameful prostitution of time, *but* I have frequently found when I have become more intimate with them, that they themselves practised that which in public they condemned'. Because what may be suitable luxury to the hardy and disciplined mind of the student would be very injurious to the weak and ignorant Christian.

A lady in Manchester, I have been told, highly disapproved of the general character of light literature, but thought that there were some works of imagination which might be suitable for her daughters, and therefore, to discover these, *she read herself indiscriminately whatever* fell from the press lest they, poor creatures, should have any put into their hands than those which her wisdom pronounced prudent and beneficial.

My Father has long been in the habit of reading fiction. I myself have perused many, but my 'many' I conceive will be 'few' compared with the quantities which the morbid appetite of the confirmed 'Dreamer' devours.

I have abstained in a great measure lest I should be carried away by 'the contagion' and lose that taste for solid, substantial inquiry which it is pre-eminently desirable to cultivate. I am especially delighted with those of a maritime character. Hence Marryat, Cooper[71] &c. possess to me commanding interest.

67. A light hearted novel by the Irish author Charles Lever (1806 – 1872), published in 1837. Lever edited the *Dublin University Magazine* 1842–5. His novels consist largely of 'vivid, rollicking

pictures of military life and of the hard-drinking fox-hunting Irish society of his day', P. Harvey, *Oxford Companion to English Literature,* 4th ed., (1967), p. 475.

68. A very lively and amusing sea story by Michael Scott (1789 – 1835), published in *Blackwood's Magazine* 1834 – 1835 and in book form from 1836. Scott, who put much of his own personal experiences in the West Indies into his stories, also wrote *Tom Cringle's Log,* (*Blackwoods* 1829 – 1833; book ed. 1835), which is mentioned in the diary p. 84 below.

69. Evangelical attitudes regarding the reading of fiction were moving in a liberal direction in John Young's day though older attitudes persisted, especially in public and where influence on the young and impressionable was under discussion. As late as 1855 an article in the *Primitive Methodist Juvenile Magazine* declared that 'the popular novels of our day are, to a great extent, written by men who are known to be lax in principle, and loose in life'. Novels are condemned as presenting 'vice and virtue in false colours', producing 'a vain turn of mind', and of diverting money from more worthy causes. Novel-reading is time 'wasted on trifles' and so on, (p. 174 ff.).

70. By 1843, when J.Y. was writing, Dickens had published *Sketches by Boz* (1836–7), *Pickwick Papers* (in monthly numbers beginning 1836), *Oliver Twist* (in *Bentley's Miscellany* 1837–8), *Nicholas Nickleby* (1838–9), *The Old Curiosity Shop* and *Barnaby Rudge* (1840–1). *Martin Chuzzlewit* was advertised in the *Newcastle Chronicle* of 24 December 1842 as commencing publication in 20 monthly parts in January 1843. William Harrison Ainsworth (1805 – 1882) edited *Bentley's Miscellany* 1840 – 1842 and *Ainsworth's Magazine* 1842 – 1853. By 1843 he had published several novels, most of a historical character, including *Jack Sheppard* (1839), *The Tower of London* (1840), *Old St. Paul's* (1841), *Guy Fawkes* (1841). The novels of Edward Bulwer-Lytton (1803 – 1873) published by 1843 included *Falkland* (1827), *The Last Days of Pompeii* (1834), *Ernest Maltravers* (1837), and *Zanoni* (1842).

The periodicals mentioned here by J.Y. are the *Dublin University Magazine,* a literary and philosophical review, published 1833 – 1877; *Blackwood's Edinburgh Magazine,* begun in 1817 by William Blackwood; *Bentley's Miscellany,* published 1837 – 1868, edited by Dickens and Harrison Ainsworth *inter al.*

71. Captain Frederick Marryat (1792 – 1848) had published by 1843, among other books, *Mr Midshipman Easy,* (1836), and *Masterman Ready,* (1841). His novels and yarns for boys were very popular, full of action, adventure and humour. James Fenimore Cooper (1789 – 1851), the American writer, would be known to John Young by his novels, e.g. *The Last of the Mohicans,* (1826), *The Pathfinder,* (1840), and also by his scholarly *History of the Navy of the United States of America,* (1839). Cooper served in the navy 1806 – 1811.

My knowledge of naval affairs

The United Service Journal always chains me to its details of the sea and land service. When I take up the daily Shipping Gazette, the very thing I notice is the information under the classification 'Navy'. For so long as I have paid attention to this subject that I am familiar with the names, rates, and complements of the ships on service, and when they return into ordinary I feel as though I had parted with an acquaintance. Indeed anything connected with Naval Architecture, manoeuvres, movements, improvements, &c. &c. is a source of unfailing interest. Whether my attainments in these matters may prove useful in some day remains, like futurity itself, obscure and dark.[72]

72. On J.Y's naval knowledge and interests in later life we learn from his obituary, *Sunderland Echo* 21 October 1904, that he took an especial interest in the naval defences of Britain and corresponded on this matter with leading statesmen.

Mr. Keene's sermon

Monday, April 24th 1843.

Rose on Sabbath weary and depressed. Alas mortality!, this shroud of flesh which smothers one's kindliest aspirations. The Sabbath instead of being a day of joyful relaxation is often a burden, because the confinement and labour of the preceding night encroaches on my necessary rest, and produces dulness and stupidity during the season of spiritual comfort and refreshment. I heard Mr. Keene† at Brougham St.† from 'I will look unto the Lord, I will wait for the God of my salvation. My God will hear', Micah [Micah 7:7]. A very delightful sermon. I sat near the pulpit. I always can understand, appreciate and profit [more] under a discourse when I am seated near to the speaker than when I am at a distance. The straining to hear interrupts the attention, and confuses the mind. Gaze on the countenance of the preacher as each thought is successively thrown out, and you are irresistibly brought under the influence of similar feelings. After dinner I went down to Keene's to request him to proceed and conduct the Lovefeast as my father was very unwell.

Mr. Mules† (who was going to preach Missionary Sermons at Hylton)† and he were at dinner. I saw his Todd's *'Index Rerum'* which I had long wished to look at. I have procured it this morning from his lodgings and intend to have one made like it. We went to B. St. together. But I did not go to the Lovefeast. I started off across the Bridge and enjoyed a pleasant walk along the North Shore.

At night I heard Mr. Keene again from 'At the time of this ignorance God winked at' &c. and following verse [Acts 17:30–31]. Walked home with Anne and at ½ past 9 o'clock went to bed being distressed with a severe headache.

I have by divine mercy once more been brought to commence another week of my probationary career. Oh that it may be given 'to reading to exhortation and doctrine' [I Tim 4:13]; the closet, the bible, there lie my weapons, which can bring 'into captivity every thought unto the obedience of Christ' [II Cor. 10:5].

Give testaments to little boys at Monkwearmouth

Last time I preached at Monkwearmouth† I felt interested in two little boys who were present and requested them to come over and see me. They called today when I presented them will a small Testament each. May the Lord grant that the gospel through this humble attempt may prove their salvation. Their names were Robert and John Bulmer.

'Cruise of the Midge'

Thursday April 27, 1843

Tuesday and Wednesday I worked freely all day except some time in the morning to read the Bible, and yesterday to the finishing of vol. II of the *Cruise of the Midge* which I got after dinner, and ended this evening.

I was delighted with the humour and imagery of this highly descriptive and beautifully graphic tale. I have read some time ago the kindred production of the same author 'Tom Cringle's Log'.[73] This morning I peeped into the Westminster Review[74] for February 1843.

73. See p. 82 above note 68.

74. A journal launched in 1824 by Jeremy Bentham and James Mill as the organ of the philosophical radicals (Utilitarians). By 1843 W.E. Hickson was editor.

Sabbath Walking

Sunday April 30th

Having been working late almost every night last week (until ½ past eleven) I felt exceedingly tired and depressed last night. This morning I lay until 9 o'clock and then walked down to S.D. St. School. I find that they have brought the boys upstairs amongst the girls. This was resolved at a Teachers' Committee meeting on Monday last.

I then went a couple of miles along the sands. On returning I was reprimanded by my father 'for setting a bad example, and neglecting a positive duty'. I have done this occasionally because I believe it to be absolutely necessary for the maintenance of health. Considering the severe incarceration of the week, from the nature of my business, and further from the necessity I am under of giving of nights and mornings to study, I am compelled to appear somewhat out of decent regularity.

Self Denial a condition of Study

In fact I must give up moral or at least intellectual improvement and preparation for usefulness if I do not deny myself of idle chit chat, amusements, parties and even to some extent that constant and frequent attendance upon the means of grace which it would otherwise be my delight to bestow. For the cultivation of the mind time is essential. A Sabbath afternoon occasionally is not sufficient. It must be the diligent improvement of daily opportunities. But the confinement consequent upon a continuous attention first to business, and then to study, brings the poor frail body to the Saturday night broken down and exhausted. Therefore something must be done on Sunday to restore and brace the system in healthy vigour, that it may be able successfully to encounter the duties of the ensuing week. The object of religion and religious principles is moral and spiritual improvement, but this depends on mental culture and the capacity of the mind or a healthful development of the brain, and the vigour of the brain is the issue of a sound and healthy physical organisation, and this again upon an obedience to those laws which Divine wisdom has appointed to promote and secure its acquisition, so that in promoting and labouring to retain the health of the body I am but laying the only foundation upon which the superstructure of efficiency of mind and enlargement of soul can be reached. Truly a 'man's enemies are those of his own household' [Matt. 10:36*] and in the words of a reviewer in the Westminster Review, the greatest and most formidable opponent a man has to engage who wishes to give his life to the noble pursuit of wisdom is *The Demon of Domestic arrangements, and habits'.*

Is it nothing to abandon the quiet lounge by the cheerful fireside, to sit up late, or to rise early, to debar oneself of a thousand little gratifications pleasing to weak humanity? Am I less susceptible of the calm delight of social intercourse than others? Does it require no effort to constrain a languid frame and jaded mind to return to its pursuits rather than indulge the idle stroll of the time-destroying flow of loose and indefinite conversations? Happy the man who can throw off such temptations, who can easily withdraw himself and, alone and solitary, and perhaps often comfortless, pursue the path which wisdom directs, which constructs and rears on the sacrifice of present pleasure a glorious though often apparently indefinite future of substantial happiness. Oh to be able at once to snap assunder the last thread which connects me with sensuality, and the allurements of the world. For many years I have puzzled and perplexed myself with schemes and resolutions of methodical study and diligent investigation, but to [see them] vanish before the stern and unbending face of social position. I have carefully reviewed my habits, and striven to secure their reformation. The practice of late reading and the acquisition of the habit of early rising has time after time occupied my mind and yet has never been completely successful.

Habits: Eating, Sleeping

The philosophy of diet and dietetics has taken no inconsiderable thought. Sometimes I have perplexed myself with doubts as to the propriety of eating this and of drinking that – and after all here I am, having learnt that it is quantity and regularity [which] are more important elements of health than quality and discrimination.

I propose especially, because I feel more deeply its necessity, to labour to acquire the habit of early rising. It would be invaluable – more than hundreds of pounds.

It is folly to be constantly thinking but of the future; the question which ought to suggest itself to my mind is *'What can I do this day?'*

May Divine mercy and love be my salvation and everlasting home, for Christ's sake!

Skinner's Aids to Preaching

Monday May 1st 1843

The first day of another week, of another month. O that when I come to review this month it may afford satisfaction and thankfulness, far surpassing that which is now part of the past.

Yesterday after dinner I came down to my little back room at the shop and lighted a fire, and after having written the previous remarks sat down and read that part of *Skinner's Aids to Preaching*[75] which treats of 'Mental Discipline', 'Studies of a Preacher', 'Power in Speaking', 'Doctrinal Preaching'.

This writer's observations are of a very superior and comprehensive character. His standard of excellence in the Ministry is much higher than generally entertained but not greater than he demonstrates to be reasonable and necessary. My mind was particularly interested and blessed by the encouragement he would give to the student, by such considerations as these. 'Ordinary healthy mind is capable of infinite improvement. There is no degree of excellence to which the student may not justly aspire. The height of intellectual cultivation attained by the greatest luminaries of the day is not so great as might be achieved by an ordinary mind by indomitable perseverance'. The student who is consecrated to his studies by the highest religious motive and personal holiness has the best guarantee for success.

The remarks on the 'Studies of a preacher', and 'Power in Speaking' are worthy of the most serious attention, and especially the last.

I find by my own experience, and have long entertained the opinion, that the Science of public speaking is far too slightingly regarded. Many appear ashamed to be known to take any pains to acquire a just gesture or correct enunciation.

I knew a young man of whom it was reported that he practised his movement before a large mirror – and great was the wrath and indignation and contempt expressed by his brethren in labour. I have myself disregarded the common sentiment and acted upon my own conviction.

When younger I had, I fancied, a tolerable voice, but 3 years of affliction left me weak in body, and feeble in utterance. Now, four years ago I commenced a system of exercise which was partly suggested to my mind by Combe's *Principles of Physiology* 'applied to the preservation of Health'.[76] In addition to the little walking I could obtain, I accustomed myself to whirl a small iron bar. I remember that two years ago I was easily exhausted, but my strength improved until I could toss and whirl my 'Iron Pestle' of 11 lbs with ease and little exhaustion. Thus my chest has been expanded and strengthened, my limbs have increased in elasticity and vigour, that now I, who for months moved on crutches, can walk my dozen miles, and deliver my two discourses with comparative ease.

I am confident that I owe my recovery from an apparently hopeless state principally to my personal perseverance in the execution of my own views and plans for the recovery of my health.

All the medicine prescribed by my medical attendant was simply tonics and purgatives. Judicious and careful exercise, and relaxation, with seabathing, were my grand restoratives.

75. Thomas Harvey Skinner *Aids to Preaching and Hearing,* (New York, 1839; London, 1840), part of Ward's Library of Standard Divinity. Skinner published other writings in the 1840s and 1850s on preaching, public speaking, education and religion.

76. See p. 14 note 8 on Andrew Combe.

Improvement of Voice

My voice has improved – why? Because I have given labour and thought to the subject. Reading aloud at home, speaking aloud on the sea-shore – by these two modes conjoined to careful pulpit exercises my voice is wonderfully improved in strength, clearness and inflection.

Westminster Review

I have been instructed, and stimulated by the perusal of some articles in this review last week: an admirable article on Dr. Arnold late of Rugby, Sir Lytton Bulwer's works and genius. These articles are worthy of perusal.

Last night I heard Mr Mules, 'Happy is that people who have the God of Jacob' &c. [Psalm 146:5*. See also psalm 144:15], after which I returned to my domicile and read until 9 o'clock.

Saturday May 6th

Monday night

Tuesday night I prepared to attend Class but was seized with so violent a toothache, that I was compelled to walk the floor in agony until 10 o'clock when I went home and sat up till 12 o'clock reading 'Fraser's Magazine'[77].

77. *Fraser's Magazine for Town and Country*, (London), 1830 – 1882. Founded by William Maginn and Hugh Fraser. Early contributors included Carlyle, Coleridge, Harrison Ainsworth *et al.*

Wine question

Business engaged my attention on Wednesday until night when I went to call Wm Dixon† to take him to the Leaders' Meeting to be present at the discussion of a proposition brought forward by Mr. Smirke, last meeting, for the introduction of unfermented wine to the ordinance of the Lord's Supper – he was not present. Mr. Peters† in the chair. It was finally, after 'the talk', moved by S. [blank], 2nd by Brother Milsom, that it be used alternately in the Chapels. The ground on which the meeting assented was that of charity, the apostolic principle that we ought neither to eat or drink aught that make our brother offend[ed]. This was Mr Peters' view. W. Dixon did not vote.

On Thursday what spare time I had I devoted to preparation for preaching at Rainton† on Sunday. My sister Anne took tea with me this afternoon. We had a long and interesting confab. until 7 o'clock. Mr & Mrs White† went to Newcastle this afternoon in their carriage. I sent a parcel of Spice Nuts[78] over by them for Mrs John Muschamp,† my dear old friend and cousin, with a note to say that I often 'think and pray' for Anne Tuer as one of my best and earliest friends. 'God bless you, and may I be ever worthy of your esteem'. I say Amen, Amen.

On Friday – continued preparation for preaching, read some of the *Quarterly Review*[79] for Feby. 1843. Read the *United Service Mag.* for Feby. 1843. At night was at work with business until ¼ to 11 o'clock. In the afternoon Messrs. Keene† and Heywood† chatted an hour and a half with me. O this waste of time.

78. These were the gingerbread nuts for which John Young became famous, though contrary to a statement in his obituary he did not invent them. It was a custom in Sunderland for a basket of the nuts to be thrown to the crowd at the opening of the Sunderland fairs in May and October. See other references p. 150 below under 9 – 11 Oct. 1843, also J.Y's obituary, *Sunderland Echo* 21 Oct. 1904; and *Antiquities of Sunderland* 21 (1954) 47 for a reference to gingerbread nuts in the 1790s. The *Sunderland Year Book* 1912, p. 39, has an interesting account on this subject. Referring to the old Sunderland fairs, the last of which was held in 1868, the writer says : 'Gingerbread nuts were in great demand during these holiday times amongst the grown-up portion of the community and one well-known establishment in High Street conducted by Mr John Young did a roaring trade in these comestibles during the fair week. His premises were brilliantly illuminated with gas designs from the roof and windows and it is said that many tons of these sweets were annually disposed of in pound and half-pound packages as presents to sweethearts and friends. They were sold at the rate of 8d. and 10d. per pound so that the turnover in his shop must have reached a high figure. Mr. Young had many rivals in the gingerbread nut trade and his popularity as the premier purveyor of them continued until long after the abolition of the fair.' School children were given a half-day holiday for the fairs and workers claimed the same. The fair ground was the stretch of High Street east of Sans Street so that John Young's first shop† was very strategically placed for sales, being in that very vicinity of High Street. The nuts were also thrown to onlookers at certain

points during the perambulation of the Sunderland parish boundaries in the 1840s : J.W. Summers, *History and Antiquities of Sunderland,* (1858), pp. 57, 61.

79. *The Quarterly Review,* London, 1809 – 1925. Founded by John Murray (1778 – 1843) as a Tory rival to the *Edinburgh Review,* though intended to be run on 'liberal, conciliatory and impartial lines'. Sir Walter Scott was a strong supporter of the venture and contributed to the *Review,* which was edited by his son-in-law J.G. Lockhart between 1825 and 1853.

Preach at Rainton (Middle)

Monday May 8th

Went to bed on Saturday night at two o'clock. Rose at ¼ past 7 and proceeded to the gig. I drove the gig out to Middle Rainton† with Messrs. Elliott and Hillary. They left me taking the gig with them to Hetton† where Elliott had to preach, and Hillary returned back to Collier Row† to his appointment. I had a little difficulty in finding the Chapel. I stopped at a door and said to a woman – in her dishabils – 'Where is (if you please) the Wesleyan Assocn. Chapel?' 'Ah don't know, but there's a woman lives next door mebbe knows'. She walked with me to the next door and called of the other person and I repeated the question. While she appeared to be considering, the first party said 'O it'll be the teetotalers ye want, or the Seceders – 'Ay' said I 'that's it'. Just then the woman of the house said, 'O there's Tommy Dixon he'll tell ye'. I knew Tommy in his Ranters coat, and small clothes with gaiters so I posted up to him. He took me to his son and then to Mr. Birkbeck.

I preached at 10 o'clock from 2 Tim: 2nd ch. 11.12.13 verses. I felt comfortable. Dined with Birkbeck. The rain poured all afternoon. Mr B. intended to take me to visit the members but owing to the rain we could not get. Nevertheless I was obliged to go and seek a place for the performance of a natural function. What inconvenience we often undergo for want of such accommodation.

I preached at night with great fervour and softening of hearts. Praise God. Text John v. 40. I enlarged much on several points of this, I think with improvements that I have not in my manuscript. Messrs. Dixon, Birkbeck, and Nesbitt prayed, divine grace came down, I was constrained to cry

Halleluia! I have not felt so well for a long period. Supped at Mr. B's., prayed with them and walked down the Rainton Road, met the gig, and got safely home by ½ past 9 o'clock.

Coble to Clatchiff

I rose this morning at ½ past six. Read a Psalm. Mind composed, and cheerful. Opened shop at 7 o'clock. Breakfasted, having been up in the newsroom about 20 m. Just when I was done breakfast, Mr. Keene† came and said, 'Now you must come with us on to the water – Mr. Peters,† the Misses Peters, Mr. Hodgson,† and a lady named Miss Clark stopping with Mr. P. and Miss Wilson are going to have a little pull. I can't pull so you must come'. Said I, 'We cannot leave business'. 'Oh' said Mr. K., 'We are not going to be more than an hour, we shall be back before 10 o'clock; come you must'. 'Well' said I 'if you will not be more I might venture, so I'll come down directly'. I went down and we pulled up very pleasantly as far as Clatchiff rock.† We landed and ascended to the top, where we had a very delightful view. Mr K. and I scrambled up the rough surface of the rock but were obliged to return. We might have done but it is folly to run risks.

Domestic Trial

We came down very sweetly and arrived at the Ferry Boat landing at about ½ past 11 o'clock. This was later than I anticipated. Arrived at the shop, found all well. Sent up to the house and received the following note.—

Dear John, Monday morning.

As you are so independent as to be able to leave your shop at business hours to take pleasure, there can be no further need to lodge with me gratis. Be so obliging therefore as to provide yourself lodgings &c. &c.

Thos. B. Young

Here was food for thought. My first impulse was astonishment, my second a breath to heaven to quell the tumult of feeling. Why should passion intrude on the serenity of my mind? My ambition has been for years to acquire a command of temper, that in all circumstances I might be *'the same'.*

If I have done wrong, I thought, and if ten years of close attention to business be as nothing compared with *Three hours of absence,* if the crime is so serious, is this the *mode in which* I am to expect to be admonished?

I advised with my honest friend, Jesse Bennett,† who is acquainted with many of my concerns.

I wrote a note to Mr Peters who came up at 3 o'clock. I acquainted him confidentially with the circumstance. He said 'He felt exceedingly pained' – I said that I did not wish to act rashly, that I knew of no one of whom I could ask advice with the same freedom and confidence, that I thought it would cause much unpleasantness if I were to leave the house, giving room for evil reports and surmises, that I thought I perhaps might be more comfortable out of the house than in it, but I should wish to do nothing that I might afterwards regret. He replied 'I think you are correction in your views; it would be a great pity, it is extremely perplexing'. I said I had no doubt of my father's sincerity in his conduct. Mr. P., 'I'm glad you take such a view, I believe he does what he thinks is for the best – and then you must remember his irritability from his "present disorders" which added to his natural impetuosity makes him do things which he may afterwards regret. I consider myself implicated in the matter as I went with you and I must call and speak to him on the subject – It is very wrong'. I replied 'Sir I think it would be better not to take any notice for perhaps if you mention it things will be worse. I consider myself that the best way in my own judgement will be to take no notice at all but return home as usual, and wait to see the issue of events, for if I apologise, or write, I believe from past experience it will only make things worse, for I do not expect my father will acknowledge himself wrong, though I were to place the matter in the must justifiable light'. Mr. P. 'Certainly not, I'm glad to see you take a Christian view for you must not forget that he is your father, and now when I reflect perhaps it will be better for me to say nothing'. John Y. 'Oh sir! no – some months ago [we] had a rupture about some little nonsense, and my father

did not cross my shop doors for a couple of months'. Peters, 'Oh dear! Oh dear. However, I think you are right, just go home as usual and demean yourself as heretofore and perhaps in a little time this feeling will pass away. Your father is delicate. He will not probably live to be an old man. It is many years since he lost his wife. If he had had a wife who could have helped and softened and smoothed his habits it would have been different with him now. Your sister is going to marry, and if you go he will be left like a "lodge in a garden of cucumbers" [Isaiah 1:8]. No, you must stay by him. I am glad you have the piety to make the attempt'.
J.Y.: 'Well Sir, if I was to give way to my natural feelings I would act very differently. I do not make a merit of diligence in business but I think my attention has been very different.'
Mr P.: 'Yes according to my observation very different, *very different* and if it were not so this is not the way to mend matters'.

J.Y.: 'I have no doubt but that my Father will say if I do not act upon his command that I have not the 'spirit of a louse' but it is harder to bear these things than to resent them'.
Mr. P.: 'Oh never you mind that, you must not think of that, I know it is hard to bear, but I believe your judgement will convince you that the other is the wiser, the more Christian course. I'll call and see you tomorrow and we'll see how things will turn out'.

Sunday at Shop

Tuesday May 16th

Nothing extraordinary has occurred. I proceeded home and conducted myself as usual. The week has been a very busy one owing to the Fair.[80] I have had tolerable health. Some blessed seasons of refreshment in spiritual strength.

On Sabbath I walked on the sands from 10 o'clock to ½ past 1. I came back to my shop, kindled a fire, and read the remainder of Skinner's *'Aids to Preaching'.* I heard Mr Keene† at night from 'A strong man armed keepeth his goods' &c. &c. [Luke 11:21*] at Brougham Street.† After service I returned to the 'retreat' to finish my reading. On

Monday morning it was near eight before I woke and got to business. This will not do. Messrs Mules & Keene spent an hour with me this morning.

80. The holding of the two fairs in Sunderland was a tradition going back at least to the seventeenth century, Fordyce ii, 479

Harry Lorrequer

At night I procured 'Harry Lorrequer' and read from 8 o'clock to 12 o'clock, finished the two volumes this day. Ah if more substantial acquirements could be digested with the same rapidity how different would be my scanty pretensions to literature and ability.

Thursday May 25th

On Sabbath I preached at Southwick† from 2 Tim 2. 11. 12.13. In consequence of Monkwearmouth† preaching room being given up I remained at home all night.

It rained very heavily all day and has continued until this moment. I heard Mr. Horsman the Town Missionary[81] preach at Brougham Street† from the 'Ten Virgins'. He was there in consequence of Mr. Mules† being unwell. Mr. Mules on Wednesday had a Polypus cut out of his nostril by a surgeon at Shields.

81. The Sunderland Town Mission, founded in July 1839, was an inter-denominational evangelical organisation intended to promote religious work among those who were not prepared to avail themselves of any of the 'means of grace' offered by the various churches and chapels in the town. It employed several agents including Mr Horsman. Their task was to visit the homes of the working classes, distribute tracts, and preach both in houses and in the open air. The Mission's officers were mainly Methodist by persuasion, (Andrew White, John Young's uncle, being President, and William Muschamp, whose brother married John's cousin Ann Tuer, one of the secretaries), but it was supported by several denominations. The minute book of the Mission covering the years 1839 – 1843 is in the Tyne and Wear Archives reference 1032/205. The Mission was dissolved in 1843 with liabilities of £112, including £30 owed to one of the agents. The debts were apportioned between the denominations supporting the Mission, with the Wesleyans bearing the major part. The W.M.A. does not seem to have been connected officially with the Mission.

Whately's Logic

I have had Whately's *Logic*[82] from the Subscription Library† and have been much gratified in its review. I have but as it were 'looked into it' for I am obliged to accommodate Father by returning it immediately. It is clear and masterly in its exhibition of the Sciences. I shall return to it by and by.

82. Richard Whately (1787 – 1863), Fellow of Oriel College Oxford 1811, Professor of Political Economy 1829, Archbishop of Dublin 1831, *Elements of Logic,* (1826).

Arminian Magazine

On Sunday evening I turned over the last vol. of the Arminian Magazine[83] of Mr. Wesley. A great deal of matter curious and interesting. I should wish to have a glance through the lot.

Praise be to God I have this week enjoyed health of body, clearness of mind and some freedom at prayers. Was at Class on Tuesday, Mr. Lewins led it.

83. *The Arminian Magazine consisting of extracts and original translations on universal redemption* was launched as a monthly magazine by John Wesley in 1778. From 1798 – 1821 it was published as the *Methodist Magazine,* and later as the *Wesleyan Methodist Magazine.*

Mesmerism

There has been during the last week a surprising interest excited in the town by certain lectures, and experiments on the science of 'Mesmerism'.[84] Messrs. Williams, Gamsby, Dobson, and others have had large audiences. Having not studied the subject I am unprepared to form an opinion. A friend observed it 'was more credulous to believe it an imposture than to receive its truth' because having witnessed the experiments he could not conceive the possibility of the patients simulating the phenomena. This friend (Mr. Wm. Coxon) assured me that he himself had mesmerised three females at Donkin's (The Bridge Hotel).† How then could he doubt!

84. Demonstrations of mesmerism, linked with phrenology and referred to as phreno-mesmerism, went on in Sunderland throughout the month of May 1843, primarily in the Lecture Room at the Athenaeum.† There was considerable public exitement and a number of leading citizens, A.J. Moore among them, were involved in the demonstrations. *Sunderland Herald* 12 May, 26 May 1843. There is a vivid account by Francis Kilvert of a demonstration of phreno-mesmerism at Weston-super-Mare in 1872; presumably those in Sunderland in 1843 were similar. *Kilvert's Diary*, ed. W. Plomer, Penguin edition (1977) pp. 210–212.

Mrs. Todd. My visits to London

Mrs Todd of London is now here. Her husband Capt. Todd is on a voyage to Hobart Town from whence she herself has but recently returned. Some years ago when very ill I went to London by sea, and was very hospitably entertained at her house. This visit was repeated two years afterwards, for the same purpose, the last visit being in the year 1838.

Mr Todd formerly commanded one of the London Line of New York Packets. At her house on my first visit when I sailed in the 'Viscount Melbourne', [Captain] Metcalfe. I was at her house three weeks and had excellent opportunities of visiting a large part of the great city, and its splendid institutions. During my last visit with the 'Duke of Cleveland', Capt. Gilchrist, I was only with her about 8 days, and being unable to walk without crutches my perambulations did not extend beyond the neighbourhood of Hackney where Mrs T. resided in Green Street. At my first visit she lived in Sydney Street, Commercial Road. If there is any place in the world where I should like better than another to reside it is in the environs of London. Is it possible that this wish should ever be accomplished? Oh! to be beside the great central fountain of movement, commercial and intellectual.

Here I am pinned to a business which threatens to ruin my not too vigorous constitution and give no hope of amelioration. With the godliness of the gospel of Jesus embodied in my life, no matter where my lot shall be case, 'all will work together for good' [Romans 8:28]. Happiness if not at present so perfect as may be agreeable to my desires, shall in Heaven be consummated. Then will the cry break forth 'He hath done all things well' [Mark 7:37].

Preach at Shiney Row and Philadelphia

Monday May 29th

Saturday the Misses Harrisons, Master John Harrison,† and Mr Keene† were present in my back room. They tea'd at our house.

On Sunday morning, according to arrangements, Mr Keene called and we proceeded by Chester Lane and railway to Philadelphia[85].

It was a very beautiful day. I called to see my sister Anne before I went out. She has been very unwell. We reached Harrisons about ½ past 12 o'clock. Mr. K. and I took coffee by ourselves in the little room. I had complained of Mr. H's hospitality in constraining me to eat such quantities of meat, pudding &c. and that it prevented freedom of thought &c.

Mr Harrison said now, 'What sermons we may expect from these gentlemen! How the Shiney Row† and Philadelphia† people will be electrified, Ha! Ha! Ha!, the coffee beans must bring forth something sublime'.

Nevertheless it was agreeable to escape the conversation of the dinner table, and feel the calmness and serenity of uninterrupted thought. I preached from John V, 40 and felt more comfortable than at any previous period. Finding some books under the seat of the pulpit I laid them beneath the stool and contrived to raise myself higher. It is indeed so elevated above the people, and so deep in the sides that it is exceedingly disagreeable to gaze down upon the people.

Mr T. Stevenson a preacher amongst the New Connexion friends was present and Miss Rutherford, Misses M. & S. Harrison and Miss Rutherford accompanied me to Shiney Row.

After, I had a discussion with Mr. H. on Mesmerism, and Phreno-Mesmerism. He denounced the doctrine as Infidelity, and Socialism. I stated many facts, and adduced strong evidence, but did not attempt to press my views.

When I entered Shiney Row Chapel I felt much depressed, such vapid deadness, and indifference, not a spark of heavenly feeling. I strove to shake it off, I cried to God, and after the delivery of the introduction the incubus disappeared, and I felt liberty and delight in the delivery of my discourse. It is wonderful the vast influence of *little matters* on the mind. I spoke from II Peter I. ch. 5.6.7 verses. Halleluia! for this mercy, O that some sinner may be brought to the feet of Jesus.

I called, and saw Mr and Mrs Smurthwaite (late Miss Ann Hays), and then returned to Philadelphia with the Misses H. I waited for Mr Stevenson and we came home together. The night was fine, and our way was beguiled with agreeable conversation. Arrived at 20m to 12 o'clock. Happy I am that the labour and responsibility of the Sabbath is gone never to return.[86].

I had some conversation with Miss H. on her marriage, and strongly urged the propriety of her consenting to be married at the South Durham Street Chapel.† It will be infamous to sneak into a Parish Church to be united by some ungodly priest, disgraceful to Mr Keene's† character as a Dissenting minister and an insult to the Society with which he is connected.[87] I must not forget that Miss Mar. Harrison desired me to write something in her album. I shall not write doggerel poetry, this is supreme folly. Every man who takes a pen to scrawl in an album fancies he must write some sentimental verses. It is bad policy. For 100 that can scribble decent prose is there one poet.

85. The railway referred to here is the Newbottle (Lambton) Colliery waggonway,† from Philadelphia and adjacent collieries to the Wear at Sunderland. John Young must mean that he and Keene walked along the railway, not that they travelled as passengers. Waggonways were convenient routes for pedestrian preachers but could be dangerous. Two Primitive Methodist preachers were killed by coal trucks on the Hetton waggonway† in February 1831, *Primitive Methodist Magazine* 1831, 274–6, 343–4.
86. He means that preaching is no longer an anxious burden to him.
87. The Marriage and Registration Acts of 1836, in force from 1 March 1837, permitted marriages at properly licensed nonconformist chapels, with the minister of the chapel officiating in the presence of a registrar. Before 1837 most dissenters had to be married at their local parish church by the incumbent of the parish. Some had objected strongly to this regulation, though not all nonconformists took this attitude – many Wesleyans for instance were content to be married at church. The W.M.A., with its strong dissenting sympathies, believed its members should

avail themselves of their new freedom and be married at their own chapels, and J.Y. expresses this point of view regarding the forthcoming marriage of Miss Harrison and Aquila Keene. The matter was particularly acute since a minister was involved. It would seem that the bride's family wanted a marriage in church, perhaps for social reasons, and the ceremony took place at St Michael's, Houghton-le-Spring, see p. 138 below. Bunker Hill, where the Harrisons lived, was in Houghton parish at that time. Aquila Keene obviously acquiesced, and in this, as in his willingness to partake of alcohol, he adopted a more liberal attitude than most of his members. The W.M.A. had licensed the Durham Street Tabernacle for marriages; J.Y.'s sister Ophelia was married there to John Dixon, see p. 130 below.

Brevity of Life

Thursday June 1st

Month after month is sliding imperceptibly away. I have felt much impressed for some time with the 'brevity of life', so short for all its great and noble purposes. One is apt at times to think, what is the profit of all this labour, mental and bodily, one must soon pass away. And why consume life in striving to get riches and knowledge, when the probability is I may be cut off in the very midst, and, to a certainty, at no remote period? 'Let us eat, drink, and be merry for tomorrow we die'. [Luke 12: 19-20]. Is this life the beginning and the close of man's career? If so, even then mere ambition and emulation would, I believe, lead me to strive for distinction and esteem. But when I remember that the moments of life give their impress to the ages of eternity, I cannot, I durst not, I will not, suffer my existence that precious responsibility, those vast obligations in which I am involved, to pass without some effort, however wayward and fearful, to secure the Elysium of repose and joy, the fruition of eternal life which awaits those who give the present to the self denial of virtue.

Motives to Exertion

My attention at present is more especially directed to the formation of good habits. Early rising, constant diligence in business, the redemption of every moment. A thousand times I have resolved, and a thousand times I have grown careless, and indifferent. Oh, for perseverance, to bow at the throne of mercy and cry, 'Lord, vouchsafe Thy spirit to guide and restrain my poor foolish heart'.

Father's attack of Spasms

Wednesday June 7th 1843.

Thursday and Friday last I occupied in committing a few thoughts to paper on the Philosophy of Education. Saturday, I did not feel particularly disposed for study, (study did I say, it is impossible on such a day of business), nevertheless there are intervals though of brief duration when I snatch a moment's thought, but in this day I was interrupted by one, and another, until all my little fragments were consumed.

On Sunday I rose at ½ past 7 o'clock. I had retired to rest about 2 o'clock in the morning, having got home from the shop about ½ past 12 on the preceding night. I did not go to chapel but sat down to study a little. About eleven my Father called me up stairs. He was suddenly attacked very violently with what I immediately recognised to be a spasmodic affection. I ran down to my shop and mixed a draught, of aethir, Laudanum and Magnes. Carb.[88] On returning I could hear his groans before the opening of the door. I instantly administered the draught, and persuaded him to allow me to run for Dr. Brown.

When I came back I found him completely relieved, to my great satisfaction. It had left him he said 'Like a shot!' The doctor arrived, pronounced the attack to have arisen from the irritation existing in the bowels and stomach, recommended the repetition of the draught occasionally, which he stated to be a very proper combination, and wrote me a prescription to prepare a box of ointment to cool the piles.

88. Laudanum and ether were presumably used here to relieve pain, and magnesium carbonate as a purgative.

First Sermon at South Shields

In the afternoon I walked down to the School in South Durham Street† and called upon Mrs Nesbitt, returning about ½ past 3. I took tea with Mrs Todd, and my father, and at 5 o'clock proceeded per Railway† to South Shields.† Went to Mr Moffat, Currier, remained about 15m for prayer and reflection, and then proceeded to Salem Chapel. After greeting the friends in the vestry, I ascended the pulpit stairs with rather a heavy heart. My depression was not diminished when I stood up and gave out:

'Come sinners to the gospel feast;
Let every soul be Jesu's guest;
Ye need not one be left behind,
For God hath bidden all mankind.'[89]

I looked around the numerous and intelligent audience and involuntarily asked myself 'What am I that I should instruct this people?'. I felt myself in a degree an intruder, and casting my mind about to gather confidence, I first thought of one, and then of another who were in the habit of addressing this congregation, instituting a comparison between them and myself. I laboured hard in prayer to get hold of the spirit of God, but felt as though I cried to no purpose.

Thank God when I gave out my text (from John V. 40v.) I felt my strength renewed, and by divine mercy was enabled to speak with better success than I had anticipated. Mr Bennett† had kindly walked over to hear me. I took him with me to Mr Moffat's to supper, and we returned together by railway. Thus the labour of another Sabbath closed. O to reach that heavenly rest, the Sabbath of God.

Monday morning dawned and I felt myself little worse for last night. This being Whit-monday we closed at ½ past 12 o'clock. I remained at the shop until near four when, going home, Mr Keene† called of me and, Mr Peters† coming up with us, we walked to Southwick.† Here a tea party was held.

Owing to the extraordinary rain which has prevailed upwards of a fortnight there was no person from the town. Some came over from Ballast Hills,† and Deptford†, and perhaps we mustered about 40. After tea we held our meeting. Mr Peters requested me to take the chair but I refused. We then proposed, and elected, Mr K. into that honourable position. Our three selves being the only persons in the singing pew. After Mr K's address I spoke about 25 minutes. I never felt so uncomfortable on any occasion. Not having had any experience as an extempore speaker, I have no self-possession. I had intended to have gone to Painshaw† to attend a concert there held. In fact I had arranged when at Philadelphia† and Shiney Row† for that purpose. This I explained to my Father, and reiterated all the persuasion and hints I possibly could, but without avail. Nothing would satisfy him but 'You must go to Southwick', and therefore I was obliged to take up my cross and march thither.

In the afternoon I put down on a scrap of paper the heads of the various remarks which I had down in my little paper on Education, and taking it out I strove to enlarge, and mould this into some sort of a speech, but I felt the dread consciousness of its unsuitability. What could I do? Gladly would I have thrown myself upon the current of spontaneous thought but timidity withheld me. I talked about the Philosophy of Education, Geology, and Phrenology, with other matters, and happy was I at last to sit down. Mr Peters succeeded. He spoke with his usual tact, and adaptiveness. My mind calmed down at last and when I prayed before we came away, I breathed a sigh for gracious influence.

89. By Charles Wesley. Hymn number 2 in J. Wesley's *Collection.*

Mr Peters' kindness

As we returned we had much conversation about public speaking. They thought I wanted to be too exact and particular, saying I must be content to do badly to learn to do well, that it was not to be supposed than any one unaccustomed to public speaking could please himself. Finally Mr Peters on taking leave said, 'We need not tell you we take a special interest in your welfare, a more than ordinary concern, and therefore we shall always be glad to see you wherever we are, and give you every opportunity to speak,' &c. &c.

This in mind, I felt grateful. May I some day be enabled to show some substantial gratitude.

'Bible in Spain'

Tuesday

This afternoon we kept holidays as before. I read a good part this morning of Borrow's 'Bible in Spain',[90] one of the most interesting books written by one of the most extraordinary men I ever read. O that the church of Jesus were blessed with emissaries of the same noble, talented, and independent character. Such labourers would shake the Kingdom of darkness to the very basis. Lord send labourers into thy vineyard. In the afternoon I went down to W. Dixon's† and had a long chat.

90. George Borrow (1803 – 1891), traveller, linguist, agent for the British and Foreign Society in Russia, Spain, Portugal and Morocco, published *The Bible in Spain* in 1843, the year in which John Young read it; it made him suddenly famous.

Gratuitous tea at Brougham Street Chapel

At ½ past 5 o'clock I found myself in Brougham Street School.† A tea was this evening given gratuitously to the Leaders, Preachers, Singing Choir, Prayer Leaders, tract distributors, Sunday school teachers, and Superintendents who are actively engaged at Brougham Street Chapel.

About 75 or 80 sat down. Mrs Moore, Mrs Wilson, and Taylor presided at the three tables.

Everything was nice, and comfortable. I sat with Mr Coxon, Mr Peters,† Mrs P. and Mrs Todd, & felt quite at home. Tea done, Mr T.B. Young was elected chairman on the motion of Mr Peters. After a few appropriate remarks Mr Peters addressed us in a very interesting, and powerful manner. Afterwards Messrs Moore, Skilbeck, Eggars,† Macklin and myself. The choir occasionally in the intervals sang pieces. Messrs Wilson† & Coxon were loudly called for, but refused to speak. Mr Keene left at an early hour to give tickets to six classes at S.D. St.†

Upon the whole every person appeared highly gratified. This tea will be paid for by a private and special contribution amongst a few friends.

Reflections

This day (Wednesday) Mr Keene† sat with me ¾ of an hour after dinner, and smoked a cigar. Mr Coxon also and Bennett† took a good deal of time up, and with business the day has passed, and it is now ½ past 9 o'clock.

I desire to give diligence to consecrate my every moment to God in prayer, in reading his word, in the constant furtherance of every wise thought and holy resolution. Merciful Parent of a poor helpless sinner, suffer me not utterly to be abandoned to the fiend of Hell. Snap the chains by which he would bind me in the embrace of the body of death. Let me arise in thy strength and grasp thy full salvation. Amen.

Lieut. Eyre's Afghanistan. Cooper's letters

Monday June 12th

Thursday and Friday I read parts of Campbell's 'Pulpit Eloquence'.[91] Thursday evening I spent a couple of hours in looking through Lieutenant Eyre's 'Afghanistan Campaign'[92] – a most horrible, blundering and diabolical affair – written with apparent impartiality and truth, Lieut. Eyre having been personally present at the transaction he narrates.

On Friday night I read after supper *United Service Magazine* for March, and then looked over Cooper's 'Letters from England'.[93] Cooper the American novelist. One of the most egotistical productions that I ever saw. Poor man! So inflated with imaginary importance that with jaundiced eyes he placed upon every little trifle a fanciful signification from which he draws still more absurd conclusions.

In all his works he manifests a spirit of hatred and a wish to depreciate everything English. This is peculiarly the case with these Letters. His praise is doled out as though constrained, and then it is edged round by every possibility and probability which he can rake together to detract from his reluctant confession. American glory, The Stars and the Stripes fluttering o'er the red cross of St. George, is what he delights to conjecture. His 'Naval History of the young Republic' is peculiarly distinguished by this unhappy mania. If we are to credit the notice of the *Edinburgh Review,* it has seduced him far from the path of candour and truth.

Mr James' examination of the American Statement of the late war[94] I have read, and I do think he proved in the most able manner that these statements are exaggerations of the most barefaced and impudent character. I believe that there will be no lasting goodwill existing in the minds of the masses of the American people until the vicissitudes of another war shall have taught them civility and respect. Awful would be such a calamity, yet I have long entertained the impression that a collision before many years roll by is inevitable.

91. George Campbell, *Lectures on Systematic Theology and Pulpit Eloquence* (London, 1807).
92. Sir Vincent Eyre (1811 – 1881), Commissary of Ordnance to the Kabul Field Force 1839, surrendered as hostage to Akbar Khan 1842, rescued by General Pollock 1843. The book referred to is *The Military Operation at Cabul which ended in the retreat and destruction of the British Army January 1842 with a journal of imprisonment in Afghanistan by Vincent Eyre,* edited E. Eyre, (London, 1843).
93. John Young appears to be referring to James Fenimore Cooper's 'Letter to his Countrymen', included in his *Gleanings in Europe : England with sketches of Society in the Metropolis,* (London, 1837).
94. William James (died 1827), a lawyer in Jamaica, detained as prisoner in the U.S.A. 1812 during the Anglo-American War, escaped, published a number of works on naval and military history : *An Enquiry into the merit of the principal Naval actions between Great Britain and the U.S.A.,* (1816); *A Full and Correct Account of the Chief Naval Occurrences of the late war between Great Britain and the U.S.A.,* (1817); *A Full and Correct account of the military occurences of the late war between Great Britain and the U.S.A.,* (1818); *A Naval History of Great Britain 1793 – 1820* (1822 – 24).

Possibilities of War. Circassia, America, Russia & France

Many years I have been accustomed to speculate on the varied aspects of political affairs. At one time threatened with a Russian War, at another period the fanatic ambition of Thiers[95] portended a French struggle, then America and India and China, have successively occupied public attention, but still we have come thus far unscathed, and under the good providence of God we shall yet triumph.

The elements of discord are but hushed into an unnatural sleep; there needs but a spark to ignite the world. The continued efforts of Russia to crush the Circassian mountaineers have long enlisted my sympathies.[96] I have marked the progress of the struggle, witnessed the undaunted perseverance and intrepid bravery of her people until I have longed to be enabled in some way to contribute to their defence. And at this very moment the fierce and sanguinary warfare exists in all its fury. Oh, that some hand were raised to stay the oppressor.

Saturday 10th June 1843. At intervals the perusal of Test. and P. Eloquence.[97] On returning home I sat up until 2 o'clock reading *United Service Magazine* for June, 1843.

95. Adolphe Thiers (1797 – 1877), who as Prime Minister of France in 1836 and again in 1840 endeavoured to pursue a bellicose foreign policy, directed in part against Britain.
96. Russian aggression against the Circassians (Caucasians) began in the early eighteenth century under Peter the Great. The final subjugation of these independent mountain tribes occupied Russia for many years, and indeed it was not until the late 1860s that opposition was mainly stifled. Incidents in these campaigns were referred to in the press at the time of John Young's diary.
97. He appears to be referring to G. Campbell, *Systematic Theology and Pulpit Eloquence*, (London, 1807).

West of Shields

Sunday (11th June 1843), rose at 9 o'clock having been disordered in the stomach and bowels the greater part of last week, I still felt a degree of heaviness and inactivity. At Brougham Street† heard Mr Keene† preach from Corinth [ians] – the cross of Christ to the Jews a stumbling block and to the Gentiles foolishness [I Cor. 1:23]. A most excellent discourse. In the afternoon visited Brougham St. School and then heard West of Shields preach from 'Henceforth there is laid up for me a crown of righteousness' &c. [II Tim. 4:8].

West possesses material out of which a Preacher may be formed, though much diligence and application will be necessary to secure even ordinary respectability. Let a young man throw himself on his own resources, think for himself, strive to make those ideas which may be presented to his mind in the strictest sense part of his own intellectual strength, and there is no danger but that he will find the faculties of his mind to unfold themselves and put forth a vigour to which he himself had been hitherto unconscious.

Visit to Mr J. Cormack

After the sermon I popped out and called upon Mr Moore† and spent ½ an hour in conversation about sundries. Tea secured, I went to pay a visit to Mr Josiah Cormack† my old school master, now at the gate of death, just waiting the dismission of his spirit to another world. 'Well John' said he, 'I'm glad to see you, I've thought of you whilst laying here, and wished to see you'. 'You wished to see me?' 'Yes,' said I. 'Well then, our desire has been mutual, I want to tell you that the gospel which I have preached unto others, is now my hope and consolation. Glory to God for the blessed gospel'. I remained about 1 hour and we had much interesting conversation. He said, 'I trust you are still placing your confidence in the gospel', I replied that I felt its power, that it was my only hope and my greatest desire to hold fast and go forward. J.C. – 'Praise the Lord it is our Salvation. I have thought of my past life since I was 5 years old while I have laid here, and have seen something of goodness, but alas! with many a dark spot upon my horizon. Yet now I have no trust in anything but the gospel, nothing that I am, nothing that I have been, or done. It is all my hope for this hour of need, the gospel.'

He then inquired kindly after our family, naming its individuals. He said, 'I have thought of my intercourse with you, for we have been thrown a good deal together, and I do not know that there is anything which I regret'. I replied that those recollections were associated in my mind with nothing but pleasurable and grateful retrospect. There had been nothing which I could remember which I could regret. 'Well' said he, 'though I do not remember anything of moment in that way, still important things were not so distinctly brought before our attention. I therefore now wish to speak of them as being at this moment my chief joy.'

He then said that he had always felt a more particular interest in me, because he thought I resembled himself in disposition, being affable and frank. 'I', said he, 'have thought much on the propriety of the attention which you know I have always given to the language. I have shut myself out from gratification of general reading to a great extent, but still I do not regard the time as altogether thrown away. It has given stability to my judgement, and I have had the satisfaction of believing and receiving my opinions from the evidence of my own senses, and not from the authority of other men. I am familiar with the Hebrew, Greek, Latin, and a little French, and can translate any passage in the Sacred volume at sight in these languages; indeed the critical study of the Scriptures has been almost a passion with me, as you will have observed.'

'I do not desire to be a young man again. Life is but a dream and a very troublesome one. How different one feels now, after experience of the reality, from the hopes and fancied prospects of youth.'

He spoke of his visit to the castle of the late Lord Durham,[98] how he had felt when he surveyed its grandeur and luxurious comforts. He asked where the family chapel was, and heard that they never assembled to worship their Creator. He said that when he visited Raby Castle he had been pleased on being shown the Hall where its habitants had been accustomed to assemble for prayer, remarking that he believed that religion was more identified with men's thoughts and feelings 2 or 300 years ago than now in ordinary life. 'Ah!' said he, 'what difference is there between Lord Durham and myself now, we are both about to be placed on one common level. I do not think he was a religious man. Few men have been more flattered and honoured in their day. Perhaps he did a good turn for this country in the affair of Canada, but what does it avail now? All his known vanity and pride are brought alike to the dust. Poor man! What is he now?' Mr C. said, 'We are far more ignorant than we think we are. There is very little we know.'

We then had some conversation on the present position of the gospel. The probabilities of the world's salvation. He said he believed that Jesus should come, but whether in the Millenarian[99] sense or the reverse he could not affirm. He had read the Bible through with his eye on Millenarian dogma but could not discover it so plainly revealed as they asserted.

He desired me to pray, and then urged me to call again as often as opportunity afforded. Here was stretched on the bed of death a man of blameless life, who in his quiet and unostentatious sphere has exemplified the noble quality of Christian patience, humility and modesty. This minister of Jesus could gather no consolation from the review of his personal labours, no plea to demand of justice the bliss of Heaven. The atonement was felt to be his only refuge and, happy to have such a hope, he now looks to death as the gate of Life.

May I thus die! May I now live so that death, whenever it may come, shall be welcomed as the forerunner of eternal joy. 'So teach us to number our days that we may apply our hearts unto wisdom.' [Psalm 90:12].

98. Lord Durham's castle was Lambton Castle.† Raby Castle was the ancient Neville stronghold, near Staindrop, later seat of the Vane family, dukes of Cleveland.

99. The belief that the Kingdom of God would be established on earth for a 'millenium' before the final termination of all earthly things. There was disagreement among millenarians as to whether the Second Coming of Christ would precede or follow the Millenium. In the early nineteenth century there was an upsurge of apocalyptic and millenarian doctrines in Great Britain, especially among the Irvingites, Mormons *et al.* but also affecting many more orthodox believers. See J.F.C. Harrison, *The Second Coming : Popular Millenarianism 1780 – 1850,* (1979).

Dr. Conquest's Bible

I remained in the house the whole of the night. I examined Dr. Conquest's 'New Edition of the Bible with 20,000 emendations.'[1] Afterwards consulted Clarke, Wesley, Benson & Burkitt[2] on the meaning of some portions of the Scripture which I have thought of preaching from.

1. John Tricker Conquest (1789 – 1855), a medical doctor, *The Holy Bible containing the Authorised version of the Old and New Testaments with many thousand emendations;* a people's edition was published London, 1840s.

2. On Adam Clark see p. 52 above note 43; John Wesley, *Explanatory Notes on the New Testament,* (1754); Joseph Benson, *The Holy Bible, with notes by the Revd J. Benson,* (1810); William Burkitt, *Expository Notes with practical observations on the New Testament of our Lord and Saviour Jesus Christ wherein the sacred text is at large recited and the sense explained,* 11th ed. 1739.

South Durham Street Sunday School Committee

Monday (June 12th, 1843)

This day occupied with business. In the evening attended a Teachers Committee Meeting of the South Durham Street School.† A large attendance. Mr. Dowson in the chair. Nothing of moment. Read the *Athenaeum* for May on return. Particularly struck by the statements of the New York correspondent respecting the cheap reprints of English popular works in America, and also those of the new and depraved French School of Romance.

Sermonise. Cooper's Letters

Tuesday (June 13th, 1843)

Began this day to sermonise afresh. O for the spirit of Christian perseverance, and love. Attended class at night and afterwards walked on the sands with W. Dixon.† Read parts of the 3rd vol. of Cooper's Letters, and retired to rest at ½ past 12 o'clock.

Monday (June 19th, 1843)

In three weeks I have laboured under a disagreeable fit of indigestion. Lassitude and langour have fastened upon my faculties and therefore my attempts at study have been fruitless and unprofitable. I have sat down and read, but the mind could not interest itself in the matter. I have sat down pen in hand to think and write, but nothing could I conceive which I durst place on paper. Business has suffered. Time has passed and carried with it no burden of improvement. Spiritual taste has depreciated. Spiritual habits neglected. Idle conversation and, tenfold more deleterious in its consequences, foolish, vain and sinful thoughts, have dissipated the mind and have left the painful consciousness of guilt before God. Oh to come afresh to the 'precious blood'. To roll the burden of a sinsick soul on the Atonement of Jesus. Oh to sit in examination on my heart, its most secret movements, its intricate mazes of deluding fancies. When the spirit of God gives divine light what horrid revelations are disclosed.

Self Delusion

I have often persuaded myself into the belief that I am a sincere, straightforward decent sort of character. I have flattered myself that others will entertain the same opinion of me. Thus I have lived to a fearful extent on the approbation of a vain heart. How dangerous. What alarming and unsuspected self-righteousness. Instead of every moment maintaining the conviction of my unworthiness, and realizing a saving knowledge of God's unlimited mercy and present adoption, thus to build upon the loose and sandy basis of imaginary goodness. Eternal Praise to God that I am not abandoned to the vileness of corrupt nature. Mercy, supreme, unchangeable is still willing to receive. O God I come. I come to thee. 'To whom should I go?' [John 6:68*]. Despise not my humble cry from the brink of death. I have sinned against thee. I have polluted that heart which I sacredly vowed to consecrate to thee. Return in thy love. Consume its sinfulness. And may I this moment feel the whisper of forgiveness and rejoice in the confidence of a reconciled Redeemer – Hear for the sake of Jesus. Amen!!

Preach at Hylton

On Thursday morning I bathed for the first time this year, at Hendon†. Saturday retired to rest, much fatigued about 1 o'clock. Rose in the morning at ½ past 7, walked after breakfast round by Hendon. Remained in the house to study during chapel hours, and started at 5m. to 1 o'clock for Hylton.†

I felt exceedingly unwell this morning. Arrived at 5m to 2, met Mr. Haswell at the chapel door. Went into Mrs Wilson's to take a drink of water. Preached from II Peter 1 ch., 5.6.7., with great labour and langour. Tea'd with Mr. Ball, and preached again at 6 o'clock from John v. 40. A good company, and considerable seriousness. We had an excellent prayer meeting at the close of the service, after which I went with Ball and Vincent Hodgson to visit an old woman who, having been a member of Society for some time, and enjoyed religion, had latterly after a severe illness fallen into the persuasion that 'her day of grace had gone by, and mercy was beyond her reach'. We prayed, and I talked and urged upon her the Salvation of the gospel, to the utmost of my ability without any seeming impression. I got her to try to try to pray for herself and, blessed be God, whilst she was looking to Jesus she was enabled to lay hold and regain her confidence. Her name is Mrs. Margaret Reay.

Road from Hylton

Supp'd at Ball's. He set me down the road. We had a good deal of conversation, and then talked very confidentially. Before he left me we saw two lads standing beside a farm door. One of them said 'Are ye going to Sunderland, Sir?' 'Yes', said I. 'Why', said they 'we darnet go. We were gaen down the road and there was a great black thing run out of the dike, and looked in our faces, and when we ran back again it came out of the dike right above us and went past like lightning'. I was amused. They appeared terrified. 'Why', said Ball. 'I suppose you've spent your Sunday badly, and your consciences are frightening you'. 'No Sir'. said one 'we've only been to see my brother at Hylton'.

Talk to Boys

I came home with them and it was a good opportunity to drop a word of advice. I held familiar conversation with them. Their names were Smith, and Wm. Rippon. Smith was a carpenter with Rotheram at Hylton, and was 16 years of age. Father dead, living with his mother opposite the Iron Factory in Hylton Lane, just above Hartley's.[3] Had been a Sunday School scholar at a village beside Sedgefield,[4] but had made little improvement, but was now attending a night school.

Wm Rippon, 16 years old, was a sailor apprentice in Mr. Harris' 'Atlantic'. Had also been a S.S. Scholar, lived in Walton Lane with his step-mother, both his parents being dead. I gave them all the counsel I could think suitable, in Religion, Morals, and Mental Improvement. Lord may this seed bring forth an abundant harvest.

June 19th 1843

3. The Bishopwearmouth Iron Works of which the proprietors were Messrs White, Panton and Kirk, all Wesleyans. The Whites were relatives of John Young – see Introduction p. xiv above. James Hartley (1811 – 1886) founded the Wear Glass Works at Millfield, Sunderland, in 1836. He soon established a world-wide reputation for his products. A Wesleyan till 1853, he then joined the Church of England. Brockie pp. 450–459.
4. A large village about ten miles south-east of Durham city.

Resolutions

Friday (June 23rd)

I am almost miserable because I feel time to be slipping by with a swift and scarcely stealthy tread. O to arrest its progress, to do something before those precious hours disappear for ever. I have now and then indulged in the delights of cigar smoking. I must give it up. There is another thing, drinking too much tea and coffee and eating supper; and going to bed late. If I overcome these I shall do well. Lord in the strength of thy grace I resolve to:–

1st Resolution. Retire to rest as early after 10 o'clock as possible, in order to rise sooner in the morning.

2nd Resolution. Not to smoke any Cigars (except they are given me).

3rd Resolution. Not to exceed 3 cups for Breakfast, and 2 at tea.

4th Resolution. Not to eat any supper without there be positive necessity.

I propose to endeavour to hold these firm until the expiration of our present preachers' plan.[5]

5. The Sunderland W.M.A. preaching plans were published every three months. Reckoning from one which has survived it looks as though John Young was setting himself a trial period of four to five weeks.

Visit Jobson

Monday (June 26th 1843)

Sabbath morning I walked towards Ryhope.† After dinner visited a poor man called Jobson. Then proceeded to South Durham Street† Lovefeast. Mrs Todd, Mrs Pearson, Miss Young and Mr. John Dixon† and Mr [blank] from Hull took tea with us. I went to South Durham Street† and heard Mr. Peters† from vii ch. Acts, 38 verse. Stayed at the Prayer Meeting, and then walked up to Brougham Street† with Mr & Mrs Peters who went to see the corpse of John Harker our late chapel keeper who died last night. He had a violent inflammation of the lungs and Frank Thomson his doctor not having visited him until the evening of the 2nd day, though sent for, and then he merely sent him a mixture not calling again for some time. In consequence Mr Mordey† was sent for who declared the disease to have made too great progress to be subdued. F. Thomson is Harker's Box Doctor.[6]

I called upon Mrs Muschamp† and Anne Young [John's sister] at Frederick Lodge,† and remained until 10 o'clock. The Misses Dixon called while I was there.

6. Presumably this is a reference to medical provision paid for weekly by subscriptions to a Friendly Society or Sickness Club.

Wickenden's death

Mr. Wickenden died on Saturday night. Mrs Todd left here to embark at Shields for Hull on her way to London this morning.[7]

I pray God to give me grace to serve him with reverence and love that I may 'so run as to obtain' [I Cor. 9:24].

'Weaker than a bruised reed
Thy help I every moment need.'

7. The Shields and Newcastle Navigation Company operated steamers from Newcastle to Hull on Tuesday and Thursday mornings, calling at Sunderland when the weather permitted. See advertisements in the *Newcastle Chronicle* and the *Sunderland Herald.* On Mrs. Todd, see p. 97 above.

My Mind, Its dulness

My mental faculties appear to have suffered a partial eclipse, as I have not been able to concentrate my attention on any subject and patiently think it out. Quantities of time have thus perished. Oh for a mighty outbreak of intense ardour to give that persevering, untiring energy which will enable me to break the trammels which fetter my happier aspiration, that my thoughts may arise clothed with vigorous and healthful power of sentiment and expression. Oh that I may feel a revulsion, a return of those sacred hours of natural inspiration, when thought crowded upon thought, and appeared to struggle for the mastery. When the difficulty was not to spend hours of laborious exhaustion to gather together a few scattered ideas and clothe them with the semblance of unity of design, but rather to select, to cull, to prune and repress the luxuriance of fancy's brilliance.

My Mind. Its strength. Is it improved?

Is it possible that my mental powers are impaired already. May not a great part of the difficulty of concentrated thought arise from the little attention which I have given of late to compository exercise. What so essential as diligent practice to give facility in arrangement and thought. Now I have not written more than one sermon these 9 or 10 months. Is it therefore surprising that I should have lost during so long a period of inactivity something of the aptitude which my previous labours had conferred. I will return to my desk and to my pen. But my visit must not be at the intervals of months. I remember that after I had written some sermon, within 3 months, instead of feeling that my fund of expression had worn out, and my novelty of thought expended, I felt as though the volcano within had been stirred, that its transient effects and casual exertions were but the struggles of a confined spirit which sought to burst forth in the wild and inexpressible energy of freedom. Freedom of thought, Freedom of imagination. Uncontrollable, delightful, joyous freedom.

My Mind. May it rise in power

Come back my own spirit. Revisit, reanimate the wanderer. Give me once again the light heart, the happy eye, that blessed sensation of weariless activity. Come to my heart thou loved, though most strange, habitant. Let me arise and shake off the accumulated depression of months and days.

Let the bright flash of intellect assert its wild, unawed supremacy. Shall vile matter clog thy noble purpose? Must the fitful rage of brutish propensities sit as an incubus on thy brighter and holier ascension? Break asunder the iron band. Dash to the earth in extreme prostration the baneful reptile that would draw from thy vitals the life of Heaven. Trample its strength to death, and spring forth exposed to the light of day in native grandeur. Rush to the gate of immortality. Let thy eye rest on its portal, let every difficulty and barrier but give an impetus to thy flight to the realm of Glory.

Coronation Day. Van Amburgh

Friday (June 30th)

The close of the last day of June. What have I done this month? Dare I review its treasury of recollections? Let alone. Let not bitter regret poison the desire of useful activity.

Tuesday, I attended class. On Monday evening I believe I walked on the sand with W.D. Wednesday morning Mr. Van Amburgh came into town this morning driving his long 'bus with eight horses containing his band.[8] Owing to this, and today being the Coronation day,[9] we kept holiday after 12 o'clock.

In the afternoon I called for Mr Keene† at Mrs Surtees', intending to take him to the Van Amburgh Pavilion. Found him absent in the country. Saw Mules† & Heywood.† Proceeded to the Pavilion and was pleased and interested. Van Amburgh did not proceed to his accustomed lengths in exciting his trained animals. Was especially pleased with the sagacity of the Elephants.

8. Van Amburgh's Circus, or 'Exhibition' as it was referred to in the press reports, performed 28–30 June 1843 in a large marquee in a field adjoining Norfolk Street, Sunderland, *Sunderland Herald* 30 June 1843.
9. The fifth anniversary of Queen Victoria's coronation on 28 June 1838.

Sunday School Tea at South Durham Street

At the termination of the exhibition I looked in at the

Borough News Room, and then went to the S.S. Tea party at South Durham Street† School. About 200 children present who were supplied with a potful of tea, and a spice wig each. About 100 Adults. After tea S. Hodgson,† without waiting for the regular election of a chairman and opening of the meeting, began his talk and spoke about an hour in a very loose and indiscreet style – *par consequence* it was near eight when he sat down and when I rose, and said, 'The friends will perceive that it is now high time that the meeting be opened in the usual, regular, and systematic method I therefore respectfully propose that our able, indefatigable and respectable friend Mr. Wm. Dixon† take the chair'. Mr Bruce seconded the motion, which, being unanimously carried, Mr Dixon opened the meeting about 10m. to 8 o'clock.

After an appropriate address of 8 or 10 m. he called Mr Eggars,† who spoke ¼ of an hour. After singing again Mr Heywood† spoke about the same length.

Dine with A. White, Esq.

On Sunday June [recte July] 2nd I heard Mr Peters† preach in the morning, and then walked to Tunstall Lodge,† and dined with Mr White.† I remained until 5 o'clock, and after taking tea proceeded with young A. White home again. Being fatigued and unwell I did not go to worship.

Tuesday I had a delightful class meeting. Monday was our Quarterly Meeting, when Mr Heywood† received notice to return home, and father with Peters† was elected delegates to the next Annual Assembly.

Some unpleasantness arose from this circumstance. Father being first elected, and no disposition to send another party being evinced, he said that if the Quarterly Meeting would send Mr Peters he would pay his own expenses. Mr Peters refused to go in that manner because he thought it was foisting him on the Assembly in a dishonourable way. Father being offended at the rejection of his offer got up, and left the meeting.

Mr Coxon then proposed that the meeting proceed to the election of another delegate, when the lot fell upon Mr Peters, and he consented to go.

Preach at Shiney Row

Tuesday (July 11th)

Sabbath day I left Sunderland by Railway, at 8 o'clock, and arrived at Painshaw† about 9.[10] Went to Mr Peter Bailey's, had some breakfast, chatted an hour, and then to Shiney Row.† Called upon Mr Robert Potter, I then went over to Philadelphia,† where I remained to preach. Dined on coffee with Mrs Harrison† in the little room. Preached from II Tim. 2. 11.12.13. Before tea I had a delightful stroll in the garden with Miss H. and Mr & Mrs Harrison. Miss Harrison, little Margaret, came over to Shiney Row† with me. I preached from XC Psalm 12v. Supped with Mr Smurthwaite. Mr. Ralph Elliott and Thos. Potter came and smoked their pipes and discussed sundries. Mr Wanless, his movements, and dissatisfaction with the Association at Shiney Row, &c.

After calling at Harrison's for Mr Thos. Stevenson of the New Connexion, who supplied Mr Henderson's appointments at Shiney Row and Philadelphia, we came away about 10 o'clock and arrived home by 12 o'clock, having enjoyed one of the most pleasant days which I have experienced in the country.

Last evening I slept at Frederick [Tunstall partly erased] Lodge, in consequence of Miss Young coming down to superintend the establishment's revisal.[11] Today, this moment, I look to God. Oh for mighty faith that will bring salvation.

10. From Monkwearmouth† station, via the Brandling Junction† and Durham Junction Railways.†

11. John Young appears to mean that his sister Anne, who lived with the Whites, came down to stay at 3 Nile Street† to organise the changes that would arise from Ophelia Young's marriage to John Dixon.† Anne and John Young seem to have exchanged beds for the night.

Class Meeting, Excitement

Monday (July 17th)

On Tuesday, July 11, I had a glorious and refreshing time at the Class meeting. There was great excitement. I have often been surprised by the immense influence which the singing of a new and striking tune has produced for the first time. Mr G. Longstaff began a new divine song, 'Worthy the Lamb'. I should think that we sang it with increasing interest for half an hour. When I got my hat to come away, and turned around to say goodnight to G.L., I was surprised at the spectacle of a young girl named Isabella Thomson rolling about in a chair in a most extraordinary state of agitation. Two females held her hands, and one her head. Her eyes were shut, but her constant and unremitting cry was 'Halleluia, Lord, Love,' &c. This was a case of pure mental excitement, induced by the wonderful unity of prayer and thanksgiving which pervaded and blessed our little meeting. I gave full vent to my feeling this night, and cried at the utmost stretch of my lungs, 'Glory,' 'Come' 'Save' &c. &c. What an indifference, almost amounting to a repugnance I have felt towards these meetings when in a certain state of the mind, and again I have luxuriated in their wildness when my soul has been deeply affected with divine and melting grace. On Friday evening I found Mr Shoebotham† of Dundee at home in the evening.

Preach Missionary Service at Seaham

Sabbath (July 16th)

I left Sunderland by omnibus for Seaham.† Found out Mr. John Storey. He was at the Wesleyan Meth. Chapel hearing a sermon preached to the Oddfellows[12] by Mr Punshon† of Sunderland. I had a walk on the sands, and on returning met Mr Storey and Mr Thos. Stalker. Dined with Mr Storey. Present Mr Hogg of Newcastle, and another party, brothers-in-law to Mr Storey. Preached at 2 o'clock from V John 40 v. Punshon of the W[esleyan] Connexion was there. Had a cup of tea and returned per omnibus. Beautiful day. This service was for the Missionary purposes, for which bills were published. Mr James Thomson preaching at night.

12. A very extensive benevolent society, with many lodges in England including the North East. The Oddfellows were originally secretive and ritualistic in character but a new stage began in 1813 with the inauguration of the Independent Order of Oddfellows (Manchester Unity), which shared all the characteristics of a thoroughly respec-

table Friendly Society. The Sunderland lodge had adopted the name 'The Loyal Andrew White's Lodge' by 1838, see handbill in the possession of the Sunderland Antiquarian Society. By the time of J.Y's diary some at least of the Oddfellows were teetotallers, Richardson v, 254.

Shoebotham Preaches

I heard Mr Shoebotham† of Dundee preach at Brougham Street.† Tuesday we had our Anniversaries in continuation of last Sunday when we had Pearson from Hull. Text CXIX Psalm 126 v. 'It is time Lord for thee to work; for they have made void thy law.' Mr S. preached an hour and a half. Called at Mr. Moore's and had a little chat, and then returning home conversed with Mr S. after supper until near 12 o'clock. Talked about preaching, the soul, mind, Phrenology, Mesmerism, Phreno-Mesmerism, and sundries.

Monday (July 24th)

Mr Shoebotham left us on Thursday July 20th, morning. He proceeds to Darlington, Manchester, Liverpool, Glasgow. Master John Harrison sailed the same morning in the Brig 'Symetry', Capt. Brown, for Quebec, belonging to Messrs Greenwell & Sons.

I intended to have gone to Painshaw,† Philadelphia† and Shiney Row† yesterday by the 8 o'clock train[13] but my father disapproved of it. I felt this very hard for I had agreed 2 months ago to visit the good people that day. I submitted to his wishes. Mr. Keene† being very unwell I had agreed to preach for him at Painshaw at 10½ o'clock, Mr. Henderson taking his appointment at Shiney Row at 2 o'clock.

13. See p. 119 note 10. Philadelphia and Shiney Row would have to be reached on foot, after alighting from the train at Penshaw.

Reduction of Preachers' Salaries

Mr. Keene proceeded with Mr. Peters† to our Annual Assembly this morning at 8 o'clock. There exists a probability of a proposal being brought forward at this meeting by the Cornish people for the reduction of the preachers' salaries.[14] This is much to be regretted. Its inevitable effect must be to drive from us the ablest and most respectable of our preachers.

Their salaries being already low enough, it is impossible that they can submit to any considerable reduction. And it is certain that it will prevent any accession of strength to our ministry. Talent will find its value in the market of the church. And though I am adverse to giving fat livings to a servant of the cross of Jesus, still I am persuaded that a man of capacity will not feel himself to be using his judgement in the way which his responsibility to his Divine Maker would indicate when he voluntarily places himself in circumstances which will require the most anxious economy to live, and leave nothing to devote to the noble purpose of mental cultivation that he may not loiter in the rear of the advancing science and civilisation of the world.

14. The stripends of W.M.A. ministers in full connexion were reduced to £80 per annum in 1844, and those of probationers to £55, Beckerlegge 1957, p. 28. Whether this was a result of the move by the Cornish W.M.A. members is not clear. The W.M.A. suffered a severe loss of members that year and economic stringencies were needed.

Necessity of Ministerial Learning

Never was there a period when there existed a greater necessity for a superior class of men to march in the van of the armies of the church. If the infidelity of society is to be combatted, and the truths of the gospel are to be illustrated and defended from the attack of perverted ingenuity, no effort ought to be considered too great, no self denial too difficult to provide the Captains of the Host of the Lord with material and ammunition to enable them to extend the knowledge of the truth in its simple grandeur as revealed from Heaven.

On Sunday morning I walked out as far as Ryhope† on the seashore when it came on a tremendous squall of wind from the N. East with rain. It was with great difficulty I got home drenched. In three hours it subsided.

How I spent my time

In the afternoon I sat in the house reading Dr. A. Clarke's Commentary on Genesis. During the past week I had been reading the book of Genesis in Dr. Conquest's Bible. I propose going on in this way conscientiously. Last week I read 2 vols. of a novel called the 'British Admiral' by a Naval Officer published about the beginning of the present century, the Monthly Review for May, some part of Dr. Kitchiner's 'Art of Prolonging and Invigorating Health', very amusing, Mason's 'Self-Knowledge'. &c. &c.[15]

The great object at which I must aim is the conservation of Health, to mentain [sic] constantly vigour of mind, and elasticity of frame. Temperance, Diet, Exercise, and throw Physic to the dogs.

On Sunday evening I heard my Father preach from the 'Laodicean Church' [Rev. 3 : 14-22]; this is the last of a series of lectures which he has been delivering on the seven churches of Asia. We had a famous prayer meeting after the Service.

Thursday (July 27th)

Yesterday morning my father left home for Leeds to attend the Annual Assembly. Sister Anne came down, and stayed all night with us. We sat up until 1 o'clock holding consultations &c. about Ophelia's wedding.

15. *The Monthly Review or Literary Journal, a periodical work giving account of new books, pamphlets etc.,* (London), 1749 – 1845. William Kitchiner, *The Art of Invigorating and Prolonging Life by food, clothes, sleep etc.,* (2nd ed., 1821). Kitchiner wrote much on similar topics; he obviously had a sense of humour: one of his books was called *The Shilling Kitchener or Oracle of Cookery for the Million,* (1861). John Mason, an eighteenth-century nonconformist minister, *Self Knowledge – a treatise showing the nature and benefit of that important science and the way to obtain it. Intermixed with various reflections and observations on human nature,* (1745).

Reading Anne's letters

Anne was sorting a large bundle of letters, which she had received from different parties in earlier days. I got a number and intend to beguile an hour some day in their examination and assortment.

On Monday night I walked with W. Dixon† along the sands, until near 11 o'clock. We had much conversation on various curious subjects. Also on the marriage of my sister Ophelia with J. Dixon,† which we agreed in predicting to be very unpromising. I firmly believe it will not be a happy union.

On Tuesday July 25th. I attended class. Had a tolerable time; stayed some time in Dean's discussing with G. Fenton, W.D. and Dean the duty and necessity of church communion.

My Reading, – Mason's 'Self-Knowledge', 'Physical Theory of Another Life' by the author of the 'Natural History of Enthusiasm',[16] and Creuze's 'Naval Architecture'.[17]

16. Isaac Taylor (1787 – 1865), *The Natural History of Enthusiasm,* (1829); *The Physical Theory of another Life,* (1836). Taylor, an artist and engraver, wrote extensively on religious questions, and was very highly regarded as a lay theologian, especially by non-conformists. However Monsignor Ronald Knox describes *The Natural History of Enthusiasm,* Taylor's best known work, as 'probably the most uniformly dull book ever written': R. Knox, *Enthusiasm,* (1950), pp. 6–7.

17. W. Morgan and A. Creuze conducted a London periodical called *Papers on Naval Architecture and other subjects connected with naval science,* from 1826 for a few years, and then re-appearing in 1865. See also A. Murray, *The Theory and Practice of Ship building with portions of the treatise on naval architecture by A.F.B. Creuze,* (Edinburgh, 1851).

Review of Spiritual Career

Tuesday (August 1st, 1843)

'We all do fade, as a leaf, and our iniquities like the wind have carried us away' [Isaiah 64:6*]. Such is the expression of my heart. I feel disposed to sit in judgement upon myself and for a moment to scrutinize my conduct and affection, to see my complete portraiture delineated and reflected in the word of God. How natural and easy to feel a fancied composure and self-gratulation in pouring forth the confession 'I am a sinner', but how seldom I realize a deep, full, clear and abiding conviction of my natural depravity.

I see clearly that it is just possible to be a great stranger at home, to be very ignorant of one's true character, to build on fancied attainments, and rejoice in an imaginary exemption from the error of frail mortality. I declare I feel positively ashamed of myself. I seem now to stand at an angle from whence I survey an area of my heart of which I have been utterly ignorant. I have long believed that I possessed a very accurate acquaintance with my mental and spiritual character, that I knew precisely its weak and strong points, where there existed an assailable bastion and where its rampart was impregnable.

I have flattered myself that 'pride', 'vanity', 'ambition' formed no element in my disposition, but the other day light appeared to shine in a moody instant upon a part of my mode of intercourse with others revealing apparent motives which had they been remarked by others I should have strenuously denied, and probably attributed the insinuation to captious vision or malignant detraction. Now I see that I ought to 'abhor myself, and repent'. Tonight I feel impressed with the infinite purity and holy obligation of the gospel precepts. What peace!, what joy! might I have realised had I continously lived to God, but 'I have done things which I ought not to have done, and left undone those things which I ought to have done'.[18] Alas how true! How delightfully glided away the two or three years following the hour of emancipation, what power over sin, what confidence in God. Temptation was lightly regarded, duty was a pleasure, prayer a luxury, the study of the scripture ecstatic delight. But now how doleful and . . . . is the discharge of my master's wishes, how onerous is prayer, how stupid and dull the reading of the Bible. Then I longed for the moment when business would permit me to pour my tale of love and confiding joy into the ear of infinite mercy, now I would fain excuse my conscience with a few muttered words of bitter mockery, the mere semblance of devotion.

I am not willing to abandon the struggle. It is thy Life, Life, thy precious undying Life that is at stake. Would thou subject thyself to hell's misery to gain the gilded day? I must now be thine! but oh, memory tells of bygone vows, olden resolutions, and with their recollection is linked their fate. Broken, despised, forgotten. This destroys my confidence. What security have I that the latter shall not be as the former, and greater in iniquity. Oh were it not that I cannot erase from my memory the Omnipotent decree, 'My Grace is sufficient for Thee' [II Cor. 12:9]. As well might I just once perish, but no. I know that I need but to throw myself on the clemency of Jesus, again to receive Grace to help 'in time of need' [Hewbrews 4:16].

18. From A General Confession, part of Morning and Evening Prayer in the Book of Common Prayer of the Church of England, familiar to Methodists as a result, in part, of Wesley's adaptation of Matins for Methodist use.

Letter from Mr. Peters

Friday (August 4th 1843)

I had a letter from Mr. Peters† this week requesting me to undertake the responsibility of filling up his appointments at Middle Renton,† Collier Row† and Houghton.† We have at present great difficulty in getting any place supplied. There is such an indifferent spirit abroad among many that they care not if places are utterly neglected. I find that Hetton† has been disappointed of a preacher for three successive Sabbaths, and now John Dixon† refuses to take his work at Shiney Row† and Philadelphia.† I am determined to do my utmost to prevent these places being left without.

Thursday (August 10th, 1843)

My heart positively sinks under the depression which results from the conviction that time and opportunities, rich, precious, and fruitful are passing away. Lost! Lost! Lost! Oh God save. Let thy light transform my heart. I am so subject first to bodily indispositions as indigestion &c. and secondly to interruptions from business that it appears absolutely impossible to give that diligent attention to studious advancement that is necessary and desirable. I believe I am sincere in my desire for intellectual improvement, I believe conscientiously that from my inmost soul I prefer it to all other distinctions. I am perhaps desirous of a respectable standing in Society, still more of the esteem of others, the result of superior mental ability. But after all, I do believe that I am perhaps more solidly and materially influenced by a conviction of the actual superiority of all that belongs to our immortal principle, than by any of the more sordid and selfish motives. These may be useful as adjunctive stimulants, but the other as the primary element and source of action. The one is the steam, the expansive power of which drives the piston; the other no higher place than the mere oil which renders the friction of the parts more easy, and comfortable.

Physical debility the foe of mental activity

How much of my mortal weakness and spiritual inactivity arises from the frailty of my tenement, who can say? How much of the happiness of the heavenly world will consist in the unembarrassed, the free development of the mind, without clay, without any interruptive and repressing material body? The mortality of that crust will be for ever destroyed, and from its destruction will arise the nobler, purer and immortal frame, whose movements will be as spontaneous and without weariness.

Preach at Shields

Friday 11th (August, 1843)

On Sunday last I took a short walk in the morning; after dinner left by the 2 o'clock train for Shields.† Heard Mr. Moore of Carville preach in Salem. Got tea with Mr Moffat, and preached in Salem from XC Psalm 12v. So teach &c. Good congregation. Couldn't get my voice clear. Returned by the half past eight o'clock train. Found Sister Anne at home. Monday night, I had a walk. Tuesday night, I attended class for the first time we have met in the new vestry. Wednesday night, Mr. W. Dixon† came up to the shop and remained discussing business till ¼ to 11 o'clock.

I wrote this week to Newcastle for one 'Index Rerum' and five blank books carrying out my proposed system of memorandum and compositions. I borrowed an Index Rerum of Mr Aq. Keene† which I sent over for a pattern.

Father's return

Father returned from Conference yesterday morning, having been at Gloucester since leaving the Assembly. I am thankful he has returned in health and spirits.

Bathing

I have 'Bathed' in the sea every day this week, and am beginning to find considerable benefit from the persevering ablutions. I wish to learn to be a skilful swimmer. I can swim 20 or 30 feet, and then I weary. I gather every time more confidence and I am certain that a little diligent practice will speedily enable me to acquire such a facility in the noble art of flotation as will prove the probable means of safety in the event of any sudden and unexpected casualty. Life is full of changeful events. Now here, and now there. Upheaved and driven by the ocean surge from one extremity of the earth unto the other. Who therefore can confidently predict what may be the path which, in the passage of time, he may be called to transverse, and which may demand resources and attainments that if in possession may command safety and success, but if unknown may ensure destruction.

I must give myself a little to serious thought. I must have some sermons and skeletons prepared for I am decidedly behindhand. The Lord give me grace, mercy and peace for Christ's sake. Amen.

Letter to Brother William

Tuesday (August 15th)

On Friday afternoon last I went to bathe, there was much swell. I incautiously let myself down into a place where it was deep, and then striking out my arms and limbs to swim towards the shore, I found myself amongst a mass of floating seaweed, which rendered it extremely difficult to make any progress. I may thank the confidence that I have acquired lately for my extrication. Praise God who is the source of all mercy.

Saturday was an extremely warm day and in the shop I was thoroughly fatigued. I received a letter from Brother Wm. dated from 'The Thorney Close'.† I have this day written in reply, and have not forgotten to plead earnestly with him on the necessity of his instant devotion to Christ. He is about to sail from Cardiff for Petersburgh.

Scottish Non-Intrusionist Preachers. Preach at Deptford

Last Sunday I had Mr Peter's† appointments to supply, and this Sunday I have had Mr Keene's† viz; Deptford,† Ayre's Quay† and Southwick.† I have had great trouble, great waste of time on the attempt, and finally, though very inconvenient, I was obliged to preach at Deptford myself and persuaded J. Cooke for the Ballast Hills [Ayre's Quay], and G. Elliott for Southwick.† In the afternoon I was so much exhausted that I lay down; in the evening I went to St. George's Chapel† in Villiers St., to hear Mr Paterson of Glasgow preach on behalf of the Scottish Non-Intrusionists.[19] A real Scotchman, considerable talent, and much abrupt energy. I then popped up to our Brougham St.† prayer meeting, stayed 15m. and then returned. After family worship, and father had retired to rest, I smoked a cigar beside Anne and Ophelia whilst we discussed the matter of Ophelia's marriage.

19. The 'Non-Intrusionists' were those Scots who opposed the system by which Church of Scotland ministerial appointments were made by right of patronage. They believed that it was a fundamental right of the Church that no minister should be 'intruded' on any congregation contrary to the will of the people. This grievance, part of a wider concern for freedom from excessive and unspiritual State control, came to a head at the General Assembly of the Church of Scotland in May 1843, the outcome being that 474 ministers seceded and formed the Free Church of Scotland. The Free Churchmen found much sympathy among nonconformists south of the Border. The *Sunderland Herald* 26 May 1843, carried long reports on 'The Secession of the Non-Intrusionists', and on the first meeting of the Free Presbyterian Assembly. The *Newcastle Chronicle* 27 May 1843, reported in some detail the meeting of the General Assembly at which the secession occurred; and the proprietors of the paper, Thomas and James Hodgson, launched a monthly journal in July 1843 entitled the *English Non-Intrusionist : Northern Lights on Southern Latitudes,* which apparently proved popular in the north east. A delegation of Scots representing the 'Free Presbyterian Church of Scotland', visited the north east in August 1843, and services and meetings were held at Sunderland on 13th and 15th August, and at South Shields and Newcastle. Dr. N. Paterson, referred to as Mr by J.Y., preached on the Sunday evening in Sunderland, and spoke on the Tuesday at the Sans Street Wesleyan chapel† when a resolution was passed in support of the Free Church and collections made on their behalf. *Newcastle Chronicle* 19th August 1843 and *Sunderland Herald* 18th August

1843. Wesleyan attitudes to the Scots Disruption are carefully analysed in A.J. Hayes and D.A. Gowland, *Scottish Methodism in the Early Victorian Period,* (1981), pp. 14–21. Interesting older accounts of this episode of Scots history can be read in L. Walker, *Chapters from the History of the Free Church of Scotland,* (Edinburgh, 1895), and in P. Bayne, *The Free Church of Scotland,* (Edinburgh, 1894).

Marriage of Ophelia

On Monday I rose at ½ past 5 o'clock, went with Thos.[20] to bathe, returned to breakfast and, after having visited the shop, walked to the Tabernacle† to witness the celebration of my sister Ophelia's marriage with Mr John Dixon,† chemist & druggist of this place. Mr Dixon, his father, and Mr T.B. Young were present with myself, Thos. and Anne. Mrs. Nesbitt, also the Miss Bells, Mrs Peters. These with some few strangers who came in at the opening of the doors were all.

The Revd John Peters† conducted the ceremony. After its conclusion J.D. and I walked down to Wm. D's at 10 o'clock. Mr and Mrs Dixon, myself, Thos. and Anne with Mr J. Tuer† went over to Newcastle to dine with Mr John Muschamp.† We returned at 4 o'clock, leaving Mr & Mrs D. to pursue their way to Shotley[21] to spend a few days. Thus the die is cast, and this affair long spoken of and expected is numbered amongst the things that were.

May the God of all grace grant that this affair may be sanctified by His spirit, and blessing to their present and eternal salvation.

20. J.Y.'s younger brother Thomas, then aged 21.
21. A once-attractive spa in north-west Durham on the river Derwent, whose popularity declined with the advent of industrial developments in the vicinity. Fordyce ii, 700–701.

Review of my Religion

Friday (Aug 18th, 1843)

I have just risen from prayer. Prayer! Seldom indeed do I continue in a wrestling frame. Few are my visits to God in secret; and yet that is the great pillar of the Christian life. What decided spiritual habits do I possess or enjoy? What symptoms exist which in themselves form unquestionable evidence of the quality of my piety? Is religion truly the grand object of my pursuit? Why then so little of peaceful contentment, and calm resignation? How much of petty vanity, and littleness of mind?

I see at present (O that it might continue) that I live and act, eat and drink, without consciousness of the Divine Presence. If my spiritual taste is to be judged by my reading of God's word, and delight in its perusal; if my frequent attention to the reading of books of a religious or practical character be a test, what is my position? It just occurs to my memory that I have not even thought to ask divine mercy on a single meal today. When I rise in the morning is it with a feeling of thankfulness, and is my prayer literally the offering of the heart or the mere formal discharge of an irksome duty? And during the day does my spirit ever recur to its connection with Jesus, and the Cross? Alas! And yet if I were asked, 'Do you believe that as a professor of religion you are the 'Temple of God'? I scarce know what I would say. My mind the Temple of God; whence then this discontentedness, and dissatisfaction? Hundreds around are by no means so favourably situated as myself, and yet I am constantly indulging in thoughts of an anxious and distrustful character.

My mind the temple of God. Whence this proneness to sensual gratification, the indulgence of the lust of the eye, the tongue, the ear? Why this delight in foolish conversation, in imaginary bluntness and slang? I remember when I first entered the kingdom of Christ, how swiftly I ran, and I devoutly believed that nought on earth could possibly shake my devotion to the cause. Had any person told me then that I should so easily, in after years, become a prey to sinful thoughts and actions, surely I would have pitied their ignorance of the strength of my piety. I then believed that no temptation or possible combination of circumstances could ever break in upon my consecration to God. But now where is my fear of the Holy One of Israel? If I sit under the word of God, it is rather to gratify my curiosity as a critic, than to be edified and humbled as a sinner.

Truly I believe this moment that could I but fully comprehend my folly and sin, I would be astonished at the kindness and Love of God in preserving me from utterly, and for ever losing all desire, all thought, of religious duty and sactifying grace. But of what use are these lamentations, and regrets? Am I to live and die in this deplorable state? Is no divine counsel to raise my depression, and move my stubbornness? Every hour, the experience of every day has taught me, 'Thou canst not serve God, and mammon' [Matt. 6:24]. O my soul wilt thou now decide? If thy reverence for the name of a crucified Saviour be a delusive veneration for a human martyr. If the story of the cross is an imposition on thy credulity, and in truthfulness sustains no relation to thy present or future destinites. If the myriads who have lived in its fear and died in its hope, whose lives, in the rush of passion and the torrent of feeling, have been curbed and guided by its rules, and who have forsaken the earth not with melancholy and gloomy despair but with a soul reposing in a calm and bright confidence that the sorrow of death was but the portal of Heaven. If all thy past convictions and deep impressions, thy penitent remorse, thy ecstasy of joy, were but the creatures of a confused, and morbid mind. If there be no bright or holy Intelligence from whom and by whom all existence came, whose mighty power has hung the vast orbs of light, the incomprehensible systems of suns and stars. If their tale of wisdom, of goodness, and love, with its deep echo in the heart of man, is but a Dream of nothing, risen in the mind from no substantial being, then give to nothing thy disturbed and fearful dream. What canst thou gain, what canst thou lose? But dare ye affirm your past folly, your present misery? Will ye proclaim your rejection of the Gospel of Jesus?

Necessity of Decision

It cannot be! Every nerve and fibre of thy body trembles with the profound persuasion of thy immortality, immortality given thee by a God and designed to prove a source of unfading joy. Immortality lost by sin. Immortality brought to light by the Gospel. O then wilt thou return? Return to the dictate of reason, the judgement of the understanding, the command of God. Return I must, return I will. O thou merciful and just God. If thou shouldest mark iniquity who should stand? But there is forgiveness with that thou mayst be feared and plenteous redemption that Thou mayest be sought. [Psalm 130 : 3-7*]

Prayer for Continued Mercy

Blessed be thy holy name thou hast not dealt with us according to our sins, nor rewarded us according to our iniquities [Psalm 103:10] else darkness and death had covered me in misery and despair. Abandon not thy servant [cp. Psalm 27:9]. Let not thine anger abide for ever [cp. Ps. 103:9 and Micah 7:18]. Return O Lord, how long, and let it repent thee concerning thy servant [Ps. 90:13]. Cause thy face to shine upon me [Psalm 31:16 etc.]. Lighten mine eyes lest I sleep the sleep of Death [Ps. 13:3]. May I awake into thy likeness [cp. Romans 6:5], lest iniquity prove my ruin [cp. Ezek. 18:30]. O that my days might be spent in thy praise [cp. Ps. 90:14]. Forget not the intercession of Him who is seated at thy right hand [Hebrews 7:25 and 8:1]. Hath he not suffered, the just for the unjust, to bring us to God? [I Peter 3:18]. Lord to whom should I go, thou only has the words of eternal life [John 6:68]. I cannot live and die a prey to sin. Deliver me from its baneful influence. May thy good spirit extinguish every evil desire, destroy every corrupt thought and sanctify me throughout, body, soul, and spirit, so that whether I live, I may live to thee, whether I die, I may die to thee, that whether living, or dying I may be thine [Romans 14:18*].

Let every moment be given to the accomplishment of the great end of life – the advancement of thy Glory, and finally through Redeeming mercy may I be presented faultless before the presence of thy glory with exceeding joy for Christ's sake. Amen [Jude 24].

Preach at Hylton

Monday (Aug. 21st, 1843)

Saturday was a busy and warm day. At night I was obliged to put off my shirt to enable me to move briskly, and talk blithely to customers. It is of the first moment to manifest a cheerful activity. I aim at this. The spirit of conciliation and good humour. I flatter myself that no small portion of the support I have heretofore received is attributed to my endeavour to acquire a pleasing method of conversational business.

On Sunday morning I rose about 8 o'clock. Reviewed my sermons during the morning. Washed myself with cold water, and soap over the whole surface of my body. Left home about ¼ to 1 o'clock. It came on a very heavy shower of rain which continued until I reached Hylton.† Changed my trousers, and dried my boots, coat and hat at Wilson's. Preached at 2 o'clock from 2 Tim. 2. 11,12,13 &c. Felt rather hampered for want of a clear voice. Got tea at Wilson's. Some little good-tempered bickering between Wilson and his [wife] as to whether coffee or tea should be used. Wilson thought there was nothing like coffee. His wife said it was only 16d kind, and therefore not good enough for a stranger. However her tea was very poor stuff. I took a walk down the waterside, in a shady lane towards Clatchiff.† Smoked a cigar, sat upon a railway and calmly looked upon the smile of nature. The sun shone brighter, the grass looked more fresh and green, the birds sang more merrily after the passing away of the rain. It was pleasant to saunter in easy relaxation, though I had to turn over in thought the subject for the evening service.

On returning I found Messrs Ball, Milner, Haswell, &c. had a good deal of conversation with them on Preaching, Talent, good sermons and bad. Fine spun, high-flown language, and plain common sense.

The discussion was begun by Mr Wilson, whose drift I afterwards discovered was no less than to reprove me for 'Shooting over the heads of the poor people'. He was, I think, alone in his opinion amongst the brethren there present. Most of them did not appear to rate the intelligence of the Hylton people so low. Now I devoutly believed that my sermon in the afternoon was (at least in my fancy) simple, very simple, in its language and design; and yet he thought it above the apprehension of the ignorant. To this, and much more of a like nature, I replied that I was much obliged for the admonition; that I believed it to proceed from a friendly feeling that if a young man learnt his defects, and all young men must have 'many errors, the growth of carelessness, or habit,' he could only be corrected by the kind remark of a friend. Therefore friendship was shown to be real when a person looked malice and passion in the face, and fearlessly told the truth. That for myself I would continue to do just to the best of my ability, discharge my duty as I could, and then if the people don't like it let it be so.

I preached at 6 o'clock from XC Ps. 12 v. 'So teach us' &c. I called upon Wilson to pray. Whilst he addressed the throne of grace in a very happy way I took off my stock, in order to be able to preach with greater ease and strength in my voice. It had a happy effect. I never had my voice with such strength, power, and fluency of expression. I spoke for about 1 hour and 10m., longer than at any previous period. I was enabled to bring forward many ideas and illustrations not previously prepared. We had an excellent prayer meeting. I got a basin of milk at Wilson's. After prayer I left about 10m past 9 o'clock. A very fine mild night. Two young women accompanied me, who are members of the Hylton Society, but having gone recently to Sunderland to live were returning from seeing their friends. Their names were Julia Mason, living with Chalmers the schoolmaster, and Margaret Southron in Burleigh Street. We reached home about 10m. past 10 o'clock. And then to bed. O Lord may the labours of this day not be utterly and for ever unfruitful. May some poor sinner be guided to thee, the Saviour of souls. Amen.

Business

Tuesday (Aug. 29th, 1843)

My attention during the last week has been absorbed by 'business'. My thoughts have dwelt almost exclusively on the grand theme of the business man, getting money, the soonest and easiest way to 'Brass'. Devising plans and schemes for the extension of connection and trade. Not that I am wholly absorbed by the desire of wealth, but because I entertain the idea that, while we are at work we should work, not simply stand behind the counter and receive the halfpence which by chance may tumble in, but to think deeply and seriously by what means one's business may be extended so as to yield the largest possible return.

At this instant as I write I am troubled with a bad toothache, and have my mouth stuffed with cotton and creosote.

I am on the 'look out' constantly for information on business matters. I make it a point to learn something from every person with whom I come in contact. I draw them out in conversation on those subjects with which I have reason to think they are especially acquainted.

Travellers, representatives of Commercial Houses, Manufacturers, Ship masters, Seamen, brokers, tradesmen generally, and even workpeople of all descriptions, from all these something of interest and value may be gathered by an observing mind. Information thus obtained may not appear of much present utility, but it is impossible to say how important it may prove as passing days bring the mind to the contemplation of new scenes, and present openings for further and more lucrative occupation.

By this means also, as lanes or paths are opened to view, we discover not only those which are the most profitable, but the particular road that is most congenial to the talent and temper of the mind.

The pursuits of commerce, the conduction of heavy and extensive business transactions, convey to the uninitiated an impression that there must be something very mysterious and complicated in its arrangement, requiring on the part of its conductors very extraordinary sagacity and enterprise. When therefore we are brought to understand the simple management of the affair we are surprised at this simplicity, and inspired with the confidence necessary to enable ourselves to enter into its walk. I am resolved to do my utmost to better my position in Society, and under the blessing of the good Providence of God what should prevent me (as others before) rising to a higher and more comfortable station in the world?

My mind in the moment of reflection is always returning to the thought that Time, the hours of youthful vigour, are so rapidly passing away without substantial and commensurate improvement. Here's the Grand Reason. 'The spirit is willing but the flesh is weak' [Matt. 26:41]. If I were the habitant of a body so constituted that to will were to perform, I should run to the goal of truth, and purity with undeviating alacrity. But here's the misery 'Death hath entered the world' [cp. Romans 5:12].

Time flies; my leisure for this little duty will soon be past, so I must finish the record of the week.

Business so filled the days that Sabbath was my first freedom. In the morning having been at the shop until near 1 o'clock in the morning, I lay 'till 9 o'clock.

Preach at Stafford Street

I heard Mr Henderson of the New Connexion preach at Brougham Street† at ½ 10, from 'Learn from me for I am meek and lowly' &c. [Matt. 11:29]. On coming out I called and prayed with Mrs Taylor who had a child last Monday. After dinner I shut myself up in the attic, thought over my subject for the night. Sought to invest it with new interest, and appropriate to it new ideas. At ½ past 2 o'clock after looking into the S. School and saying 'How do you do?' to Mr W. Dixon,† and S. Hodgson,† I went into class. Mr Mules gave us our tickets. I came away at 4 o'clock and took tea with Mr John Dixon. At 6 o'clock I preached at the Stafford Street New Connexion Chapel[22] for Mr Thos. Stevenson. Subject of discourse XC Ps. 12 verse. I had considerable difficulty in speaking, and did not possess mental liberty. After service I walked on the moor with Thos. Stevenson and then went up to the vestry.

22. A chapel, probably a rented room, in the east end of Sunderland, belonging to the Methodist New Connexion.

Prayer Meeting

The New Vestry was crowded with people who appeared to be influenced by a good feeling. I did not stay long but, having shown my 'Physog', popped out, and proceeded to stretch my limbs up High Street to Brougham Street† Prayer Meeting. There I found my father, T.R. Wilson,† and Mr Keene† engaged in conversational exhortation, and prayer with a number of young females professedly under religious impressions. I detest the practice which is so common, viz., that kneeling down alongside of young females, placing the arm over their shoulders and then introducing the face in the closest possible approximation to that of the female, for the professed object of 'familiar exhortation'. Familiar truly! But a familiarity from which I am persuaded a virtuous, modest and sensitive nature must shrink.

Philadelphia

Monday (Sept. 11th, 1843)

It is a singular that last week should not have given one entry for my journal. On Sunday Sept. 3rd I went out with J. Hutchison and J. Thomson into the country in the gig. We picked up Mr Thos. Stevenson on the road. He and I getting out together, went down to Philadelphia.† I looked into the New Connexion Chapel, and then called at Bunker's Hill.† Saw Mrs Keene, late Marianne Harrison,† who was married to the Revd. Aquila Keene† on the preceding Thursday at Houghton le Spring Church.

Mr. Keene being our 2nd preacher the fact of his going to the Established Church to be married has given considerable umbrage to many of our members who protest against what they term a deviation from the principles which Dissenters ought to reserve.

At 2 o'clock I walked down to Chapel, opened the service and Mr Stevenson preached from the parable of the rich man who said 'Soul take thine ease' [Luke 12:19]. Mr Stevenson took tea with us. We had to give the health of the bride, Mr S. in a glass of wine, myself with a piece of cake. I have been a teetotaler for 8 years, and I am still convinced of its necessity and reasonableness. We had much interesting conversation at the tea table. I retired to the recess in the garden, smoked a cigar, and studied my sermon.

Shiney Row

I preached at Shiney Row† at 6 o'clock from XI ch. of Ecclesiastes 4 v. Two of the Potters set me over to the brook [the Herrington Burn†]. I had supper with Mrs Harrison, Mrs Keene and Miss Sarah. I felt exceedingly happy, after the labour of the day, calmly and socially to enjoy the refreshment provided, doubly refreshing from the kindness and attention of the entertainers.

Mrs H. said, 'I never look in your face Mr John, without

pride and gratitude, to think how ill you were at one time, and how different now'. 'I am much obliged for your sympathy', I replied, 'I have great reason to be thankful.' Mrs H., 'Why did you not preach, Mr. John, I felt it to be a great disappointment'. 'Really', said Mrs Keene 'you must not disappoint us again; there is such a difference between Mr S. and you. In giving out the hymn, what a change.' 'I thought', said Miss Sarah, 'that Mr John had sat down on purpose to let us see the difference between himself and Mr Stevenson.' What could I say to remarks which savoured much of flattery, but yet were uttered in such a simple, natural, and spontaneous manner as to incline me to believe that they were sincere?

I know something of myself, my abilities &c. There exists perhaps some partiality towards me as the son of an old friend, and where people love the preacher for his own sake, mere talent will fail to accomplish so great an interest. Many other remarks in a similar strain I might put down, but I forbear. True this record is for my own eye, nevertheless I shirk from placing on paper what savours of egotistical vanity.

I design however, when I begin a new Journal, then to lay bare the 'Heart'. To narrate truthfully those motives, secret influences and desires. What is an autobiography without these? And when I succeed in portraying them in their successive interests before the mind I shall feel astonished. Durst I really place on paper the truth? Humanity, how frail! Must I add another link to the chain of evidence which forces me to believe that many weaknesses may exist with general integrity of purpose? Perhaps I may tread the path of ingenuousness until I stumble upon something which I would fain pass by without acknowledgement. Whose being, if felt, would make me despise myself.

Mr Stevenson called for me at Mr H's. By the way, Mr H. by my advice went to bed after dinner. Having got cold the previous night he was very much troubled with langour and headache. I prayed before I came away. Called in the village for a young man named Hall. The whole road home I was distracted with the toothache. Rendered incapable of conversation. Happy when I had the floor of my father's house. The pain continued until I believe after three o'clock in the morning. What a malady is this!

Mysteries of Udolpho

The Week has been filled up with business &c. No time to study, no reading. On Friday I read the 'Mysteries of Udolpho' by Mrs Radcliffe,[23] to relieve my frame from langour and fatigue which rendered mental labour impossible.

The heat of the days has been most excessive. I cannot bear up against it. I stripped myself of my shirt several times of late to give ease.

Sept. 10th. Sunday, I heard Mr Heywood† preach from 'Christ a Physician'. In the afternoon I walked out, and in the evening remained in the house.

I now begin the week. May it be more fruitful than its predecessors. Amen for Christ's sake.

23. Mrs Ann Radcliffe (1764 – 1823), *The Mysteries of Udolpho, a romance interspersed with some pieces of poetry,* (London, 1794).

Preach at Seaham

Saturday (Sept. 23rd)

On Sunday last walked out past Ryhope,† and then taking the omnibus proceeded to Seaham.† Dined with Mr Storey, and preached at 2 o'clock from 2 ch 2 Tim. 11,12,13 &c. Walked on the sand at the conclusion of the service to review my sermon for the evening. Mr Bennett came out and had tea with me at Storey's, and accompanied me home at night. I preached from XC Ps. 12v. Mr. Storey and Mr. Stalker set us on the road. We came through Ryhope Dene.† It was very dark, and the southern sky glowed with rapidly succeeding flashes of lightning. Still the road was calm and pleasing, though I was very weary, and jaded. Next to a good conscience nothing shortens a lonely walk so much as a cheerful companion.

This week and last also I have been severely visited by the toothache and indigestion. What hours are passed in slow, harrassing tediousness when the body, the muscular system, is incapable of vigorous action.

Flight of Time.
Oh, Misery.

Oh Misery, Oh Misery, Young in years, yet getting old, and time knocking me on the head, and every knock rendering me less able to fulfil my destiny according to design. Merciful Father, give unto me health to sustain the efforts of the mind to enable me to get on and on, and still to cry 'On', for ever on. I thirst to slake the parching dryness of the grasping of an immortal spirit in the fulness of truth. Let me plunge into the depths, and find that I am bathing in the dew of eternal life. Oh! I could go mad, mad, mad. I could weep tears of blood to think of the martyrdom of my hopes. I would break the chain at once and wing my path to the gate of life, but this frail tenement, this poor body, ever and anon must be plastered and propped.

Preach at Brougham Street

Wednesday (Sept. 27th, 1843)

I never intended to preach in Brougham Street† on Sunday last in the afternoon. This I named to my father. 'Oh!' said he, 'I suppose you won't preach because so few will be there on account of the Lovefeast at S.D.St.† However, I'll take care that it shall be given out, and then if you don't go, people will know why.' Rather than have such a slur on my character I went. My true reason for not wishing to go is simply this. Some thought, or I fancied that they thought, that I was ambitious of figuring off in the large chapels, and therefore I secretly resolved not to enter those pulpits at present.

My principle and conviction is that I will attain my true level in a little time, with patience. For indeed I am resigned to the Divine Providence, and in that sense conscientiously believe that whatever is, is best. Why should I shove myself forward? I was dragged into preaching by the solicitations of the church, and if I move onward I long ago determined that it should not be by my personal efforts to place myself before the eye of the public, but from the sentiment of the Church.

I should find more pleasure in studious retirement from public duty, but I must not, because it is duty. Time will creep on, and if I am careful to improve my advantages, and treasure up with a diligent hand the wisdom which will reward perseverance by and by, I shall rise to usefulness of a more substantial and extended character than could possibly result from any presumptious and precocious attempt to step in advance of my true influence.

I preached from V John 40 v. Scarcely at any former period did I experience such difficulty in speaking, arising just from the weakness of the voice, and 2ndly from the S. School Children who disturbed the service by their intolerable noise and clamour. My work however was done. My consolation I did my duty, and my reflection if in this case I am dissatisfied with myself, another time I shall do better. In the evening I heard Mr Keene† preach, and returning home looked into Harris' 'Christian Union'.[24]

Still distracted with the pain in my face, which prevents my progress in any labour.

24. John Harris D.D., *Union : or the Divided Church made one*, (London, c.1837). Harris was a Congregationalist, and Principal of New College, London. He published many sermons, tracts and pamphlets.

Old woman died on my premises

On Monday morning as usual I read the Times, Sun, Gazette. After breakfast, whilst my lads were at their breakfast, an old woman came into the shop, and sat down upon a chair with an appearance of feebleness. I said 'Well what does thou want this morning'? She replied 'Oh! I wish I had not come out this morning, I feel very poorly'. I said, 'Well you had better tell us what you want and get home as soon as possible'. She made no answer; in attempting to set a little basket which she carried on the floor she suddenly tumbled off the chair. I ran round the counter. A woman coming into the shop, named Mrs Madison of Little Villiers Street, I said 'Here's a poor woman taken a fit, lend us a hand to lift her up'. At the same moment perceiving an acquaintance, Gabriel Reay of Nile Street, standing across the road I waved him over. He lifted the old woman on to the chair. He said, 'She's going.' I replied, 'I'm afraid so'. I immediately sent Mrs Madison for Mr Potts the surgeon.[25]

Mrs Madison returned in about 4 minutes. The instant she saw the poor woman she said, 'Oh dear she's gone! She's dead.' In two minutes Mr Potts arrived and confirmed the fact. Mr Potts, G. Reay, Mrs Madison and myself lifted her into my back room and laid her on the sofa. Mrs Madison asked for a piece of linen to tie her [? champs or chaufs]. I should never have thought of it. So much for experience.

Mr. Potts gave information at the police station and presently an inspector and one of his men arrived. The rumour soon spread and brought crowds to the door. A woman named Mrs Marley of Numbers Garth identified the body as that of Mrs Ellen Masterman, a widow resident in Burleigh Street. The body was removed to her daughter's, Mrs Donnison, Stamps Lane.

25. John Potts, surgeon, lived at 139 High Street, Sunderland.

Inquest on old woman who died in my shop

An inquest was held on Tuesday morning at 9 o'clock in narrow Flag Lane† at a Public House named Millar's. I was summoned as a witness before the jury and Mr Maynard the Coroner. After oath I gave my statement, which was taken down by the coroner. He asked me particularly, 'What in your opinion caused her death?' I replied, 'I have no opinion, it being impossible to form an opinion without an examination.' 'I know,' said he, 'that the fact cannot be known without doubt unless a post mortem examination take place, but I simply want your opinion.' I answered that Dr Green, and Mr Parker the surgeon had looked at the body and thought she had died of disease of the heart, and therefore if I were guided by medical authority I might suppose the same. He put it down as my opinion that she died of disease of the heart. What the verdict of the jury was I strangely enough have not yet heard.

I have read this week Blackwood's Magazine for July and August. There is always much of interesting matter in this periodical. The Quarterly Review for May 1843 I have read with special pleasure. Articles, 'Sir Charles Bell', 'Francis Horner', 'Theodore Hook', present an extemely interesting and instructive view of the characters, and lives of these great men. I always feel refreshed and cheered after the reading of these Reviews. There is such a stream of clear thought and invaluable information as cannot fail to interest the mind.

Monday (Oct. 2nd, 1843)

I thank thee O Lord God that though I have been very treacherous, very unfaithful, in the path of the holy truth, thou hast not suffered thy wrath to kindle against me [cp. Psalm 124:3] but I am yet within the covenant mercies of Jesus and may still look with confidence to the cup for [? : of] salvation [Psalm 116:13]. Salvation – what is not signified by the term? Salvation from everything that can cause the human spirit to groan because of misery. Salvation to raise us from the degradation of enmity in the heart to realize peace, happiness, and heaven. Jesus, appear. Let me feel my alliance with thy influence. Perish every unholy desire. Consume every sinful thought. Dwell in, fill my heart.

Religious Reflections

On Saturday I felt more seriously disposed than usual. On Sunday I lay in bed until ½ past 10 o'clock. I have been very unwell of late. Dressed, and lay down on the bed, and read Henry's 'Pleasures of Religion'.[26] I am certain that if I possessed more closely the mind of Christ, the preparation for the sanctuary would be more blessed, and blessing. If my heart were in with the truth of God, I should feel for souls, and thus feeling sinners would tremble. Oh for a spirit of prayer! How delightful to know myself right in the work. True I have temptations, and they are heavy, they are powerful, but here is the proof of my sincerity, this the test of my faithfulness to my master, that I am willing to suffer, willing to endure affliction to approve myself a good soldier of Jesus Christ [II Tim. 2:3]. He that will be a friend of the world is an enemy of God. That is a plain and universal principle. How can I mistake? Only, the heart is so deceitful, that it returns to its delusions and rejoices in its folly. I must come to Christ, in his word, in prayer, in faith, and then experience will prove her ways to be ways of pleasantness and her paths peace [Prov. 3:17].

Godliness with contentment is great gain [I Tim. 6:6].

On Sunday after dinner I walked out, called at Dean's, Mr J. Dixon's,† then walked on the moor. Enjoyed the cool refreshing breeze. I met Mr Heywood.† We walked to Silver Street together. Passed a poor man holding forth on the great topics, the 'Suffrage', 'Equal rights', 'Justice', &c. &c. Poor philanthropist. Better return diligently to his last and his leather, than attempt to cobble the Constitution.

26. Matthew Henry (1662 – 1714), *The Pleasantness of a Religious Life opened and prov'd and recommended to the consideration of all, particularly young people,* (London, 1714), appears to be the book referred to; it is not in the British Library Catalogue of Printed Books, but there is a copy in the John Rylands University Library of Manchester.

Mr. T.B. Young preaches at Silver Street

Arriving at the New Chapel in Silver Street I was astonished to find it crowded with people. My father preached from 'Who then is willing this day to consecrate himself to God?' [I Chron. 29:5*]. My Father preached with great liberty and influence. He sang three successive times during the sermon, at each division.

This was the opening of a new place of worship. It formerly was a Sailcloth Manufactory,[27] but having been taken at a rental of about £13.10/– per annum by Messrs. T.B. Young and Milner, they have been at the expense of placing Pulpit, Trims, Pews, &c. and painting out so that it now presents a very decent comfortable appearance, a very chapel. I remained in the back room or vestry, and came out at the conclusion of the Sermon.

It was announced by Mr Heywood that I should preach next Sabbath at ½ past 2 o'clock. The Lord help me! I was distracted with this pain in my face. After tea lay down, and feeling better rose for Brougham Street.† Heard Mr Mules† preach from CXL Ps., v [blank] 'prisoners of the Lord.'[28] Partook of the Sacrament at the close of the Sermon, and then going home with Mr Wm. Moore went into his house, and chatted for a while.

On Monday felt better. Engaged with business and harrassed the whole day.

On Tuesday evening I went down to Silver Street with Mr W. Dixon† and Mr Milner. Mr. D. put the numbers on the pews.[29]

27. It is a sign of the advancing development of steam power for ships that a sail cloth workshop should be closed and converted for worship. T.B. Young, as a sail-maker, presumably experienced commercial difficulties himself, and his emigration in 1852 may have been caused by the decline in his trade. Other factors could have been at work however, including the collapse of the 'Methodist Bank' 1851–2.
28. There is no verse number given and the reference is confusing.
29. For the purpose of pew-renting, which was general in Methodist chapels at the time of John Young's diary.

Income Tax Examination

Monday (Oct. 9th, 1843)

Last Thursday I was engaged part of the day in drawing up a statement to lay before the surveyor of the Income Tax and the Commissioners at Durham.[30]

I have been much flurried and hurried by business this week – business rendered uncomfortable by exhaustion of mind and body.

On Friday morning I left by the Brandling Junction Railway for Durham.[31]

In the railway carriage I met a number of shopkeepers on a similar errand to myself. The mutual chattering and complaining was very amusing. Some insisted that their neighbours must have informed of them as they could never have asked questions which implied a knowledge of the business they did. And deep were the murmurs of displeasure against the parties whom they supposed guilty of such conduct.

Had I time I could amuse myself by recounting sundry amusing incidents. Arrived at Durham. I met several parties who had their backs placed against the gate of admission in order to secure an early time. By dint of running I got there before the rest of our freighted bus. 'Hello are you here?' was a general exclamation. 'Why here's a confounded mess' was the reply. The door keeper arrived and then what an undignified crush and rush across the court up the stairs. Vigorous were the snatches of outstretched hands to seize the tickets. By a disregard of needless courtesy I gained and kept the top. Kerss the Blacksmith and I grasped the same ticket, and in our mutual unwillingness to leave hold, we each retained a portion. Luckily on mine the figure 3 appeared.

Mr Ray (Wm.) and Mr Bruce the grocer were next me.

Great was the rumours and surmises respecting the treatment to be received at the hand of – the **Tribunal.** Numbers arrived immediately and those who came half an hour later than we were getting Nos. 37–50–55. No. 1 was called and emerged from the dread door while dozens of anxious eyes scrutinised his countenance as though it afforded some indication of the climate within the Sanctum. No. 2 entered. The door keeper cried 'Let No 3 hold himself in readiness. Where is No 3? 'Is No. 3 here?' 'Here, I am No. 3' said I.

A meeting having to be held in the large room in which we were assembled we had to descend again into the Court. There I paced waiting the exit of No. 3 [recte 2]. He came. I immediately, hat in hand, entered the room of fate.

Mr Fawcett was seated at the side of a large green table and Mr Hays the clerk on the other side with two commissioners.

'What is you name?' said the Surveyor. 'John Young sir.' 'What is your profession?' 'Chemist and Grocer sir.' 'Have you brought any statement?' I then drew from my waistcoat pocket my paper, and handed it to him. 'Is this all?' said he. 'I don't like this way of making returns. It is not satisfactory. You should have come prepared with an account of your stock, cash etc. and taking the balance we should have seen how you were situated at once.' He gave the paper across the table to Mr Fox the Commissioner.

'What's this?' said Fox. I explained. He also objected to the manner of statement as not being satisfactory.

I had simply given in the amount turned over in the year and the percentage profit with a deduction of expenses. I had considerable difficulty in persuading them that I was right. They made numerous inquiries. 'How I lived?' Kept my family? Household expenses?'

Fawcett the Surveyor says: 'Nay, haven't you 75% upon many of your articles and 50 upon others?' 'Yes sir' I replied 'but it is so occasionally that we regard it as a "very windfall".'

I answered all queries with the most conciliatory courtesy and finding the surveyor and his clerk inclined to set me back to take stock I talked as much as possible to the Commissioners.

'But' says Fox 'how do you make out this 30%, you might have said 25 or 20.'

I told them that having taken stock last year, and averaged my profits for the balance of the year, I had taken that as the criterion by which to judge the profits of this.

What need I say more – I got through. 'You' said they 'may pass through this year, but next year you must take your stock and come here with a clear statement.' 'All right.'

I waited of Ray and Bruce and we then went to a Coffee House and took Ham and Coffee and laughed over our adventures. Poor Bruce was made to pay and Ray came off clear. Left Durham about 12 o'clock in Ray's phaeton and came home very pleasantly by 2 o'clock. So this affair is done.

30. B.E.V. Sabine, *History of Income Tax*, (1966) gives a number of points which corroborate the account which follows, especially regarding the relative roles of the Commissioners and the Surveyor. The tax in question of 7d in the £, was imposed by Peel in his budget of 1842. Those with incomes below £150 p.a. were exempt, and judging from the outcome of the tribunal described by John Young he must have persuaded the commissioners that he was in that category. There was a good deal of popular animus against this tax, and the Sunderland Corporation at its meeting on 1 February 1843 passed a petition to be put to both Houses of Parliament protesting that the tax was 'harsh and oppressive in operation, exposing many whose incomes do not amount to £150 per year to annoyance, delay, and in innumerable instances to heavy pecuniary losses; that it is inquisitorial and vexatious in its machinery, exposing the private affairs of those within its range to numerous local officers appointed for carrying it into operation, and that in its spirit and details it is repugnant to the feelings of Englishmen, and being essentially a war tax it ought not to be inflicted on the nation at that period when Great Britain and the world are emphatically at peace'. Tyne and Wear Archives, Minute Books of Sunderland Corporation, i 312. I owe this reference to Mr John Pearson. The wars alluded to here were those with China, the 'Opium War' 1839–42, and Afghanistan, 1838 – 1842.

31. See p. 196 below note 3. J.Y. presumably left by the 8 o'clock train from Monkwearmouth. It is notable that J.Y. did not travel to Durham on the direct Durham and Sunderland Railway.†

Preach at Silver Street

Sunday (Oct. 8th)

After breakfast took a walk on the sands, thought over my subject for the afternoon. Enjoyed the cool breeze, and calmness of the morning. Conjured up several new ideas and placed them on paper, went to the shop, smoked a cigar, threw my arms about, studied my subject, returned home and dinner, dressed, washed myself with cold water over the whole of my body, drank a cup of coffee. After these preparations went to Silver Street and preached with great liberty and abounding command of language from II Peter I vv 5.6.7. Felt well. Lord in the work. Anxiety to make an inroad on the heart but preached too long. One hour and ten minutes. I have heard of it since. Very foolish. Must amend.

Took tea at Mrs Nesbitt's with Mr Tuer,† and Mr and Mrs John Dixon.†

S. Hodgson's Sermon at Brougham Street

At Brougham Street† I heard Simson Hodgson† preach from 'Now is Christ risen from the dead, and become the first fruits of them that slept.' [I Cor. 15:20]. If I have any judgement in these matters a greater blunder in preaching was never perpetrated. The oratory of the attempt was miserable. Plenty of noise, but no just estimate and correct distribution of its modulations.

The material was more beyond description, masses of long, flowing, graphic, flowery words strung together for the evident purpose of display. Strung together so loosely and illogically as often to involve contradictions of the most glaring character.

After he had attempted to establish the fact of the resurrection of Jesus, by the testimony of Josephus, the improbable conduct of the guard and Jewish rulers, the change of the Sabbath, testimony of heathen antiquity, Eusebius, Origen, Tertullian and others & after having from them, and other evidence, proved, he said, the fact of the resurrection, he then proceeded to undo all that he had done and say that all these, mentioning them successively, may have been erroneous or false. But there was another grand, complete, and sufficient evidence, 'You feel he is risen.' 'Brother do you feel he is risen?' Sister do you feel he is risen?' But enough.

After chapel I walked with G. Elliott as far as Tunstall Hills.† A beautiful moonlight night. We discussed S. Hodgson's sermon &c.

Being a preacher myself it becomes me to be exceedingly circumspect in speaking of my brethren, lest that which is said in frankness and sincerity be placed to the account of malice or envy, which would inevitably prove the case.

On returning home, and conversing with father at the supper table, he expressed precisely the same opinion, and said, 'Let this be a warning to you never to talk about things which you don't understand.' I told him that it was my invariable rule never to give utterance to anything whatever unless I am well assured of its correctness, to refrain from any allusion to things of which I entertained a doubt.

Manufacture Spice Nuts

On Monday Oct. 9th I felt only indifferently well, and was kept constantly engaged in attending to the Manufacture of Spice Nuts for the fair. Had Mr Bennett employed, Monday and Tuesday.

On Tuesday G. Elliott, Bennett† and I baked some nuts ourselves at night in the front warehouse.

On Wednesday Oct. 11th I was in the shop very late wrapping up Spice Nuts. G. Elliott assisting.

Bodily Depression

I have had a very severe cold, and attendant exhaustion, lassitude, debility, &c. During Wednesday night it blew a complete gale of wind. In the morning the first news was five vessels in shore, and alas! one or two have since been known to have foundered, bodies washing up &c.

This cold dreary storm completely spoiled the fair day.

On Friday Oct. 12 [recte 13] the weather improved. And Saturday it was still finer. I was kept in the shop till about midnight all these three nights, to say nothing of the three previous nights working till 11 or ½ past 10 o'clock. Oh dear, it is killing work. Shopkeeping with confinement like mine is ruinous to the constitution.

I have lately just been in a state of bodily and mental nothingness. Here is Business to attend, Business which will admit no delay, and it must be done.

I do pray that Divine Providence may open out my way to more time and greater willingness to give myself to the Cause.

Today being Sunday Oct. 14th [recte 15th] I am a little better; I lay in bed this morning until 12 o'clock. After dinner walked to Ophelia's and from there to Frederick Lodge† to see Anne. There I had tea. Yesterday I spoke to Mr John Eggars† to go to Southwick† for me tonight, and today, Mr Cook having agreed to go, I called at the Brougham Street Chapel† Keeper's and left a message for Mr Eggars not to go.

Tonight I am seated in the back parlour penning my Journal, and scheming how best I shall be able to save, and improve, time. How to begin, and conduct the coming week.

Influence of Temptation

Sunday (Oct 22nd)

This morning I have laboured under strong excitement, and temptation. I advanced so far in the broad road, that I had begun to persuade myself that the object of my wishes was perfectly legitimate. Ah! how it is our subtil foe withdraws one's heart from piety. What is conviction and knowledge before the grasp of passion unless divine grace interpose? It is but the writhing of the lamb in the ruthless paws of [the] lion of the forest.

But for restraining grace I had long ere now forsaken the Church and religion, and plunged headlong into the gulf of sin. I am here. What a mercy. But what are my pretensions to holiness of heart. Even at this moment, does not some secret passion or wild desire lurk in the hidden corner? Shall I now drag it to the light, brand its iniquity, and proclaim my freedom from its influence? The power O Lord is thine. Let it come! And Now!!! Such is the frailty of my heart. Alas! led once and again to pant after sinful pleasure. Oh! that the Spirit of Christ might come, and break the bond of evil, and let that Love which casteth out all fear possess my soul wholly and entirely.

I thank God for the returning indications of health. His mercy has caused the symptoms of disease to vanish. What misery is it to pass along life weighed to the earth by pain, and corruption.

The last week I have lost time, and enjoyment, because of disorder.

On Monday, Tuesday, and Wednesday nights Mr Keene† slept at our house.

Conversation with Mr. Keene. Obstacles to study

I sat up with him late each night. I had much agreeable and interesting conversation. We spoke freely to each other of our respective situations, and prospects. Particularly we had conversation on the disadvantages we laboured under from the want of thorough scholastic education. We agreed in believing it to be essential to enable us to achieve any decent acquirements, and respectable usefulness. We freely spoke of our mutual want of time for study, a want arising in Mr Keene's case from the fact of his incessant occupation in the discharge of the active duties of the ministry, and in my own from possible, nay undoubtedly, more constant attention to business affairs. Engaged in the conduction of the business of Chemist & Druggist, on my individual responsibility, my time is completely and entirely occupied, either in actual manual labour, or the superintendence of the trade. Had I begun business in happier times, had I possessed resources to have maintained additional assistance in the business, then possibly I might have had greater liberty, but as it is with unparalleled dulness and stagnation, with immense competition in commerce, with small and slender resources, it requires the utmost attention, the most persevering diligence, and the strictest economy of time and money to enable one to hold on one's way with honest integrity.

Thus situated, where the time for mental culture? And then, over, above, and beyond all this, let the day be finished, let there be one, two or three hours at its conclusion, what is their value? The fact is, so exhausted, borne down, and overpressed do I feel myself that I am unable from sheer fatigue to apply myself to improvement, confined am I from that light and exercise which is so necessary to the conservation of the health, that I do not even get from my shop once in the week to take a meal.

Bad Health and Business Great Obstacles to Study

What shall I say as to the anxiety of mind engendered by the presence of difficulties? But no Christian should be anxious. Good! but there must be a certain degree of anxious care, or otherwise be not surprised if ruin forms the pillowy couch of the easy man. In Health, business and all its details is easy, nay a positive gratification, but in that nervous lassitude which is the result of this abominable galley-slave confinement the care of business becomes a burden, a curse, and conjoined with ill health, beget a feverish, a fretful, anxious discontent, a dissatisfaction, arising from the conviction that there is business which must be done, but which you cannot do as you would wish because of your shattered frame.

Here is an immolation of any fancied schemes for intellectual improvement. Here the Grave of my cherished and ambitious hopes of distinction which should be the child of studious labour. Years ago I revalued my plans to be accomplished now. This Now is the witness of their frustration.

But shall I go down to the earth without some effort to shake off this apparently crushing load? What can I do?

Estimate of Mental Power

Amongst other notions I have long felt desirous at some period or other to obtain a Collegiate Education. Eh! What! Yes a College Curriculum of Study. Were I to mention this to many how their lips would curl with derision at my presumption. Never mind, John Young, you are conscious of the stirrings of mind. Mind! Immortal mind.

Who shall arrest its progress, if decision of character nerve its grasp, and the eternal principle of love prove the Achilles tendon of the unwearied foot whose advance is ever onward, onward? I claim no high powers of mind, the brilliant genius, the profound, the comprehensive grasp of nature's prodigy. Ordinary capacity, a mediocrity of capability, a desire to know, to learn. If indeed my path were ever opened out to enter the halls of Science, what injury would I sustain? Surely a three years drilling might somewhat weld and fuse my sluggish brain, strike some latent spark of fire from the slumbering mass. Surely it might in some degree increase my ability in more mature years to push onward the chariot of truth and love. Doubtless it would, other circumstances being equal, supposing that I possess physical vigour. I feel no hesitations whatever in the opinion that I should, in the phrase, 'make something out'.

My Character formed

My Character is not to form. I am not a silly boy, new-fangled with the world's temptations; the desire which the revolutions of years has fostered, the desire to learn, is not likely to be all at once, and for ever extinguished, by a mere entrance in a University, and therefore I am warranted in the conclusion that with ordinary perseverance I shall not fail of acquiring considerable learning.

Oh! the reflection is insupportable to me, that entertaining the high view which I must ever hold of the superiority of knowledge over all other pursuits and objects in life, that I nevertheless should lose my life, mar my existence, burn my hopes, rush through this into the other world a fool, ay a fool!

We create our fortune

Well! my destiny in so far as it can be controlled, rests in my own hands. I believe that every man is in a certain sense the creator of his own fortune. True, 'one man is born with a silver spoon in his mouth, and another with a wooden ladle', and this principle or fact finds its attestation in numerous instances where genius or talent and learning and favourable opportunities are alike important to provide success. Whereas how many born blunderers blunder in a marvellous way into 'high places' and 'comfortable things'.

Having thus recorded my honest convictions, I next ask myself — Situated as you say you are what do you propose to do? That's the question. And to its solution I devote some pages.

My Position in Business

Being at present in business on my own account, it is obvious that I cannot go to a College without its abandonment.

It is two years and a half since I commenced. During that period I have had great difficulties to contend against, arising principally from pecuniary embarrassment. I had no money of my own, and therefore received from others assistance. That money thus borrowed, must be repaid. A considerable amount has already been withdrawn. In the Drug trade it requires the flow of time to establish a connexion.

I am now just beginning to feel easy, and to be cheered by improving prospects. I am no longer dunned by men wanting money for whom I have nothing. Thank God for an escape from such misery.

If therefore I now give up business, I resign the whole of my fruits of two years and a half of anxiety, and that at the threshold of success after having pioneered the road. I resign also with almost no resources to carry me through a College Education. Therefore without help come from some other quarter I would act imprudently in its resignation. Help will not come from another quarter, without Divine Providence raise a friend.

If then I go to College it cannot be at present.

My wisdom will therefore consist in finding out 1 how I shall hasten the time of emancipation? and 2 in seeing what I can do with my present opportunities to facilitate my progress when there?

I. What can I do now?

The Principles of Language, and of number, are the foundations on which true learning must be laid. If I were now to go to College, this would be my first step. Suppose one years continuous application were necessary to enable me to go forward to general branches of study, might I not now be doing something towards their acquisition?

Might I not in three years make a considerable advance? To be successful in Learning we must begin at the beginning, for on the stability and strength of the foundations depends future prosperity. Let me commence. Now, to arrange some plan which will, if slowly, yet surely carry me forward.

II. How shall I hasten the time?

It is evident that unless some kind friend should give and bequeath a certain sum for my particular and especial benefit I must depend entirely on my success in business. Two years and better than a half I have tugged like a galley slave. Weeks and months I have debarred myself from relaxation and enjoyment, to push forward the great concern. And in this labour continual lies my only hope. Oh! that divine mercy may vouchsafe life and health, if in so doing its Glory may be advanced.

Prayer for Decision

My Resolution then is this: 'I am in Business. Business, if worth doing at all, is worth doing with my strength. Therefore I will scheme and work and throw myself on the Mercy of God. Father of mercies listen unto the cry of a worm in the dust. I firmly believe thy love will accomplish and establish all things well, but oftentimes my faith wavers because of the weakness of my flesh. Oh forsake me not, but let me be brought to taste the river of thy grace, that my soul may be raised above the grossness of the earthy and for ever united in Spirit and design with the Heavenly Adam. May thy precious word be yet more sacred, more cheering, more consolatory, and whilst the corruptions within strive to drag me to the gratification of sinful desires, do thou bestow me that calm and heavenly temper, that holy resignation to thy love, which will destroy the power of sin, and lead me in 'all my ways to acknowledge thee that thou mayst direct my path'. Oh that I might be sanctified throughout, body, soul and spirit. Come Lord Jesus, forget not thy atonement, whisper forgiveness. Let the burden of guilt roll away that I may live to thee! Amen.

Book of Materials for Sermons

Friday (Oct. 27th)

I have begun one of my new blank books, and called it

'Sermons, and materials for Sermons'. This week I desire simply to put aside all formality and troublesome division into subjects, or any other method. To confine myself to a sort of journalizing of thoughts and ideas, freely, spontaneously as they arise in the mind, and then by and by I can use them up as occasion may demand.

On Tuesday evening I wrote an Introduction to a sermon on Sincerity. I had designed to finish it this week and I believe I could have done so if it were not for the bad cough and health I have at present. However I will work when I can, and believe that I sincerely desire to do to the extent of my ability, cast my 'Care on him that careth for me' [I Peter 5:7*]. The Lord help me so to do.

Sunday (Oct. 29th)

Preach at Shiney Row & Philadelphia

Wednesday (Nov. 8th)

On Sunday I called on Mrs Hodgson† about ½ past 8 o'clock and proceeded to the gig, and drove her and Mr Lewins to Herrington, where we met Mr Hodgson who took my place.

I walked through the fields to Shiney Row.† It was a fine morning. The genial air braced my shattered nerves for it was 1 o'clock when I left the shop. I sauntered leisurely along smoking a cigar, and turning over my Sermons. Going along a wallside I began to declaim aloud some new idea, and whilst vociferating with all the ceremony of gesture, suddenly a chap popped his head over the wall. His apparition cooled my ardour. I was glad to creep off. At ½ past 10 I arrived at Mrs Smurthwaite's very much fatigued. Dined on coffee. Laid on the sofa an hour after dinner and then preached in Shiney Row chapel. I felt melted down under the first prayer, text II Tim 2. 11.12.13v. I had great liberty. Took up the subject in a new light, the tears burst from my eyes as I besought them to remember the Immutability of the Divine purpose to save the world only through his Son. 'If we believe not, yet he abideth faithful; he cannot deny himself.' [II Tim. 2:13].

I had some chat with Misses Potters, took tea at Mrs Smurthwaite's, Mrs Keene there. Felt very unwell. They wished me to go home. Rested again on the sofa. Went over to Philadelphia† with Mrs Keene. Excellent congregation. Text Ecc. XI. 4v. 'He that observeth' &c. Felt well. Supped at Mr Harrison's.† Walked home with Mr Hillary.

Conflict with Excise

On Monday morning I felt better than I expected.

During the morning an Exciseman called and left a summons to appear before the Magistrates to answer a charge of having on my Premises an article capable of being mixed with pepper.

About four months ago they took a cask from me, under pretext of my using it to adulterate pepper. I never have been in the habit of adulterating my pepper, I never intend. I have consulted A. J. Moore Esq.† Attorney and I trust I shall be able to defeat the abominable effort to impose a heavy penalty upon one who is utterly unconscious of any design to defraud the Revenue, or in any way to act dishonourably.

Last night, that is Tuesday night, I went up, and consulted Mr. And. White, my uncle who is Mayor at the present time.

If they succeed in convicting me it will (without help arise from some quarter, where I know not) prove my ruin, for I cannot afford to pay £200 or £100 penalty.

My mind is at ease. My confidence is in God. Father of mercies, may thy kind wisdom overrule this matter to advance thy glory. Let me possess the spirit of meekness, and humility. May I be ambitious only to do right and leave final results to thee. For the sake of Jesus. Amen.[32]

Tuesday (Nov. 14th)

On Saturday evening when I left the shop, I was seized about 1 o'clock A.M. with a very bad toothache which continued incessantly until 11 o'clock next day. I slept none. At half past 12 I rose, dressed, went to Mr White's† thence to the Railway. I left at 2 o'clock and reached Mrs Muschamp's† in Newcastle about 3 o'clock. Got Tea, at 5 o'clock Mr. John Muschamp and I went to S. Shields.† I preached in Salem Chapel at 6 o'clock. Text II Peter I ch.

5.6.7v. Excellent time. Returned to Mrs Muschamp's at Newcastle, slept all night, and then came over to Sunderland per Rail at 8 o'clock. I feel thankful that I am much better in health. I trust it may continue. Yesterday I was troubled again with the toothache. Oh! to plough with all diligence.

I have been so unwell this summer that is has generally been near 8 or ½ past 8 before I have got to the shop. This must not be. Oh for health, for strength.

32. See Appendix I below.

APPENDIX I

JOHN YOUNG AND PEPPER ADULTERATION

John Young's shop was visited by Excise officers on 20 July 1843 and a cask containing 58 lbs. of a substance alleged to be in 'imitation of pepper' taken away. This is not mentioned in the diary under that date. The offence with which he was charged, and for which he was summoned to appear before the Sunderland Magistrates on 18 November 1843, was not one simply of food adulteration but an Excise offence since pepper was subject to a duty of 2/6 (12½p.) per pound weight. The penalty, under 59 Geo. III c. 53, sec. 22, was heavy: a fine of £100 could be charged both for possessing adulterated pepper and for holding substances which could be mixed with pepper. John Young was charged on both counts and was liable to a fine on one or both of them, hence his reference in the diary to a possible penalty of '£200 or £100'. Eleven other grocers and chemists were charged at the same time, the result of a blitz on Sunderland by the Excise men with the obvious intention of making an example of those alleged to be guilty, and of deterring other possible offenders. It is difficult now to determine the rights and wrongs of the matter. There does seem to have been considerable uncertainty or plain ignorance of the law on this point in the minds of shopkeepers. There was also confusion and contradictory opinion about whether the substances alleged to be sold in imitation of pepper were in fact held for that purpose. No doubt some were, but whether this was true in all cases is unclear. J.Y. argued through his solicitor A. J. Moore that the substance impounded was in fact Capsicum (green peppers, dried and ground) and was sold for medical purposes, and he quoted *Materia Medica* to prove his point. Capsicum does possess properties which make it serviceable both for internal and external medical use. The Magistrates may have been willing to believe him, or at least to condone the offence – two of them, Andrew and Richard White, were in fact his uncles – but under the terms of the act and faced with eleven other cases it was difficult to do any other than find John and the rest guilty. They imposed a mitigated penalty of £25 on all the parties charged, which meant that John Young, who possessed 58 lbs. of the dubious substances, received the same penalty as a widow grocer holding only 2 lbs. *Sunderland Herald* 24 Nov. 1843 and *Newcastle Chronicle* 25 Nov. 1843; the text of the report of the Magistrates' hearing as reported in the *Herald* is printed below.

Sunderland Police
Saturday, Nov. 18.

Present (on the Bench) R. Carr, Esq., (Chairman), J. Scott, E. Backhouse, Wm. Ord, J. Simpson, A. White, N. Horn, R. White, R.B. Cay, and P. Laing, Esqrs.

Adulterated Pepper
Information against Sunderland Grocers, &c.

A fortnight ago, a great number of informations were laid by the officers of Excise against grocers and druggists of this town for having in their possession for purposes of sale adulterated pepper. This being the day appointed for the hearing of those cases, the court was filled by tradesmen and others who evinced much interest in the novel and important proceedings, MR JAS. THOMPSON, the collector of Excise, conducted the cases, no professional gentlemen being employed.

JOHN YOUNG, chemist and druggist, and licensed dealer in tea, coffee, pepper, &c, was the first person called. He was charged with having in his custody and possession a certain large quantity, to wit, 58 lbs. weight of certain commodities and substances, prepared and manufactured by a certain person unknown, in imitation of pepper, contrary to the form of the statute in that case made and provided. There was a second count, charging him with having 50 lbs. weight of the above commodities mixed with 8 lbs. of pepper. This was substantially the same offence; but under each count the defendant was liable to a penalty of £100.

The following is a copy of 59 George III., c.53, section 22, under which all these cases were laid:– "And whereas commodities made in imitation of pepper have of late been sold and found in the custody and possession of various dealers in pepper, and other persons in Great Britain; be it therefore enacted, that from and after the 5th day of July, 1819, if any commodity or commodities, substance or substances, shall be prepared or manufactured by any person or persons in imitation of pepper, shall be mixed with pepper, or if any such commodity or commodities, substance or substances, alone or mixed as aforesaid, shall be kept for sale, sold or delivered, or shall be offered or exposed for sale, or shall be in the custody or possession of any dealer or dealers in, or seller or sellers of, pepper, the same, together with all pepper with which the same shall be mixed, shall be forfeited, together with the package or packages containing the same, and shall and may be seized by any officer or officers of Excise; and the person or persons preparing, manufacturing, mixing as aforesaid, selling, exposing to sale, or delivering the same, or having the same in his, her, or their custody or possession as aforesaid, shall forfeit and lose the sum of one hundred pounds."

MR A.J. MOORE appeared for the defendant.

Richard Houst, officer of Excise, deposed – I served a copy of the summons produced on the defendant personally. On the 29th July I went into Mr John Young's shop, accompanied by Benjamin Hemsley Shotland. I asked Mr. Young whether he had any ground pepper; he said he had none. I replied, I suppose you have some of what is called P.D.; he said he had. I asked him to show it to me. He sent his boy with me into the cellar, and I brought up a cask, which I told him I must seize, at the same time asking him what he did with it. He said he sold it to shopkeepers as a substitute for pepper. There were 58 lbs. in the cask. I survey Mr. Young as a trader; he has an Excise License to sell tea, coffee, pepper, and other articles. I took a sample of it, gave it to Mr. Davison, my supervisor, and it was sent by him to the Hon. Commissioner of Excise. The bulk was removed by me to the Excise Office.

Cross-examined – I will swear I asked him if he had an article called P.D. We found by his invoice it was called corrie, a copy of which I now produce. It was not capsicum. It was purchased at 45s. per cwt., 4¾d per lb. The cask was nearly three-quarters full. It is now at the Excise office.

Benjamin Hemsley Shotland, Excise office, deposed – I was present when the cask was seized. I think Mr. Young called it capsicum – it is so called in my copy of the invoice. He did not obstruct nor interfere with us at all in the discharge of our duty.

Mr. Davison, supervisor, merely proved the transmission of the sample, per mail, to the Board or Excise.

Mr. George Phillips deposed – I am analytical chemist to the Board of Excise. I received the sample produced marked with the letter II, and I have since examined the bulk of a cask at the Excise office, which I find corresponds with the sample. I could not subject it to a chemical process – my examination was a mechanical one. The results were – pepper, sawdust, red and white mustard seeds, and chillies. A very small portion of the compound was pepper. The sawdust was not the husks of pepper, but common sawdust from wood. Cross-examined – The sample was forwarded to me sealed by order of the Board. I cannot state the exact quantities of the various articles, but pepper was small compared with the others. Chillies are called capsicum; they did not preponderate. I have lately examined probably 400 samples, and in nearly every one of them I have found chillies. It is added to give heat to the palate, whilst the small quantity of pepper gives it the scent of pepper. I have never examined capsicum chemically. Mr. Phillips then explained how his examination was conducted. He first washed the compound, and then put it into a fine metal strainer; after the dust had run through he separated the particles, which he was thus enabled minutely to examine. He added that at Worcester, where he was lately, the magistrates having some doubt as to the examination, he went through the process in open court.

The Collector intimated that he should only proceed on one count of information, and it would rest with the magistrates to decide whether they would mitigate the penalty, which by another clause in the Act they had authority to reduce to £25.

MR A.J. MOORE then addressed the Bench on behalf of the defendant. After reading the section of the act which we have inserted above, he said the question for the magistrates to determine was, whether Mr. Young had in his possession an article mixed with pepper, which he intended to sell for and in imitation of pepper. He submitted with confidence to the Bench that this has not been established. He should prove that this article was purchased of a respectable house, Mr Wm. Dowson, of Leigh, and invoiced to him as capsicum. Mr. Young was a retail druggist, and it was part of his business to keep capsicum (which was much used in medical practice) on sale. He would also prove to them that this cask of capsicum was never mixed nor adulterated, that it was not mixed with pepper, nor sold as pepper, and therefore Mr. Young could not have any intention of defrauding the revenue. Had he been disposed to do so, he would have used linseed cake or some other article cheaper, instead of capsicum, to mix with pepper. If Mr. Young was convicted, why there was not a chemist and druggist in the town who kept capsicums on sale, who would be safe from Excise informations. The first witness had already been contradicted; he should call witnesses who would still further contradict his testimony; and he trusted that, under all the circumstances, the magistrates would dismiss the case.

Jesse Bennett – I have been employed occasionally as assistant to Mr. Young, and sometimes during his illness or absence have had the sole charge of his business. He sold pepper, which he never mixed with any substance. I remember when the cask of capsicums came; I did not know what they were used for, but Mr. Young told me they were used as an article in medicine. I have never any directions to sell any of it as pepper or to mix it with pepper. Probably Mr. Young does not sell more than 1 lb. of pepper each week. I do not remember selling any capsicums.

Cross-examined – I do not know what capsicums are.

Wm. Clement – I am apprentice to Mr. Young and 14 years of age. I was present when the excisemen came and asked Mr. Young if he had any article called P.D. He said no. One of the men then asked "have you any corrie?" Mr.

Young said "no; I have an article called capsicum, if that is what you want." The Exciseman then went down into the warehouse and took the cask away. During the two years and a half I have been with Mr. Young, he has never mixed anything with the pepper.

Cross-examined – Mr. Young did not tell the officer he sold it to small shopkeepers. We sold it to any person who came into the shop.

By Mr. Simpson – We ground pepper in the mortar. When it was beaten it was blacker than the samples now produced.

Mr Thompson submitted that Mr. Moore had not weakened his case. It had been proved a quantity of adulterated pepper was found in his possession, and being a licensed dealer in pepper was therefore liable to the full penalty of £100. He did not say Mr. Young mixed it, and it was not necessary to prove this to sustain the information.

The magistrates retired for a short period, and on their return the Chairman said they considered the offence proved, and convicted John Young in the mitigated penalty of £25.

MR. MOORE asked the magistrates not to issue a distress warrant until the defendant had an opportunity of memoralizing the Board of Excise.

MR. THOMPSON said he should apply at once for a distress warrant, but he would pledge himself it should not be used until an answer had been received from the Excise.

ISABELLA GREGSON was charged with having in her possession a cask containing 36 lbs. of the like article.

Mr. T. Burn, who appeared on her behalf, admitted its being found on her premises, but denied any guilty knowledge.

Mr. James Thompson, the collector, said he only charged her with having it in her possession. The Bench levied the mitigated penalty of £25.

JOHN JENNINGS was charged with having 2½ lbs. unmixed P.D. and 8 oz. mixed with pepper in his possession. He admitted the charge and was fined in the same amount.

(Nine other cases followed, and in each case a penalty of £25 was levied. In all cases memorials were presented to the Board of Excise for a remission or mitigation of the penalties.)

APPENDIX II

The Sunderland W.M.A.'s statement of principles of doctrine and discipline published in 1838 helps to explain the nature of the denomination to which John Young belonged, and illuminate certain passages in the diary in which the W.M.A. and its activities are referred to. The Association had a brief existence of some twenty years as an independent denomination. In 1857 (earlier in Sunderland) it amalgamated with the Wesleyan Reformers, another group of seceders from the Wesleyan Connexion, to form the United Methodist Free Churches. The latter were then joined with two other Methodist bodies in 1907 to form the United Methodist Church, whose members, with the Primitive Methodists, were reunited with the Wesleyans in 1932, creating the Methodist Church as it exists today.

The copy reproduced here, signed on the cover by John Young, has kindly been lent for the purpose by the Revd. Dr Oliver A. Beckerlegge.

with John Young's
Compliments

PRINCIPLES OF DOCTRINE

Oct 30 1859

AND

CHURCH DISCIPLINE

HELD BY THE

METHODISTS

OF THE

WESLEYAN ASSOCIATION

IN THE

SUNDERLAND CIRCUIT.

"The Lord is our judge, the Lord is our lawgiver, the Lord is our king; he will save us."——Isaiah, c. xxxiii. v. 22.

"Teaching them to observe all things whatsoever I have commanded you."——JESUS CHRIST. Matthew, c. xxviii. v. 20.

"Ye have received of us how ye ought to walk and to please God."——PAUL. I. Thess. c. iv. v. i.

"To the law and to the testimony, if they speak not, &c."
Isaiah, c. viii. v. 20.

Sunderland;
PRINTED BY MARWOOD, WHITE, AND CO.

1838.

PREFACE.

In publishing the "Form of Doctrine and Discipline" adopted by the societies of the Wesleyan Methodist Association in the Sunderland circuit, a favourable opportunity presents itself to place upon record, both for the information of the Christian public generally, and for the use of their own members in particular, a concise account of their origin and formation.

In April, 1836, several persons—being local preachers, leaders, or members of the Wesleyan Methodist societies in Sunderland and its vicinity—seceded from that body. Their fundamental objection to the constitution of Wesleyan Methodism, consisted in the irresponsible and irresistible power of the conference in its legislative and executive character. The conference, as is well known, consists of preachers only, to the entire exclusion of lay-members, however high in character, talent, or office in the church. From the supreme and irresponsible power of the conference, and the entire exclusion of laymen from its deliberations, many evils and grievances had originated, of which a numerous body of the members complained. Efforts to remedy those evils, and to obtain a redress of the grievances complained of, had for some time been made, in various parts of the kingdom, by those who participated in these views, but without success; whilst the ruling party in Methodism seemed determined to confirm and strengthen the authority from which these evils arose. Under these circumstances, many of the local preachers, leaders, and members of the Sunderland circuit, to the number of about 600, withdrew from the communion of the Wesleyan Methodists, and formed themselves into separate societies, under the denomination of *Wesleyan*

Seceders. These societies, whilst they held the same doctrines, and adopted the same religious usages, as the Wesleyans, in their class meetings, love feasts, &c. were founded on principles of church government which they conceived to be more in accordance with the spirit and precepts of our Lord and Saviour Jesus Christ.

They continued to stand alone, and to act independently, until August, 1837, when, having had the previous concurrence of each separate society in the circuit, they formed a union with the Wesleyan Association, at their annual assembly, held at Liverpool. The express condition of the union was, that the annual assembly should strictly adhere to the following sound and scriptural principles :—

"I. That this meeting (the annual assembly) recognises and holds as the *only and sufficient* rule of faith and practice, and also of church government, the holy scriptures of the New Testament of our Lord and Saviour Jesus Christ; and regards as matters indifferent, so far as membership with a Christian church is concerned, whatever is not manifestly enjoined in those infallible records."

"II. That the members of this association are desirous of cultivating, to the utmost of their ability, a catholic spirit; and to live on terms of the most affectionate Christian communion with all who love our Lord Jesus Christ."

"III. That it is desirable that some plan should be devised by which the different societies, separated from the Wesleyan conference, may be brought so to unite as that they may regard each other as members of one common family—professing one common faith—cultivating friendship towards each other—adopting a common token of membership—and uniting in promoting plans of general usefulness. *Each society to be at liberty to have such particular rules of church government, and as to its ministry, as such may think proper to adopt*, provided there be nothing in the rules so adopted clearly repugnant to the word of God."

The official members of these societies have been repeatedly asked for rules, and urged to publish them for the use of the members, and to produce more uniformity of practice throughout the circuit. They have delayed doing so until their principles and practice had been put to the test of experience. During the experience of two years, their opinion has been confirmed of their scriptural character and beneficial tendency. They proceeded to prepare them in the most deliberate manner. At the quarterly meeting, in December, 1837, a committee was appointed to draw up the annexed "Form of Doctrine and Discipline," which was submitted to the next quarterly meeting, in March, 1838, and was afterwards read in each society in the circuit, and received their unanimous approbation.

We cannot, on this occasion, refrain from calling the attention of our members to the goodness of God towards us. Peace and brotherly-love have eminently dwelt in all our borders. Zeal for God, and love to our fellow-men, have animated the preachers, leaders, and members; and God—even our own God—has blessed us with prosperity and increase. Our numbers at the last quarterly meeting were, 1195 members, and 84 on trial. The societies are progressing towards stability by the erection of chapels, and the consolidation of their plans of operation; and we have but "to walk by the same rule, and to mind the same thing," and the blessing of the Lord our God will be upon us, and he will establish the work of our hands.

PRELIMINARY NOTES.

1. It is not intended in the following summary to include what is commonly known amongst the Wesleyans, as the *Rules of Society*. We indeed believe those rules to comprise a very excellent compendium of Christian duty, all of which, as Mr. Wesley states, God has plainly enjoined in his written word; but we prefer referring our members to the written word itself, that they may learn the will of God in the words of God,—that the word of Christ, which is profitable for doctrine, for reproof, for correction, for instruction in righteousness, may dwell in them richly in all wisdom, and that they may be made perfect, thoroughly furnished unto all good works. For a full exhibition of Christian duty, we especially refer them to Matt. 5, 6, 7 chap.; Rom. 12, 13, 14 chap.; Gal. 5, 6 chap.; Eph. 4, 5, 6 chap.; Col. 3, 4 chap; 1st Thes. 5 chap.; Titus, 1, 3, 4 chap.; Heb. 11, 12, 13 chap.; James' Epistle; 1st Peter, 2, 3 chap.

2. It will be perceived, that in the following statement we reject all claims to legislative power on the part of ministers of the gospel, or any other persons, either in their individual or their collective capacity, as convened in councils, conferences, or assemblies.

3. It will be equally obvious, that in denying the right and competency of Christian ministers to legislate for the church, we do not thereby abridge their scriptural authority, which, as our Lord has plainly taught us by the commission he gave to

7

the apostles—the highest class of officers he evei appointed in his church—consists, 1st, of the power to make disciples, by preaching or calling sinners to repentance; and 2ndly, the power to teach and enforce the observance of whatever he commanded them.

4. In the following summary, it is proposed simply to state the leading doctrines we maintain, and an outline of the form of church goverment we have adopted, and which we believe to be according to the word of God, without entering into any proofs or arguments in support of them.

5. It may be necessary to state, that we require nothing as a term of church membership, but what God requires in his written word, namely, repentance, faith, and holiness of life and conversation. Prudential rules for the regulation of prudential and connexional affairs, we regard as of no authority further than is necessary "that all things may be done decently and in order;" and to these apply the apostolic rule, "let every man be fully persuaded in his own mind." To impose prudential rules upon a Christian society, and to require submission to them on pain of suspension from church privileges, or expulsion from the church, is plainly contrary to the word of God (see Romans, 14th chap).

DECLARATION

OF THE FAITH, CHURCH ORDER, AND DISCIPLINE OF THE WESLEYAN ASSOCIATION IN THE SUNDERLAND CIRCUIT.

We hold the following doctrines as of divine authority, and as the foundation of Christian faith

8

and practice; and the principles of church order and discipline, as hereinafter stated, as clearly deducible from the holy scriptures.

PRINCIPLES OF RELIGION, OR FORM OF DOCTRINE.

1. The scriptures of the Old Testament, as received by the Jews, and the books of the New Testament, as received by the primitive Christians from the evangelists and apostles, we believe to be divinely inspired, and of supreme authority.

2. We believe in one God, essentially wise, holy, just, and good; eternal, infinite, and immutable in all natural and moral perfections; the creator, supporter, and governor of all beings, and of all things.

3. That God is revealed in the scriptures as the Father, the Son, and the Holy Spirit; and that to each are attributed the same divine properties and perfections.

4. That man was created after the divine image, sinless, and, in his kind, perfect; but that the first man disobeyed the divine command, fell from his state of innocence and purity, and involved all his posterity in the consequences of his fall.

5. That God having graciously designed to redeem fallen man, made disclosures of his mercy, which were the grounds of faith and hope from the earliest ages.

6. That in the fulness of time the Son of God was manifested in the flesh; and, that in the person of our Lord Jesus Christ, the divine and human natures are united: so that he is truly and properly God, and truly and properly man.

7. That Jesus Christ, the Son of God, revealed, personally, by his own ministry, or by the Holy

9

Spirit in the ministry of his apostles, the whole mind of God, for our salvation; and that, having perfectly obeyed the divine law in his life, he, by his death, offered a proper, sufficient, and complete satisfaction, oblation, and sacrifice for the sins of the whole world.

8. That, after his death and resurrection, he ascended up into heaven, where, as the mediator, he ever liveth to make intercession for them that come unto God by him.

9. That the Holy Spirit is given in consequence of Christ's mediation; and that his influence is indispensably necessary to the conversion, sanctification, and final salvation of men.

10. That repentance towards God, and faith in our Lord Jesus Christ, are essential to personal salvation.

11. That justification is an act of God's free grace, whereby, for the sake of Christ, he pardoneth and absolveth all them who truly repent and unfeignedly believe his holy gospel; that a holy life is the necessary effect of a true faith in Christ; and that good works and holy tempers are the certain fruits of a vital union with him.

12. That sanctification is an entire destruction of sin in the heart—an entire conformity to the mind and image of Christ, called, in the scriptures, "perfect love;" and that this state of purity and enjoyment, it is the privilege of every believer to seek after and possess.

13. That the soul of man is immortal, and, after death, is received into happiness, or banished into misery, according to its previous state and character.

14. That Christ will come again to raise the dead, and judge the whole human race; that he

10

will separate the righteous from the wicked; will receive the former into "life everlasting," and consign the latter to everlasting punishment.

15. That there are but two sacraments in the Christian church—baptism and the Lord's supper. The first is the rite of admission into the Christian dispensation or economy; the second is to shew forth the Lord's death till he come the second time without a sin offering unto salvation.

PRINCIPLES OF CHURCH ORDER AND DISCIPLINE.

1. We hold it to be the will of Christ, that true believers should voluntarily assemble together to observe religious ordinances, to promote mutual edification and holiness, to perpetuate and propagate the gospel in the world, and to advance the glory and worship of God through Jesus Christ; and that each society of believers, having these objects in view in its formation, is properly a Christian church.

2. That the New Testament contains, either in the form of express precepts, or in the example and practice of the apostles and apostolic churches, all the principles of order and discipline requisite for the constituting and governing of Christian societies; and that human traditions, canons, and creeds, possess no authority over the faith and practice of Christians.

3. That Christ is the only head of the church; that the officers of each church under him are appointed to administer his laws impartially to all; and that the only appeal, in all questions touching religious faith and practice, is to the sacred scriptures.

4. That the New Testament authorises every

11

Christian church to elect its own officers, to manage its own affairs, and to stand responsible only to the supreme and divine head of the church, the Lord Jesus Christ.

5. That the only officers placed by the apostles over individual churches are pastors and deacons;* the number of these being dependent on the numbers of the church; and that to these, as the officers of the church, was committed respectively the administration of its spiritual and temporal concerns, subject, however, to the approbation of the church.

6. That none should be received as members of Christian churches but converted or awakened persons, who walk according to the gospel; and that none should be excluded from the fellowship of the church, but such as deny the faith of Christ, violate his laws, or refuse to submit themselves to the discipline which the word of God enjoins.

7. That the power of admission into any Christian church and rejection from it, we believe to be vested in the church itself, and to be exercised through the medium of its own officers.

8. That the power of a Christian church is purely spiritual and that the authority of ministers and officers is simply executive, not legislative; their office is to interpret and enforce the laws of Christ, not to make laws of their own; agreeably to the commission given to the apostles by

* The terms pastors, bishops, elders, and presbyters, we are of opinion all mean the same class of officers, variously endowed, some for leading or guiding the flock, others for preaching the word, and some gifted for both; and that the office of deacon is to visit the sick and poor, and to distribute the contributions of the church.

12

Jesus Christ, "teaching them," says he, "to observe all things whatsoever I have commanded you."

9. That it is the duty of Christian churches to hold communion with each other, to entertain an enlarged affection for each other as members of the same body, and to co-operate for the promotion of the Christian cause.

10. That the fellowship of every Christian church should be so liberal as to admit to communion in the Lord's supper all whose faith and piety are approved, though conscientiously differing in points of minor importance; and that this outward sign of brotherhood in Christ should be co-extensive with the brotherhood itself.

PRUDENTIAL AND CONNEXIONAL RULES.

Prudential rules for the regulation of local and circuit affairs we consider requisite, in order that all things may be done decently and in order. It is obviously the duty of Christian societies to submit to and observe the rules they have adopted; and of the constituted authorities of such societies to enforce the observance of them; but to require submission to such regulations on pain of suspension from church privileges, or expulsion from the church, is plainly contrary to the word of God.

CHURCH MEETINGS.

1. There shall be a meeting of each society once in every quarter, to be held, if convenient, on the

13

first Monday evening after each quarterly meeting, when the temporal and spiritual state of the society and circuit shall be laid before the members.

2. Each separate church, in its own meetings, shall possess the power, through its official representatives, to propose any new measures, or to suggest any alteration in the existing rules, to the quarterly meeting.

LEADERS' MEETINGS.

1. The meetings for the management of the business of each society shall consist of the preachers, stewards, leaders, and deacons of that society.

2. The business of this leaders' meeting shall be —1st, to appoint its own stewards, whose office it is to receive all class and ticket money from the leaders; 2nd, to discharge all the local expenses of the society; 3rd, to pay over the balance in hand each quarter to the circuit stewards for the maintenance of the itinerancy; 4th, to receive new members, if approved, on the recommendation of the leaders.

3. To administer church discipline, in all cases where the preliminary steps recommended in Matt. chap. xviii. v. 15, 16, 17, (which we resolve always to abide by) shall have failed: the leaders' meeting shall then examine and adjudicate on the case by the decision of the majority thereof. The person thus tried to have the right of appeal to the whole church.

4. To enquire after the sick, and see that they are visited; to fix the hours of public worship, and the order of all religious services; and, in general, to superintend and regulate all the affairs of the church.

14

5. In small societies, where the leaders' meeting shall consist of less than five members, the society shall elect the requisite number to supply the deficiency from the male members of the church.

6. That no new leader shall be appointed except with the joint concurrence of the class over which he is to be placed and the leaders' meeting.

QUARTERLY MEETING.

1. The quarterly meeting shall consist of the preachers, leaders, stewards, and trustees of the several societies included in the circuit, and be open to all accredited members.

2. It shall elect its own chairman, stewards, and secretary, who shall continue in office one year, but be eligible for re-election.

3. It shall be the business of the quarterly meeting to superintend and direct all the affairs of the circuit, particularly—1st, to determine upon the admission of any societies into connexional union; 2nd, to exclude any society that may depart from soundness of doctrine or purity of discipline; 3rd, to determine, in conjunction with the Annual Assembly upon all changes in regard to the itinerant preachers; 4th, by its steward to receive and discharge all monies belonging to the circuit; 5th, to appoint the delegates to attend the Annual Assembly; 6th, to determine matters of appeal from any particular society; 7th, to enquire into any charge brought against any itinerant preacher in regard to his character, doctrine, and ministerial abilities.

4. The chairman of the quarterly meeting shall see that the minutes of the meeting are carried into effect during the interval of the quarter.

15

PREACHERS' MEETING.

1. The whole of the preachers in the circuit shall meet once in a quarter, at such time and place as shall be published on the plan.

It shall be the business of this meeting—1st, to consider of such alterations as are needful in the quarterly plan, for the approbation of the quarterly meeting; 2nd, to enquire into any neglect of appointments; 3rd, to receive the recommendation of the leaders' meetings as to preachers and exhorters; 4th, to examine into the conduct and abilities of the brethren on trial; 5th, to enquire into any moral charge against the character of any preacher; 6th, to consider of such plans of usefulness as are likely to conduce to the prosperity and extension of the cause of God in the circuit.

2. All persons offering themselves to become preachers before they are admitted on the plan, must be recommended by the leaders' meeting of the society of which they are members, and approved by the preachers' and quarterly meetings.

3. No preacher shall be recommended to the annual assembly for the itinerancy, without the concurrent approbation of these three aforesaid meetings.

MISSIONS.

A general missionary committee shall be annually appointed by the quarterly meeting, to make arrangements for collecting subscriptions, and appointing anniversary meetings and sermons to aid the foreign and home missions of the Wesleyan Association.

SCHOOLS.

1. Every society is urgently requested to establish sunday schools in its own locality; and to

16

report the state and numbers, once a quarter, to the quarterly meeting.

2. There shall be annually appointed a circuit sunday school secretary, to keep a record of the schools, number of scholars, and to assist and advise the schools in the purchase of books, &c.

CHAPELS.

1. No new chapels to be built without the concurrence of the quarterly meeting; and each chapel to be settled on trustees, being members of society, according to the plan of the circuit trust-deed.

2. Trustees to be chosen by the societies of the place where the chapel is to be built, and to be approved of by the quarterly meeting.

3. The quarterly meeting shall annually appoint a chapel committee, who shall assist in preparing plans and specifications, arranging collections, and in promoting the erection of new chapels, and, when necessary, the liquidation of chapel debts.

Printed by Marwood, White, & Co. Sunderland.

THE YOUNGS AND SOME OF THEIR RELATIONS

John White
1764 – 1
(Ship owne
mfr etc

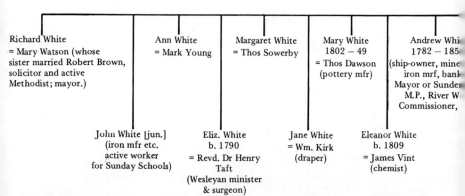

Richard White
= Mary Watson (whose
sister married Robert Brown,
solicitor and active
Methodist; mayor.)

Ann White
= Mark Young

Margaret White
= Thos Sowerby

Mary White
1802 – 49
= Thos Dawson
(pottery mfr)

Andrew Whi
1782 – 185
(ship-owner, mine
iron mrf, bank
Mayor or Sunde
M.P., River W
Commissioner,

John White [jun.]
(iron mfr etc.
active worker
for Sunday Schools)

Eliz. White
b. 1790
= Revd. Dr Henry
Taft
(Wesleyan minister
& surgeon)

Jane White
= Wm. Kirk
(draper)

Eleanor White
b. 1809
= James Vint
(chemist)

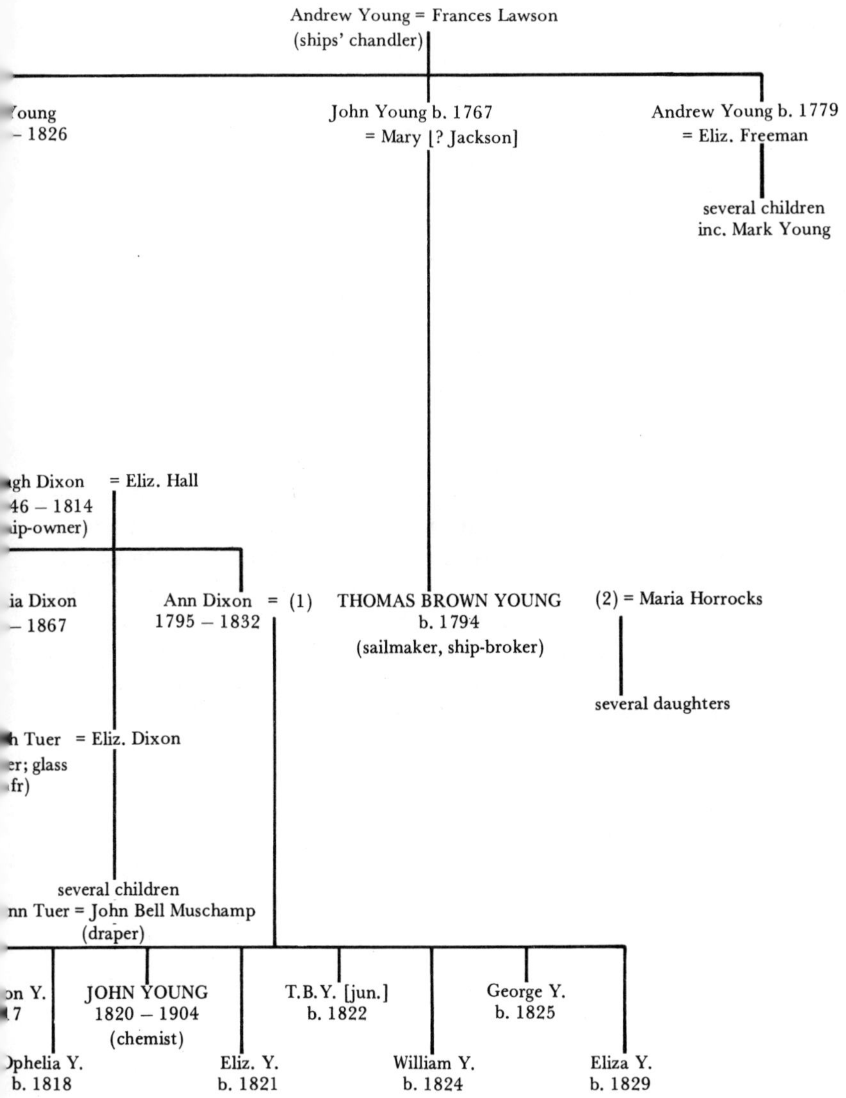
Andrew Young = Frances Lawson
(ships' chandler)
oung
– 1826
John Young b. 1767
= Mary [? Jackson]
Andrew Young b. 1779
= Eliz. Freeman
several children
inc. Mark Young
gh Dixon
46 – 1814
ip-owner)
= Eliz. Hall
ia Dixon
– 1867
Ann Dixon
1795 – 1832
= (1)
THOMAS BROWN YOUNG
b. 1794
(sailmaker, ship-broker)
(2) = Maria Horrocks
several daughters
h Tuer
er; glass
fr)
= Eliz. Dixon
several children
nn Tuer = John Bell Muschamp
(draper)
on Y.
7
JOHN YOUNG
1820 – 1904
(chemist)
T.B.Y. [jun.]
b. 1822
George Y.
b. 1825
phelia Y.
b. 1818
Eliz. Y.
b. 1821
William Y.
b. 1824
Eliza Y.
b. 1829

SUMMARY BIOGRAPHIES

1. The Backhouses were an eminent family of Quakers, with business and banking interests in Sunderland, Darlington and elsewhere. Edward Backhouse (1789 – 1860) is the member of the family referred to by John Young. He occupied a large house, Ashburn, built in the early nineteenth century on Ryhope Road, Sunderland. The gardens, apparently open to the public in the early 1840s, were part of what is now known as Backhouse Park.

2. Joseph Barker (1806 – 1875), Methodist preacher and controversialist. Served the Methodist New Connexion as a minister 1829 – 1841, including spells in Newcastle, Sunderland and Gateshead. Expelled in 1841 on doctrinal grounds. Founded 'Barkerite' congregations in Newcastle and elsewhere. Moved away from orthodox belief altogether but in later life regained his faith and joined the Primitive Methodists. See Joseph Barker, *The History and Confessions of a Man,* (1846), J.T. Barker ed., *Life of Joseph Barker,* (1880); J. Barker and W. Cooke, *Authentic Report of the Public Discussion in the Lecture Room Newcastle,* (1845). In the autumn of 1843 the Newcastle Bench somewhat reluctantly fined Barker a sum of 2/6 (12½p.) for causing an obstruction by preaching at the foot of the Grey Monument: *Newcastle Chronicle* 7 Oct. 1843. One of the two tracts by Barker which J.Y. refers to would probably be *All War Anti-Christian,* a 12-page pamphlet published in Newcastle c. 1840.

3. Jesse Bennett, a friend of John Young's referred to several times in the diary. On occasions he worked as an assistant in his shop and J.Y. sometimes left him in charge when he was absent. Bennett gave evidence on J.Y.'s behalf

when the latter was accused of selling adulterated pepper, see appendix I pp. 160-65 above. Directories show a Jesse Bennett, shopkeeper, at 6 Sunderland Street, in 1844 and 1847 and by the latter date he is also described as a sail cloth manufacturer.

4. Joseph Brown M.D. 1784 – 1868, a noted Sunderland doctor, sanitary reformer, medical author, scholar, Liberal member of the Borough Council and mayor in 1839. Directories of the 1840s describe him as 'physician' at 131 High Street. An active supporter of the Anti-Corn Law Movement. See Brockie, pp. 256–266; anon., *Public Men of the North,* (1855), pp. 124–133. He was brought up as a Quaker but later became a member of the established Church.

5. Hewitt Burnett had a business as bookseller, printer and proprietor of a circulating library on Sans Street. He later moved to premises adjacent to, or possibly above, J.Y.'s shop on High Street.

6. J.S. Cormack is described as a tea and coffee dealer, and proprietor of an academy at 13 Upper Sans Street in Directories of the early 1840s.

7. Hugh Dixon, referred to by J.Y. as his cousin, was presumably the son of a brother of J.Y.'s mother, though this is unverified. Corder's Manuscripts show a William Dixon of Derwent Street, Bishopwearmouth, who had a son Hugh born in 1819. (J.Y.'s grandfather on his mother's side was Hugh Dixon, showing that Hugh was a family name.) The 1841 Census shows young Hugh Dixon, described as a 'shipowner', living at Frederick Lodge, the home of Andrew White. White's wife was a Dixon, and Hugh was no doubt her nephew, as was J.Y.

8. John Dixon, W.M.A. lay preacher and Sunday School instructor, friend, and possibly relative, of John Young, perhaps a brother of William Dixon. Married J.Y.'s sister Ophelia, see p. 130. J.Y. and Wm Dixon confessed to private doubts about the marriage, p. 124 above. Dixon refused to take certain preaching appointments. He was a chemist with a shop on High Street, and a residence at 41 South Durham Street, 1844 *Directory*.

9. William Dixon, a close friend and possible relative of John Young, active in the W.M.A. as Sunday School teacher, Trustee and member of the Library Committee. J.Y. met him frequently for prolonged conversation and walks e.g. pp. 70, 117 above. Directories show a William Dixon, chemist, at 98/99 High Street in the early 1840s. He was a representative for Sunderland at the W.M.A. Assemblies 1855 – 1857: *W.M.A. Mag.* William Dixon and Lillyfoot accompanied John Young as a young preacher 'on trial', and would later be called on to report on him to the preachers' meeting.

10. Revd. John Dunning, a W.M.A. minister about whom little is known. He entered the ministry as a probationer 1839, and was received into full connexion in 1842 when he was serving in Whitby. The references in the diary seem to refer to a visit by him to Sunderland in April 1843, when he was in his third year at Whitby. After this term of service he apparently disappeared from Connexional records. Beckerlegge 1968, p. 71.

11. John Eggars [*recte* Eggers], a joiner, and an active member of the W.M.A. in Sunderland. With his wife Caroline and four children he emigrated with T.B. Young and others in 1852, but died on the ship and was buried at sea on Christmas Eve. See above, Introduction, p. xvii, note 11. Caroline was his second wife; his first wife Elizabeth died in 1847 aged 37, *WMA Mag.* 1848, pp. 82–4.

12. Sir John Fife (1795 – 1871), a well-known Newcastle surgeon and a leading member of the Barber Surgeon's Company; active in founding the Newcastle School of Medicine 1834; a radical, and active in civil politics; mayor of Newcastle 1838/9 and 1842/3; knighted 1840 for his action in calling out the military on 30th July 1839 to suppress a Chartist riot – an episode which cost him some popular favour. *D.N.B.;* R. Welford, *Men of Mark 'twixt Tyne and Tweed,* (1895), ii, 226–235; G. Grey Turner, *The Newcastle upon Tyne School of Medicine 1834 – 1934,* (1934), pp. 182–184.

13. John Foster (1803 – 1856), not Forster as spelt by J.Y., was a lay preacher in the Sunderland W.M.A.

Circuit. A tribute, with an account of his life by the Revd. Aquila Keene, was published in the *WMA Mag.* 1857, 325–331.

14. John Harrison, of Bunker Hill, was resident viewer (manager) of the Newbottle Colliery and a close friend of the Youngs. There are frequent references to his family in the diary, often in connection with J.Y.'s visits to Bunker Hill when preaching in that vicinity. The 1841 Census shows the family to have consisted of John aged 50, Ann his wife aged 40, and four children, Mary, whom J.Y. calls Mary Ann or Marianne, 20, Sarah 15, William 10 and Margaret 7. Marianne married the Revd. Aquila Keene, W.M.A. minister in the Sunderland circuit (see below), at Houghton-le-Spring parish church in September 1843, see above pp. 99-100, 138. Two sons, Thomas and John, not listed in the Census entry, are mentioned by John Young, see above pp. 50, 98, 121. The Harrisons were strong supporters of the W.M.A.

15. Edward [*recte* Edmund] Heywood is apparently to be identified with Edmund Heywood who became a W.M.A. minister in 1845: Beckerlegge 1968, p. 108. He came to Sunderland, as J.Y. recounts, to serve as full time missionary (lay evangelist) in the W.M.A. Sunderland Circuit, apparently replacing a Mr Clare, also mentioned by J.Y., and staying some eighteen months. J.Y.'s phrase 'Heywood of Heywood' shows that he came from Heywood in Lancashire, which is borne out by other evidence, *WMA Mag.* 1857, 489, 515.

16. Simpson (Simson) Hodgson, W.M.A. lay preacher about whose preaching and speaking John Young makes some critical remarks, see pp. 118, 149-50 above. A person of this name is found in Directories of the 1840s at 2 Nile Street Sunderland, the house next door to that where T.B. Young and John lived, described as either 'clerk' or 'agent in Lloyd's office'.

17. Revd. Aquila Keene (1816 – 1901), occasionally spelt Keane by John Young, entered the ministry of the Wesleyan Methodist Association in 1839 in Worcester, and served two spells in Sunderland in 1842 – 1845 and 1853 – 1858. He was accepted 'into full Connexion'

i.e. his probationary period was completed, in 1843, (see p. 62 n. 65 above), and he married Marianne Harrison soon afterwards. His ministerial work was largely done in the northern counties, though he finally retired at Croydon. Secretary of the (Connexional) Chapel Fund 1845, and a member of the Connexional Committee 1848–9 and 1851. Beckerlegge 1968 p. 134. There is a photograph and short account in W.R. Sunman, *History of Free Methodism in and about Newcastle upon Tyne* (1902), pp. 83–4, where Keene is described as of 'a kind and genial disposition, . . . able and much loved . . . with intellectual ability and superior power as an expository preacher'. It is interesting to note that John Young uses the title 'Reverend' in this entry. The first Assembly of the W.M.A. in 1836 had decided against this practice but the title slipped back into use and the decision was rescinded in 1845. Beckerlegge 1957, p. 20.

18. George Longstaff, a gardener, was J.Y.'s Methodist class leader, and a trustee of the Brougham Street, Bishopwearmouth, W.M.A. Tabernacle.

19. James Milne, who ran the Seamen's Mission in Sunderland, lived at 7 Frederick Street. The Sunderland Sailors' Society, which employed the missionary, was instituted in January 1843 and was supported by voluntary subscriptions on a non-sectarian basis. The missionary visited vessels, and distributed Bibles and Tracts to sailors, Fordyce ii, 461. The first anniversary of the Society, *Sunderland Herald* 24 Dec. 1843, reveals it to have had strong Methodist backing. John Peters, the W.M.A. Superintendent, was on the committee and made a speech of great length of this occasion, fervently urging support of the society. However it is certain that similar work had been going on under other auspices for a good many years before 1843. James Milne was the author of *Maritime Piety – experiences in a French Prison,* (1851), in which he is described as "Sunderland Sailor and Pastor".

20. John Moffitt, also spelt Moffat in the diary. A close friend of John Young, and fellow preacher, opened a school, but soon abandoned teaching and sailed for Demerara where he died in November 1843. His death much affected J.Y. see pp. 37–8 above.

21. Anthony John Moore, solicitor, Steward of the manor of Sunderland, Borough Councillor from 1837 and Alderman from 1853, an active promoter of public services, especially gas and water supply, mayor 1854/5 and 1855/6, Liberal in politics and an active Anti-Corn Law League supporter. Resided in Building Hill House in the early 1840s; later built Bede Tower (1853). See Fordyce ii, 484–5, and anon; *Public Men of the North,* (1855), pp. 55–59. W.T. Moore, draper, who was a trustee of the Brougham Street Tabernacle, was probably A.J. Moore's brother William who is mentioned occasionally in the diary. John Young employed A.J. Moore as his solicitor when accused of pepper adulteration, see pp. 158, 160-65 above.

22. William Mordey, surgeon, of 39 John Street, Sunderland. He became Chairman of the Sunderland and South Shields Water Company, formed in 1846; a borough councillor from 1842, and elected mayor in 1859. On the Mordey family see Isobel Mordy, *Mordey in Sunderland,* (1969), typescript in Sunderland Library.

23. Revd. Humphrey Mules, W.M.A. minister about whom little is known. He served in Liskeard 1841–2, and was appointed to Sunderland for two years 1842 – 1844, but then disappears from the Connexional records: Beckerlegge 1968, p. 116. Preaching once at Hetton he put two texts to the vote, p. 58 above. He appears to have lived in lodgings in or near South Shields, which was in the Sunderland W.M.A. circuit.

24. Ann Muschamp, née Tuer, was John Young's cousin (see p. 90 above) and wife of John Bell Muschamp who from 1842 to c. 1852 was a partner with his cousin Emerson Muschamp Bainbridge in a drapery business on Market Street, Newcastle, which was eventually to develop into a famous department store. See A. and J. Airey, *The Bainbridges of Newcastle : A Family History 1679 – 1976,* (1979), esp. pp. 45–48; A. Airey, 'The Bainbridge Family of Weardale and Newcastle', *Bulletin of the Wesley Historical Society, North East Branch* 35 (1981), 3–11; 36 (1981), 4–13; 37 (1982), 4–10. Like the Bainbridges, the Muschamps were a Weardale family. Originally Quakers, by the nineteenth century most of them

appear to have been either Wesleyan or Primitive Methodists. Three sons of John Dover Muschamp (1777 – 1858) of Westgate migrated to Sunderland: William Muschamp and John Bell Muschamp, both Wesleyans, who shared a drapery business on High Street, Sunderland, until John Bell moved to Newcastle; and Emerson Muschamp, their elder brother, who was active in many fields – iron making, as resident managing partner of the Bishopwearmouth Iron Works; railways, as a consultant engineer; farming and land management, in connection with his interests in Weardale; religion, as a deeply committed Primitive Methodist; and civic affairs, as a member of the Sunderland Town Council from its inception in 1835. Emerson died at the age of 40 in 1849. On various members of the Muschamp family, see the *Primitive Methodist Magazine* 1839, 26–31; 1849, 705–708; 1858, 699–701.

The Muschamps demonstrate the complex family, and business, connections of the leading Methodist families in Sunderland as also in Newcastle. Emerson Muschamp was E.M. Bainbridge's cousin, and also married his sister. She later married the Revd Luke Tyerman, a well-known Wesleyan scholar. It appears that Emerson Muschamp helped Bainbridge at a crucial moment in his business life and may well have been instrumental in suggesting his brother, John Bell Muschamp, as a partner to help him through the crisis. The mothers of John Young and of Ann Tuer were sisters. Ann's father Joseph Tuer was another Wesleyan draper who later became a glass manufacturer. Ann and her husband John Bell Muschamp were living on Stepney Lane, Newcastle, when John Young visited them. On some of the Methodist business families in early nineteenth-century Sunderland, see G.E. Milburn, 'Wesleyanism in Sunderland in the later eighteenth and early nineteenth centuries', *Antiquities of Sunderland* 26 (1974–76), and 27, (1977–79), esp. 27, 19–23. John M. Tuer, mentioned in the diary, was probably a son of Joseph Tuer of Sunderland and brother of Ann Muschamp. Another son, Joseph Robertson Tuer, joined James Jopling in a drapery business which was to become well known in Sunderland as Jopling & Tuer, later simply as Joplings.

25. Revd. John Peters (1795–1865), born Dunaghy, Co. Antrim, joined the W.M.A. in 1835, and entered in its ministry 1836; received into full Connexion 1837; served entirely in the northern counties and Scotland, including Sunderland 1842–4; retired 1864. President of the W.M.A. 1843 and 1851, Connexional Secretary 1847, member of the Connexional Committee 1837–63. Beckerlegge 1968 p. 182. When in Sunderland he lived at 30 South Durham Street (*Directory* 1844), next to the Chapel. A teetotaller and an active supporter of the Anti-Corn Law movement. At a meeting at Brougham Street to bid farewell to Peters in 1844 there were very warm expressions of appreciation of his ministerial work: *WMA Mag.* 1844, 375–6. A sermon by Peters is printed in the same magazine, pp. 412–417.

26. 'Punshon of Sunderland' (page 120 above) appears to be a reference to William Morley Punshon (1824 – 1881) who in later life became one of the most celebrated preachers of the mid-Victorian decades, his lectures on religious and historical themes being particularly successful. His father was a native of Sunderland, though left the town; William's boyhood years were spent in Doncaster and also in Hull where he began work for his grandfather, a timber merchant. He moved to Sunderland in 1840 to work under his uncle, Hugh Panton, who was an active Wesleyan. Though only sixteen William showed a remarkable propensity for Christian work and became a lay preacher in the Sunderland Wesleyan Circuit. It was while engaged on preaching commitments that both he and John Young found themselves at Seaham on 16 July 1843 on which occasion, as J.Y. records, Morley Punshon attended John's afternoon service. A few weeks later Punshon left Sunderland to begin theological study preparatory to entering the Wesleyan ministerial training institution at Richmond, Surrey, in 1844. See Brockie, pp. 413 – 421.

27. Revd. William Reed (1820 – 1885), born Sunderland, son of a shoemaker on High Street, local preacher at 16, minister with the W.M.A. from 1838. Buried in Bishopwearmouth cemetry. Darlington was his only north-eastern circuit, 1839 – 1841. He was President of the United Methodist

Free Church in 1862, and held a number of other appointments, including that of Connexional Editor, 1860 – 1871, when he had responsibility for the monthly *Magazine* and other connexional publications. As editor he supported the policy of full and open reporting of the debates of the annual Assembly; the report for 1861 ran to thirty four pages in the *Magazine:* see G.J. Stevenson, *Methodist Worthies,* (1884–86), vi, 960–968, Beckerlegge 1957, pp. 51–2; Beckerlegge 1968, pp. 192–3. The W.M.A. chapel in Paradise Place, Darlington was built while Reed was a young minister there – its foundation stone was laid 12 May 1840: Richardson v, 167; it was opened 28 May 1841, when T.B. Young was one of the speakers: *WMA Mag.* 1841, pp. 292–3.

28. George Rippon (1796 – 1855), W.M.A. lay preacher, founder member of the W.M.A. in South Shields. A waggon-wright by trade, killed when crushed between two coal waggons; the Revd. Aquila Keene preached a memorial sermon and wrote an obituary, *WMA Mag.* 1857 pp. 26–28.

29. Daniel K. Shoebotham was originally a Wesleyan minister, from 1827. When stationed at Dundee he left the Wesleyans to throw in his lot with a Scottish Free Methodist group which was linked with the Newcastle District of the W.M.A. in England, and he served as a W.M.A. minister in Dundee 1836 – 1840. In 1840 he and his church, known as Shoebothamites or Shufflebottamites, became Independent. Beckerlegge 1968, p. 214; Beckerlegge 1957, p. 77; also A.N. Cass, 'Developments in Dundee Methodism 1830 – 1870', *Bulletin of the Wesley Historical Society* (Scottish Branch), (2 Sept. 1973), 3–7; A.J. Hayes and D.A. Gowland, *Scottish Methodism in the Early Victorian Period,* (1981), pp. 3, 8, 83–4. In 1841 Shoebotham was invited to be one of the preachers at the opening of the Brougham Street Tabernacle, see pp. 207-8 below.

30. Revd. Law Stoney (1809 – 1884), minister of the Methodist New Connexion, which seceded from Wesleyan Methodism in 1797. The M.N.C. Zion chapel in Sunderland was built on Zion Street in the first decade

of the nineteenth century and rebuilt 1846. Stoney served in Sunderland 1841–3: Beckerlegge 1968, p. 226. There was an attempt to unite the New Connexion and the W.M.A. in the 1830s. Though this failed there seems to have been amity between the two movements in Sunderland at the time of John Young's diary.

31. Henry Taft, a physician, and Methodist minister who served the Sunderland Wesleyan Methodist circuit as one of its ministers in the period 1807 – 1809, married Andrew White's sister Elizabeth (b. 1790). The J. Taft referred to by John Young would appear to be a relative of Henry, possibly his son.

32. James Thompson, a lay preacher with the W.M.A. in Sunderland. Born in Leith, Scotland 1817, he came to Sunderland to work at a glassworks in Deptford. After hearing a sermon by T.B. Young he was converted and became a lay preacher in 1837. Died April 1846 of pulmonary disease: *WMA Mag.* 1846, 430–2.

33. John M. Tuer, see Muschamp entry above, note 24.

34. Andrew White (1792 – 1867), son of John White, a Wesleyan, (1744 – 1833), shipowner, mine owner, proprietor of the Bishopwearmouth Iron Works and of the Sunderland Joint Stock Banking Company. Helped to promote the incorporation of Sunderland 1835, and elected mayor in 1836, and again in 1837 and 1842; M.P. for Sunderland 1837 – 1841; a River Wear Commissioner. Married Ophelia, daughter of Hugh Dixon, in 1814; Ophelia's sister Ann married T.B. Young, John's father. White's religious allegiance is not clear. He was brought up a Wesleyan but appears to have been sympathetic to the Wesleyan Association. Brockie pp. 90–99, 154–160; G.E. Milburn, *Antiquities of Sunderland* 27 (1979), 18–20; Introduction pp. xiv-xv above.

35. James Williams (1811 – 1868) Sunderland Radical, Chartist, supporter of the Anti-Corn Law League, town Councillor from 1847, and sanitary reformer. Proprietor of the *Sunderland Times* from 1857. Strongly influenced by Quakerism, though later became a Unitarian. His partner in the Chartist agitations in Sunderland was

the Quaker George Binns 1815 – 1847. Both were imprisoned for six months in 1840. See Brockie pp. 267 ff.

36. Thomas Reed Wilson, a draper, trustee of the Brougham Street Chapel, lived and had his shop at 222 High Street. He later served as assistant overseer of the poor and rate-collector for Bishopwearmouth. Brockie p. 322.

37. Revd. Joseph Woolstenholme (always spelt Wolstenholme by John Young), 1800 – 1845; after serving several years as a minister with two other small Methodist groups he joined the Wesleyan Methodist Association and from 1838 worked for it as a minister in circuits in Leeds, Rochdale, Sunderland (as Superintendent), Liverpool and Todmorden: Beckerlegge 1968 p. 264.

Map of the Sunderland area showing places and features which are mentioned by John Young. It includes all the villages and towns where the Sunderland Wesleyan Methodist Association had chapels or preaching rooms. Drawn by David Orme; see Notes to Area Map.

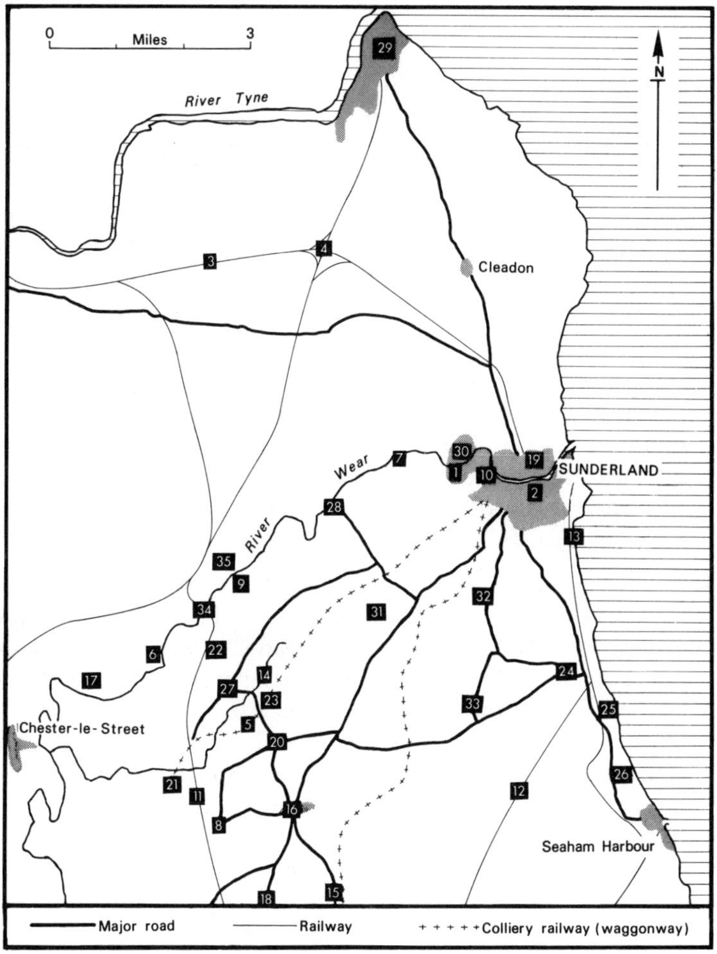

The Sunderland area

NOTES TO THE MAP

1. Ayres Quay (Ballast Hills), a developing industrial community, formerly a separate village, on the river Wear about a mile upstream from the Wear bridge in Sunderland. It was busy with bottle works, shipyards and other industrial activities at the time John Young wrote his diary, and the Jews of Sunderland had a burial ground there: Fordyce ii, 531. The W.M.A. chapel there was opened in 1839 and contained the pulpit from the old Wesleyan Chapel on Numbers Garth, Sunderland, where Wesley had preached. John Young often refers to Ayres Quay under the name of Ballast Hills.
2. Bishopwearmouth, an ancient village and parochial centre which at the time of John Young's diary was developing rapidly as a large modern urban extension to the old town of Sunderland; see Town Plan. The original parish of Bishopwearmouth was very extensive, reaching out to Ryhope, Tunstall and South Hylton.
3. The Brandling Junction Railway from Monkwearmouth to Gateshead was opened in 1839. There was no rail bridge over the River Tyne at Newcastle until the High Level Bridge of 1849 so that passengers travelling there by the Brandling Junction line had to complete the journey from Gateshead on foot or by horse-drawn vehicle. Another line of the Brandling Railway ran to South Shields, diverging from the Gateshead line at Brockley Whins junction, near Boldon. In the 1840s there were hourly services to and from all three towns, Sunderland, South Shields and Gateshead. It was possible to travel by a circuitous route to Durham from Sunderland by using the Brandling Railway to Brockley Whins, and then completing the journey on the Pontop to South Shields, and Durham Junction Railways, crossing the river Wear near Penshaw on the famous Victoria via-

duct opened in 1838. This was an alternative to the more direct route provided by the Durham and Sunderland Railway; see note 12 below. The Durham station was out of the city at that time and omnibuses were provided for the last stage of the journey.

4. Brockley Whins junction; see note 3 above.

5. Bunker Hill; see note 23 below and note 14 in the Summary Biographies.

6. Chatershaugh, a village on the north bank of the river Wear near Fatfield, with staiths for the loading of coal into keel boats. The W.M.A. had a preaching place here at the time of John Young's diary.

7. Claxheugh, 'Clatchiff' being the phonetic form of the local pronunciation, is a rocky outscrop overlooking the river Wear a short way downstream from South Hylton. By water the distance from Sunderland is a good five miles.

8. Collier Row, see note 16 below.

9. Cox Green, a small riverside community on the south bank of the Wear, with staiths for the loading of keels and other boats.

10. Deptford is situated on the south bank of the Wear, about 2 miles upstream of the main heart of Sunderland. In the 1840s it was a developing industrial community with a ropery, a glass bottle works, a copperas plant, shipyards, a paper mill, a timber yard etc: Fordyce ii, 518, 530–31. The W.M.A. chapel was opened 6 October 1838. Andrew White, at that time one of the M.P.s for the borough, officiated at the opening and presented a Bible to the chapel, which stood on George Street, situated near what is now the southern end of the present Alexandra Bridge. It was a plain brick building of two storeys. See *Sunderland Echo* 29 October 1938.

11. The Durham Junction Railway was opened in 1838 and was particularly remarkable for the fine viaduct near Penshaw, see note 3 above.

12. The Durham and Sunderland Railway, opened in 1836, was built on a route over Seaton bank top and had some

severe gradients. For the first twenty years it was entirely worked by stationary engines. It was somewhat notorious for serious accidents – see *Newcastle Chronicle* 14 January 1843, and 11 March 1843; *Sunderland Herald* 29 December 1843. Andrew White was a partner in the company operating this line.

13. Hendon, between Sunderland and Ryhope; once a popular resort, it later was to become an urban suburb of Sunderland.

14. The Herrington Burn, a small limestone beck rising near Herrington and running past Shiney Row and Burnmoor. At the latter place it is joined by other streams and takes the name of the Moors Burn, flowing via New Lambton and Lumley to the Wear at Chester-le-Street. For part of its course the Herrington Burn defines the western boundary of the old Newbottle township lands.

15. Hetton-le-Hole, a mining community created as the result of the successful sinking of pits through a deep stratum of magnesian limestone. The colliery opened in December 1821. By 1841 the population of Hetton township was 4,158; in 1801 it had been 212. The Hetton Colliery railway, which ran over Warden Law to the Wear at Sunderland, was opened in November 1822, George Stephenson being the engineer. The W.M.A. had a preaching place at Hetton at the time of John Young's diary. See Fordyce ii, 579. The Primitive Methodist chapel mentioned by John Young was built in 1824 and seated 300 worshippers. It formed part of Hetton square which included some of the first houses built by the Coal Company and was probably the first place of worship in the village. It was replaced in 1858 by the large chapel in Union Street which still stands, anon. *Union Street Methodist Church Hetton le Hole 1858 – 1958,* (1958), pp. 3–7.

16. Houghton-le-Spring and Colliery (or Collier) Row had developed rapidly with the extension of coal mining in the early nineteenth century. Between 1801 and 1841 the population of Houghton township increased from 966 to 3433: Fordyce ii, 548 ff. The 1841 Census showed 596 people in Colliery Row, the vast majority

of the employed males being miners or in trades associated with the pits. The foundation stone of the W.M.A. chapel at Houghton-le-Spring was laid by Andrew White on 3 February 1837, and he presented a pulpit Bible. Local farmers gave the stone needed for the building: Richardson iv, 340. The Colliery Row Chapel was opened in May 1838: *WMA Mag.* 1838, 315.

17. Lambton Castle, on the north bank of the Wear near Chester-le-Street, was the home of George Lambton, Earl of Durham, son of John George Lambton, 'Radical Jack', the first Earl, who died in 1840. The Lambtons' profits from their extensive collieries were evinced in the considerable enlargement and improvement of the Castle in the early nineteenth century by Ignatius Bonomi and others. Fordyce ii, 627 ff.

18. Middle Rainton, [spelt Renton by John Young in some entries], a community of colliery houses begun about 1820 to serve the Londonderry pits at Rainton: Fordyce ii, 574. The W.M.A. had a preaching place here.

19. Monkwearmouth, an ancient village and parish on the north bank of the Wear, the urban parts of which were included in the borough of Sunderland created in 1835. The old community of Monkwearmouth had been gathered in the vicinity of St Peter's church but at the time John Young was writing a new town was developing to the west, around North Bridge Street, comparable to the new building south of the river in Bishopwearmouth but on a more modest scale. The W.M.A. had a preaching place here, in which John Young preached his first sermon. It seems to have been given up by May 1843, see p. 95 above.

20. Newbottle: an ancient farming village, about six miles south-west of Sunderland and a mile north of Houghton-le-Spring. Several potteries developed there in the eighteenth and nineteenth centuries, and collieries were opened up a little way north and west of the village. See G.E. Milburn, 'Newbottle: an outline history', *Bulletin of the Durham County Local History Society*, 23 (August 1979), 12–28. See Philadelphia below.

21. New Lambton, a mining village belonging to the Earl of Durham. The W.M.A. had a preaching place here.

22. Penshaw, spelt formerly also as Painshaw or Pensher, an old village, much expanded by coal mining, situated between Sunderland and Chester-le-Street. The W.M.A. had preaching places in both New Penshaw, a colliery community, and Penshaw Staiths.

23. Philadelphia was the name given to a colliery village begun during the 1770s to serve the groups of pits (known together as Newbottle Colliery) lying half a mile to the north of Newbottle, and owned originally by John Neasham. A waggonway was built to carry coals from the pits to the Newbottle staiths on the Wear at Sunderland. It opened in 1815. In 1819 the Newbottle pits were sold to John George Lambton. Surtees writes of the miners at Philadelphia living in 'long uniform lines of low brick buildings running along each side of the public road . . . a distinct class in society, almost entirely separated from the agricultural part of the community'. Robert Surtees, *History and Antiquities of the County Palatine of Durham,* (1816–40), i, 180. A short distance away from the miners' rows stood a small community of managerial houses, named Bunker Hill (John Young calls it Bunker's hill). Both this and Philadelphia were obviously named after places associated with important developments in the American War of Independence. The W.M.A. Tabernacle at Philadelphia opened 29 October 1837, T.B. Young being one of those taking part: Richardson iv, 399. On some of the problems arising from the W.M.A. secession at Philadelphia, see W.R. Ward, *Early Victorian Methodism : The Correspondence of Jabez Bunting 1830 – 1858,* (1976), pp. 160–163.

24. Ryhope: an ancient farming village about four miles south of Sunderland, where the beaches were popular for bathing. This was before it became a colliery community, later in the nineteenth century.

25. Ryhope Dene, a small but typical example of the coastal valleys of County Durham, ending in a deep gorge through limestone cliffs.

26. Seaham, about seven miles south of Sunderland, had developed remarkably with the building of the harbour, begun in 1828 to export Lord Londonderry's coals, and the start of the construction of the new town. The Wesleyan Chapel on Tempest Place was built in 1833. The W.M.A. Tabernacle where John Young preached was erected in 1837; it was on the first floor, with a house below. Fordyce ii, 592. However the *WMA Mag.* 1840, p. 40 describes a chapel opened at Seaham in 1839.

27. Shiney Row, a colliery village a mile or so north-west of Newbottle. The Wesleyan Association secession here led to extended controversy about the ownership of the Wesleyan Chapel. *Sunderland Mirror and Houghton-le-Spring Advertiser* 15 and 22 July 1840, 22 October 1840; Panton ii, 88, 91, 107–108; iii, under years 1836–7, 1852–3; W.R. Ward, *Early Victorian Methodism,* (1976), p. 163.

28. South Hylton, or Ford, several miles upstream from Sunderland, where the W.M.A. opened a chapel in 1838, was noted for its shipyards and other industries, including pottery, copperas works and paper making. Its population increased from 602 in 1801 to 1720 in 1841. See T.F. Hunter, 'The Growth of South Hylton', *Antiquities of Sunderland* 27 (1977–9), 84–100.

29. In South Shields (population 23,337 in 1841) the W.M.A. rented the Salem Street Chapel of 1824 from the Particular Baptists as early as December 1834. G.B. Hodgson, *The Borough of South Shields,* (1903), p. 275. The chapel was later purchased by the W.M.A. and galleries were added in 1839 so that it could seat over 700. The cause at Shields was lively, being the most important in terms of numbers in the whole Sunderland circuit.

30. Southwick, in the 1840s an expanding industrial community on the north side of the river Wear several miles upstream of Sunderland, was a centre for potteries, glass making, and ship building: Fordyce ii, 539–540. J.Y. preached there often. It is not clear whether the W.M.A. place of worship at that time was a full chapel or simply a preaching room.

31. Thorney Close was a large house some three miles south-west of Sunderland, just off the Durham Road. It belonged to the White family. The ship William Wesley Young was sailing in presumably was owned by the Whites, and named after their house.

32. The Tunstall Hills are a long low limestone ridge on the south side of Sunderland and were a popular and easily accessible resort in the nineteenth century.

33. Tunstall Lodge, a fine house (still standing) between Tunstall and Burdon, was owned by Andrew White at the time of the diary. He also occupied Frederick Lodge as his town house.

34. Victoria Bridge, see notes 3 and 11 above.

35. Washington Staith, a riverside industrial hamlet which, in addition to its loading staiths, had shipbuilding yards and works for the manufacture of bricks, coke and, most notably, chemicals. There was a W.M.A. chapel here. See Fordyce ii, 741.

The plan shows the central parts of the borough of Sunderland in the 1840s, with some places relevant to John Young and his diary indicated. The borough, created in 1835, was composed of the east-end parish of Sunderland and parts of the two large older parishes of Monkwearmouth and Bishopwearmouth, which lay north and south of the river respectively. In the later eighteenth and early nineteenth centuries the part of Bishopwearmouth parish between St. Michael's church and the Sunderland parish boundary was being extensively developed as a new urban centre replacing the old heart of the town further to the east. It was in this new town that John Young lived and worked.

Drawn by David Orme, based on the town plan published in 1844 by Thomas Robson. See Notes to the Town Plan.

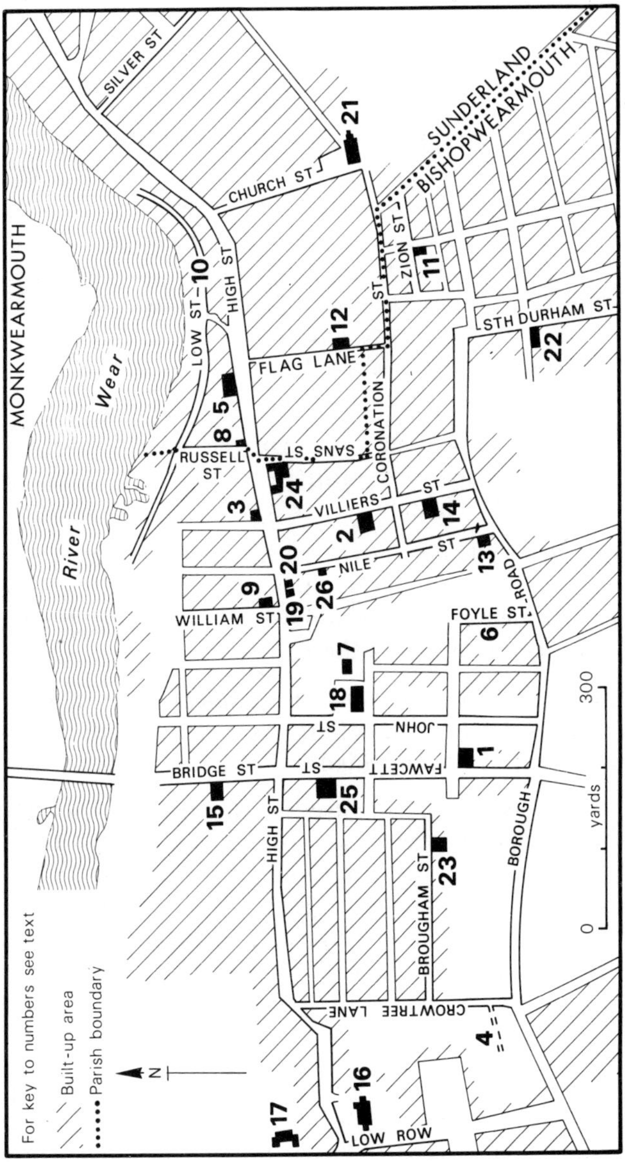

Central Sunderland

NOTES TO THE TOWN PLAN

1. The Athenaeum was opened on Fawcett Street, Sunderland, in 1841. It housed the borough museum and library (until 1879) and the library of the Sunderland Literary and Philosophical Society, as well as offering facilities for meetings and lectures. See Fordyce ii, 477. The site is now occupied by the offices of the North-Eastern Electricity Board.

2. Bethel Independent (Congregational) Chapel, Villiers Street, Bishopwearmouth, erected 1817. A burial ground adjoined the chapel.

3. The Bridge Hotel on the corner of High Street and Sunderland Street was a popular centre for public meetings; the Sunderland Anti-Corn Law Association for instance held weekly meetings there.

4. Crowtree Terrace, a short cul-de-sac of medium-sized terraced houses, not built at the time the diary was written; John Young died at No. 2 in October 1904.

5. The Exchange, High Street East, opened May 1814. It had an open piazza at ground level, constituting the Exchange area, with various public rooms around and above it, including a large news room which was used also for special gatherings and banquets. The Exchange served as Sunderland's Town Hall when the corporation was revived in 1835.

6. Foyle Street, an attractive street of terraced houses built as part of an ambitious piece of land development in the new parts of Bishopwearmouth by the Fawcett family from c. 1814. Foyle Street had houses of rather more modest size than those in the grander nearby Fawcett Street and John Street. John Young lived on Foyle Street, at No. 6 and then No. 20, in the 1850s.

7. Frederick Lodge: Andrew White's town house, situated in St. Thomas Street, said to have been "one of the most aristocratic mansions in the town, and the scene of many a gay rout . . . . It occupied the centre of artistically laid out grounds", *Sunderland Year Book* 1904 p. 37. The building no longer stands.

8. John Young's first shop, at 210 High Street East, was on the north side of High Street on the corner of Russell Street. The Crown and Thistle public house adjoined it on the east. The Sans Street Wesleyan chapel was on the opposite side of High Street, a little higher up. John Young occupied this shop from 1841 to the early 1850s. For some reason the number of the shop was changed from 210 to 209 during his occupancy. The Borough News Room was opened in a room above this shop in February 1843.

9. John Young's second shop, which was used by him from the early 1850s to probably the later 1870s, was at number 130 High Street West, on the corner of William Street. Premises to the rear, on William Street, were also used by him. This shop was in a more genteel area than the first, with attractive residential streets such as Sunniside close by. The Subscription Library was just across the road.

10. Low Street, where T.B. Young had his sail-making workshop, was mainly given over to warehouses and smaller manufactories at the time of John Young's diary.

11. Methodist New Connexion Chapel, 'Zion', which gave its name to Zion Street. The chapel dated originally from 1809, and was built to serve a congregation of seceders from Wesleyan Methodism.

12. The Primitive Methodist Chapel, Flag Lane, was erected in 1824 as the large central chapel of this denomination which was particularly strong and influential in Sunderland and its environs, being more successful than most Christian organisations in its approaches to the working class.

13. The Quaker (Society of Friends) Meeting House, Nile

Street, was erected in 1822 to replace an earlier building on High Street. The Quakers in Sunderland, though relatively few in number, were prosperous, socially active and benevolent.

14. St. George's chapel built in Villiers Street, Bishopwearmouth, in 1825, and belonging to the Presbyterian Church in England. The minister at the time of John Young's diary was Dr J.T. Paterson, not be be confused with Dr N. Paterson, of Glasgow, referred to by John Young. Presbyterianism in Sunderland was much strengthened by Scots migrants. This handsome stone building, seating 800 worshippers, was one of the most important Presbyterian chapels in the town.

15. St Mary, Roman Catholic, Bridge Street, erected in 1835. The position size, and style of this building show the growing confidence and affluence of the Catholic community in Sunderland in the 1830s.

16. St Michael, Bishopwearmouth, an ancient parish church, which had been much rebuilt in the early years of the nineteenth century. Considerable changes to the structure were made in the 1930s. John Young's two older sisters were baptised here.

17. St Michael's Rectory, a large, old, attractive residence, befitting this very affluent living. It was demolished in 1855.

18. St Thomas, Church of England, erected in John Street Bishopwearmouth 1827 – 29 as a daughter of St Michael's, to serve the new town which was being built all around it at that time. A parochial district was created in 1844.

19. The Sunderland Subscription Library was founded in 1795 by a group of local gentlemen. A new library building on High Street West was begun in 1801. By the 1850s reading members paid £1 per annum. Fordyce ii, 462; *Antiquities of Sunderland* 9, (1908), 1–48. In 1878 the library was transferred to another building, on Fawcett Street, which still survives, though not as a library.

20. The Sunderland Joint Stock Bank, the 'Methodist Bank', on High Street West, commenced business in 1836 and collapsed in 1852. See introduction p. xiv above.

21. Sunderland Parish Church, Holy Trinity, was consecrated in 1719. In the same year, by Act of Parliament, a new parish was created for the 'large and populous' town of Sunderland, which had formerly been part of Bishopwearmouth parish. The name Sunderland came in due course to be applied to the whole area made up of Sunderland proper and the urban parts of Bishopwearmouth and Monkwearmouth. John Young, and his younger brothers and sisters, were baptised at Sunderland Parish Church.

22. The Tabernacle, South Durham Street, was the first of the chapels built in Sunderland by the W.M.A. after their secession from the original Methodist Connexion. The foundation stone was laid 23 May 1836 by Andrew White, mayor and John Young's uncle; John's father, T.B. Young, gave a lengthy address on the principles of the seceders: Richardson iv, 306–7. 'Tabernacle' was the favoured name of the seceders for their places of worship. A ground plan of the chapel, now demolished, is in the Tyne and Wear archives, reference 1305/4. Both this Tabernacle and that on Brougham Street had active Sunday Schools, mentioned frequently in the diary.

23. The Tabernacle, Brougham Street, the second of the W.M.A.'s chapels in Sunderland, opened 1 June 1841, the foundation stone having been laid by A.J. Moore 8 June 1840. Preachers at the opening services were the Revds John Ely (Leeds), Dr R. Wardlaw (Glasgow), D.K. Shoebotham (Dundee) and Robert Eckett (London); and T.B. Young. Eckett was an influential connexional figure in the WMA: Beckerlegge 1968, p. 72; Gowland p. 38. On Shoebotham see p. 192 above. Dr. Ralph Wardlaw (1779 – 1853) was a well-known Scots Congregationalist, Professor of Divinity at the Congregational Theological Hall, Glasgow and author of a number of hymns. The Tabernacle on Brougham Street was 81 feet long and 57½ feet wide, with 800 or more sittings in the form of an amphitheatre. The chapel was on the first floor with a large schoolroom for 400 pupils, vestry and chapel keeper's residence beneath. The building had a mock-Gothic front, and cost £2000: *WMA Mag.* 1841

pp. 341–2; Brougham Street Trustees Cash Book: Tyne and Wear Archives 1032/251. An illustration of the chapel can be found in the *WMA Mag.* 1841 and in anon. *Fifty Years On : a short history of Thornhill Methodist Church, Sunderland.* After some alterations in 1900 it was finally closed for worship in 1902, being replaced by the Thornhill Church, near Burn Park. The old building was used for many years as a vehicle showroom but was eventually demolished.

24. The Wesleyan Methodist chapel in Sunderland on the corner of High Street and Sans Street, opened in 1793. It was a large, handsome Georgian building, befitting the central chapel of the important Sunderland Circuit. Its successor still stands on the same site but is no longer used for worship. Always known as Sans Street Chapel, it was here that T.B. Young and his family were members before the Wesleyan Association secession in the mid-1830s.

25. The Wesleyan Methodist Chapel, Fawcett Street, was built in 1836 to serve the prosperous Wesleyan families in the new town of Bishopwearmouth. After Sans Street, this was, at that time, the Wesleyans' most important central chapel south of the river Wear. It had a Gothic front, and an organ, both being significant innovations for Methodism in the 1830s.

26. The Youngs' family home, No. 3 Nile Street, at the time that John Young was writing his diary.

INDEX

Local places in Sunderland and Bishopwearmouth are indexed under their own names. The letters 'n' and 'nn' refer to editorial notes accompanying the text of the Diary. The following other abbreviations are used:

JY John Young
MNC Methodist New Connexion
PM Primitive Methodist
W Wesleyan
WMA Wesleyan Methodist Association.

The Society is indebted to Mr John A. Vickers for the compilation of the index.